2020

中国 PPP 市场透明度报告

上海财经大学 PPP 研究中心

上海财经大学出版社

图书在版编目(CIP)数据

2020中国PPP市场透明度报告/上海财经大学PPP研究中心著.—上海:上海财经大学出版社,2021.12
ISBN 978-7-5642-3936-7/F.3936

Ⅰ.①2… Ⅱ.①上… Ⅲ.①政府投资–合作–社会资本–研究报告–中国–2020 Ⅳ.①F832.48 ②F124.7

中国版本图书馆CIP数据核字(2021)第277496号

责任编辑 江 玉
封面设计 张克瑶

2020中国PPP市场透明度报告

著 作 者:上海财经大学PPP研究中心
出版发行:上海财经大学出版社有限公司
地 址:上海市中山北一路369号(邮编200083)
网 址:http: //www.sufep.com
电子邮箱:webmaster@sufep.com
经 销:全国新华书店
印刷装订:江苏凤凰数码印务有限公司
开 本:787mm×1092mm 1/16
印 张:18
字 数:290千字
版 次:2021年12月第1版
印 次:2021年12月第1次印刷
定 价:158.00元

2020
中国 PPP 市场透明度报告

课题组

方　芳　　　宗庆庆　　　石　成

内 容 提 要

PPP是Public-Private Partnerships的英文首字母缩写，译为政府和社会资本合作。当前，中国的PPP模式已经不仅仅是政府的一种市场化投融资手段，更是一次全面的、系统的公共服务供给市场化社会化改革举措，因而各界对PPP的发展都寄予厚望，希望PPP能起到引领财政体制机制改革、助力公共事业全面深化改革的作用。在这一背景下，PPP项目的规范化管理就显得尤为重要，其中PPP项目及时、完善的信息公开又是PPP项目规范化管理的基础。2017年以来，财政部连续发布的多份文件都涉及PPP项目的信息公开工作，特别是2017年初发布的《政府和社会资本合作（PPP）综合信息平台信息公开管理暂行办法》（财金〔2017〕1号），详细规定了PPP项目信息公开的各方面要求。进入2018年后，PPP项目的退库清理成为PPP管理的重心之一，2 000多个不符合管理规范的PPP项目被清理退库，同时也有不少新增项目加入PPP管理库中。进入2019年后，伴随着更多的PPP项目进入执行阶段，如何有效推动PPP项目适时公开信息的管理工作显得愈发重要。同时，公众对提高PPP项目信息质量的呼声也越来越高。2020年3月31日，财政部发布《政府与社会资本合作项目绩效管理操作指引》，全方位建立了完整的PPP绩效考核体系，明确了责任主体，将信息真实、公开、透明、质量纳入具体的考核细则。

在此背景下，上海财经大学PPP研究中心课题组继过去连续三年对PPP项目的信息公开工作进行评估后，又对截至2020年12月31日的中国PPP项目的最新信息公开状况进行了详细的评估。具体而言，课题组对2020年底财政部PPP管理库的9 662个项目的信息公开工作进行了详细评估，编制了一套“2020中国PPP市场透明度指数”。该指数囊括68个指标字段，并分为即时公开透明度指数、适时公开透明度指数，以及识别阶段、准备阶段、采购阶段和执行阶段等各阶段的透明度分指数。课题组采用层次分析法和专家打分法相结合的方法对指数进行合成：对于分指数下面的具体指标，按照专家对其重要程度的判定，设置不同的分值；而在分指数合成总指数时，则采用同类指数编制过程中常用的层次分析法，以保证指数编制方法的可靠性。最终，通过对指数具体结果的统计分析，课题组得到以下几个主要发现：

第一，2020年全国PPP市场透明度总指数为78.15，较2019年略有提高。截至2020年12月31日，全国PPP市场透明度总指数为78.15（满分100，下同），与2019年的76.19相比上升了2左右。其中即时公开透明度指数为80.37，相比2019年（79.14）上升了1.2，而适时公开透明度指数为74.67，相比2019年（71.57）上升了3。进一步对PPP项目的异质性分析表明，PPP项目透明度指数没有明显的行业差异，示范项目和非示范项目的透明度得分也差别不大。

第二，省级层面的PPP市场透明度指数稳中有升，但不同省份的PPP市场透明度指数差异有所扩大。绝大多数省份的PPP市场透明度指数在70～85之间分布，但也有少数省份的PPP市场透明度指数高于82或低于70。云南（84.98）、山东（83.72）、河北（82.99）、湖南（82.69）和江苏（82.63）位列省份榜单的前5名。

第三，多数城市PPP市场透明度指数较2019年有所提高。课题组挑选了46个PPP项目数量较多（入管理库的项目超50个）的城市，对其PPP信息公开工作进行了分析。通过和2019年PPP市场透明度指数对比可以发现，部分地级以上城市2020年的指数较2019年是大幅上升的，尤其是新疆阿克苏，其2020年总指数较2019年上升了15.39，紧随其后的是广东东莞，较2019年上升了13.62。不过，同时也可以发现，很多地级以上城市2020年的PPP市场透明度指数较2019年有所降低，尤其是贵州黔南和海南海口，2020年的总指数较2019年下降最多，分别下降了13.10和12。

第四，PPP中介机构信息公开指数跨期差异不大，中介机构透明度指数与其资历、业务量正相关。课题组分析了PPP中介机构的信息公开现状，主要得到以下几个发现：中介机构信息透明度指数平均为70.16，而在二级指数中，中介机构参与的项目信息公开得分较高，但部分中介机构网站主动公开相关信息的工作不理想，与2019年相比意愿进一步降低。进一步的分析还发现，中介机构的信息透明度指数与中介机构参与的PPP项目数量和中介机构存续年龄具有明显的正相关关系。

在指数的编制和分析过程中，课题组也提炼出了进一步改进PPP信息公开工作的一些政策建议，例如，完善“不适用”类信息和临时性重大事项信息公开的管理，进一步明确PPP信息公开的责任主体和具体分工，等等。我们希望通过进一步完善PPP信息公开和规范管理的制度来进一步提高PPP市场的信息透明度，进而助推整个PPP市场的规范化发展。

目　录

1 导　论

1.1 PPP的概念内涵与操作流程

1.1.1 PPP含义

PPP是Public Private Partnerships的英文首字母缩写，直译为政府和社会资本合作。PPP是社会资本参与基础设施和公用事业项目投资运营的一种制度创新，不同的国际组织对其均有自己不尽相同的定义。例如，亚洲开发银行认为PPP是指为开展基础设施建设和提供公共服务，公共部门和私营部门之间可能建立的一系列合作伙伴关系。联合国发展计划署认为PPP是指政府、营利性企业和非营利性组织基于某个项目而形成的相互合作关系，在这种关系中，政府并不是把项目的责任全部转移给私营部门，而是由参与合作的各方共同承担责任和融资风险。欧盟委员会认为PPP是公共部门和私人部门之间的一种合作关系，其目的是为了提供传统上由公共部门提供的公共项目或服务。世界银行则认为，PPP是私营部门和政府机构间就提供公共资产和公共服务签订的长期合同，而私营部门须承担重大风险和管理责任。而根据中国政府的定义，政府和社会资本合作模式是指政府通过特许经营权、合理定价、财政补贴等事先公开的收益约定规则，引入社会资本参与城市基础设施等公益性事业投资和运营，以利益共享和风险共担为特征，发挥双方优势，提高公共产品或服务的质量和供给效率。中国政府对PPP模式的定义与其他国际组织定义的差异主要体现在“社会资本”和“私人资本”上，在中国，社会资本覆盖范围更广，除了私人资本、境外资本等之外，还包括国有企业资本等。

综合上述几个定义，可以认为，广义上，PPP就是指政府和社会资本充分发挥各自优势，为提供公共产品或服务而建立的合作伙伴关系，这些合作通常集中于基础设施及公共服务领域。在PPP模式的合作中，政府一般采取竞争性方式选择具有投融资、运营管理能力的社会资本，双方按照平等协商原则订立合同，由社会资本提供公共服务，政府依据公共服务绩效评价结果向社会资本支付对价。具体而言，PPP通常模式是由社会资本主要负责基础设施和公用事业的项目设计、建设、运营和维护工作，承担商业和财务风险，通过政府购买、使用者付费或其他回报机制获得合理投资回报；政府主要负责公共服务及基础设施质量和价格监管，保护消费者利益，以保证公共利益最大化，并承担政策法律风险。PPP最初主要是在基础设施领域产生的制度创新，随后逐渐发展并覆盖大多数公共产品或服务领域，包括交通、能源、水利、水务等经济基础设施和科技、环保、教育、文化、体育、卫生、旅游、社会福利等社会基础设施。

1.1.2 PPP操作流程

财政部于2014年11月下发《政府和社会资本合作操作指南》，对PPP项目的全生命周期的操作规范进行了规定，对PPP项目的设计、融资、建造、运营、维护至终止移交的各环节操作流程进行了全方位规范。PPP项目操作流程可分为项目识别、项目准备、项目采购、项目执行和项目移交五个阶段（如图1-1所示）。区分这五个阶段，是PPP市场透明度指数编制工作的重要中间步骤。

图1-1 PPP项目操作流程

此外，2017年11月，财政部印发《关于规范政府和社会资本合作（PPP）综合信息平台项目库管理的通知》（财办金〔2017〕92号），对PPP项目的流程管理进一步优化，实行分类管理，将PPP项目按阶段分为项目储备清单和项目管理库。项目储备清单内的项目重点用于孵化和推介，项目管理库内的项目则要接受严格监管，确保全生命周期规范运作。对照之前的五阶段划分，储备清单主要对应识别阶段，是地方政府部门有意愿采用PPP模式的备选项目，但由于尚未完成物有所值评价和财政承受能力论证等的审核，严格而言还不能称之为PPP项目，因而属于储备库；管理库则囊括准备阶段、采购阶段、执行阶段和移交阶段，是严格按照相关管理办法进行全生命周期管理的PPP项目。

1.2 PPP市场透明度的概念内涵

就字面上的理解，信息透明度是指一个市场、公司或项目的信息公开程度。不过具体到本报告所聚焦的PPP市场透明度，则特指各责任主体（主管部门、政府授权合作方、社会资本方、中介机构等）对PPP项目信息公开的程度。从理论上讲，整个PPP市场的信息公开程度还包括项目管理方式的公开、政策文件的公开、项目各参与方的信息公开，如目前已有的PPP专家库、机构库等包含的丰富的信息，但限于数据可得性等原因，本报告中的PPP市场透明度主要指PPP项目的信息公开程度，并在此基础上汇总形成各类透明度指数。从横向看，我们主要构建了省份、城市以及行业等透明度指数。从纵向看，我们主要构建了透明度总指数、即时公开透明度指数、适时公开透明度指数以及分阶段指数。除了PPP项目信息公开程度外，本报告还专门构建分析了PPP中介机构信息透明度，将其作为专门的一章。

PPP是一个市场化的公共服务供给机制，需要与市场化相适应的管理手段和服务能力，提升PPP市场透明度就是其中重要一环。经过三年多的系统推进，PPP信息公开工作取得积极成效。全国PPP综合信息平台已成为各地强化项目管理、推进项目对接、推动项目落地的重要工具。当前，我国正加速推进PPP项目信息和政务服务信息公开，不断提升PPP管理透明度。

特别是在2017年1月，财政部金融司印发1号文，即《政府和社会资本合作（PPP）综合信息平台信息公开管理暂行办法》（财金〔2017〕1号），进一步明确PPP项目信息公开的责任主体，细化公开内容、时点和方式，确保及时充分披露入库PPP项目的基本情况、实施方案、评价论证报告、采购文件、项目合同等关键信息，并要求示范项目率先公开，确保项目在阳光下运作，强化政府监管和社会监督，推动项目规范实施。因此，该文件也是本报告评估中国PPP市场透明度的主要依据：达到该文件各项信息公开要求的PPP项目，即为信息透明度高的项目，反之，若对于该文件要求披露的信息，PPP项目没有披露，则为信息透明度低的项目。而且为了保证评估的客观、公平，凡不在该文件要求范围内的相关信息，课题组均暂不将其纳入评估范围。这是因为课题组的数据也来自财政部PPP中心的信息平台，而该信息平台的设计依据主要就是1号文。

1.3 PPP信息公开的必要性与意义

第一,改善营商环境,鼓励社会资本参与公共事业。通常而言,在政府和社会资本的合作中,政府天然处于强势地位,因此,社会资本往往对与政府的合作有顾虑。PPP更是一种社会资本先期投入、分期收回的长期投资模式,诚信政府对社会资本的参与至关重要。因此,提高PPP市场透明度,有助于打消社会资本方参与PPP项目的顾虑,营造公平、公正的市场环境。同时,提高PPP市场透明度,也有助于强化政府和企业的契约精神,铲除腐败土壤,维护廉洁高效的政府形象。

第二,促进社会和谐,增强民众的关注与信心。作为一项公共事业,而不是商业项目,PPP与民众的切身利益密切相关。一方面,PPP项目一般是为普通民众提供的公共产品与服务,建设和运行的质量直接关系到民众的切身利益;另一方面,PPP项目要么最终需要纳税人的税收来买单,要么需要使用者来付费,因而也直接关系到民众利益。因此,加大PPP信息公开力度,有助于社会公众更方便地关注、监督PPP市场和PPP项目,促进社会公众的理解和配合,也为相关工作的推进营造和谐氛围。

第三,提升供给效率,增强公共产品绩效管理。PPP项目主要应用于基础设施等公共产品与服务中,这些项目一般具有信息不对称性强、定价难等特征,因此,加强PPP项目信息公开工作,有助于各领域的专业人士科学严谨地评估PPP项目中的定价基准、财政承受能力和收费标准等问题,有助于提高公共产品与服务的科学定价。同时,PPP市场透明度的提高也有助于缓解公共产品建设和运行中的信息不对称问题,铲除内幕交易的土壤,实现国有资产的保值增值,维护纳税人和消费者的权益。最后,完善的信息公开也有助于化解地方债务风险和金融风险。

第四,提升治理水平,构建新型公共管理模式。PPP是一种市场化、社会化的公共产品与服务的供给管理模式,旨在通过改革创新,打破垄断,引入竞争机制,利用市场的专业化和创新能力,丰富公共产品与服务的供给,提高公共产品与服务的供给质量,满足人们不断增长的多样化的公共产品与服务的需求。因此,加强PPP项目信息公开对提升治理水平和构建新型公共管理模式具有重要的现实意义。早在

20世纪八九十年代，我国在基础设施建设领域就开始尝试公私合作模式，但由于制度建设缺位，导致项目“异化变形”。为了解决这些问题，在本轮推广PPP的过程中，行业主管部门从制度建设入手，按照“顶层设计+配套政策+操作指引”三位一体的思路，制定了覆盖PPP全生命周期的制度体系。完善的信息公开就是这一制度体系中不可或缺的一部分，主管部门可以以PPP信息披露为抓手，敦促地方政府以及PPP项目各个参与方更规范地参与PPP项目，进而共同促进这一新型公共管理模式的不断完善。

第五，促进PPP发展，推动全面深化改革进程。在公共服务领域推广运用PPP，是全面深化改革的一项重要任务，是推进供给侧结构性改革的一项重要举措，是实施创新驱动、发展新经济的一项重要手段。推动PPP市场发展，充分体现了依法治国和发挥市场在资源配置中的决定性作用以及更好发挥政府作用的核心精神。PPP市场的发展，推动了整个行政体制、财政体制和投融资体制的改革。因此，通过提高PPP市场透明度带来的PPP市场规范化发展，对于其他改革事业也有很大的借鉴价值。当前，中国PPP市场的信息披露工作在同类政府事务中处于领先地位，甚至在全球都处于领先地位。深入评估分析和总结PPP市场信息公开工作取得的成绩和经验，可以为其他改革事业提供有益借鉴。

第六，营造国家形象，展示中国制度自信。PPP项目各国都有所涉历，多个国际组织也非常关注各国的PPP市场。中国的PPP项目在经过多年探索之后，形成了自己的模式和风格，在很多方面都有所创新。总结分析PPP市场透明度，对于塑造中国政府开放、高效的形象，提高在国际PPP市场上的影响力和话语权，具有很大的帮助。而且，基础设施也是“一带一路”倡议中的重要组成部分，通过信息公开推动PPP规范化，有助于PPP的中国模式在“一带一路”国家和地区的推广，在输出产品和技术的同时，也输出中国的软实力。

1.4 中国PPP信息公开实践历程

自2013年我国大力推广PPP项目以来，根据党中央、国务院的部署，财政部先后出台了《政府和社会资本合作（PPP）综合信息平台信息公开管理暂行办法》（财金〔2017〕1号）、《关于规范政府和社会资本合作（PPP）综合信息平台项目库管理的通知》（财办金〔2017〕92号）和《关于进一步规范全国PPP综合信息平台项目信息管理工作的通知》（财政企函〔2018〕2号）等文件。此外，财政部统筹推进PPP改革，推进PPP项目信息公开的工作。

第一，建立了全国政府和社会资本合作（PPP）综合信息平台。2015年，财政部在国家“互联网+”行动计划指导下，构建了一个覆盖全国各地区、涉及19大领域、贯穿项目实施全过程、服务主体全覆盖的PPP综合信息平台。首先，建立了贯通“中央–省–市–县”各级财政部门的PPP项目信息采集和管理的一条通道。其次，包括了信息披露和线上管理两大平台，用来发布PPP政策法规、工作动态、项目合作、知识分享以及信息跟踪管理等，而且还满足了项目管理、交易撮合、信息服务三大功能。最后，涵盖了项目库、专家库、机构库和资料库四大核心应用数据库，其中，项目库用于收集和管理全国PPP项目的关键信息和资料，专家库和机构库用于收集和管理专家、咨询机构、社会资本、金融机构等各参与方信息，资料库用于收集和管理PPP相关政策法规、工作动态、指南手册、培训材料和经典案例等信息。

第二，建立信息披露机制。明确了PPP项目信息公开的责任主体、各阶段公开信息内容和具体要求，制定了专家库、机构库管理的规定，明确了PPP专家、咨询机构信息公开的要求。

第三，创新PPP信息披露制度。按月披露PPP项目入库和退库的信息，按季度开展PPP项目信息统计和发布。通过财政部门户网站“PPP专栏”，财政部政府和社会资本合作中心中、英文网站及微信公众号“道PPP”“中国PPP地图”手机客户端等网络媒介，实现PPP政策文件和工作动态的多点发布。目前，我国已经形成定期披露、全面披露、多方式披露的PPP项目信息公开格局。

在各方面的关心支持和共同努力下，PPP信息公开工作取得积极成效。项目库、机构库、专家库的社会影响力和认可度不断提高，已成为各地强化项目管理、推进项目对接、推动项目落地的重要抓手。项目库季报被视为PPP市场的“沪深指数”。金融机构甚至为信息公开程度更高的示范项目开辟了信贷支持的“绿色通道”。据统计，截至2020年12月末，PPP综合信息平台收录的累计在库项目10 010

个，PPP中介机构360家。网站、微信公众号等已成为PPP信息的权威发布平台。2020年3月31日，财政部发布《政府与社会资本合作项目绩效管理操作指引》，全方位建立了完整的PPP绩效考核体系，明确了责任主体，将信息真实、公开、透明、质量纳入具体的考核细则。这意味着PPP绩效管理政策的实施将更加精准有效地提升信息公开的质量。

PPP信息公开对中国PPP发展产生了积极作用。世界银行发布的2020年度《基础设施发展基准报告》从PPP准备、采购、合同管理和民间自提项目四个维度，对140个经济体的PPP政策法规建设进行了打分评价。报告指出，中国搭建了PPP基础制度框架，规范了物有所值评价、财政承受能力论证等关键环节的操作方法，制定了采购文件、工程进度等重要信息的公示制度，营造了良好的政策环境。在分数构成上，中国PPP采购得分80分（高收入经济体平均得分73分，中上收入经济体平均得分62分），位居全球前列；合同管理得分81分（高收入经济体平均得分64分，中上收入经济体平均得分64分）；PPP准备得分54分（高收入经济体平均得分50分，中上收入经济体平均得分44分）；民间自提项目得分50分（高收入经济体平均得分63分，中上收入经济体平均得分60分）。

PPP市场信息公开工作取得的成绩和经验需要总结，同时也要深入剖析有待进一步完善的内容。本评估报告旨在通过编制指数的方式，对PPP市场的透明度工作进行经验总结，分析其成绩和不足。而严谨、公正的市场透明度评估，有赖于评估方法的科学性，具体到本报告，就体现在PPP市场透明度指标体系和指数编制方法的设计上，这将是我们在第2章讨论的重点。

1.5 中国PPP市场发展基本概况[①]

按照《关于规范政府和社会资本合作综合信息平台运行的通知》（财金〔2015〕

① 本部分的数据和分析要点主要来自财政部政府和社会资本合作中心发布的全国PPP综合信息平台项目管理库2020年年报摘要。由于采样截止日期和数据缺失等原因，我们后文中纳入指数编制的样本与本部分的样本并不严格对应。

166号）要求，财政部建立了全国政府和社会资本合作（PPP）综合信息平台及项目库。本报告对PPP项目信息公开的评估就是基于该信息平台上所能获取的数据，因此，在本节，我们首先根据该平台上的数据，对中国PPP市场的基本情况进行简述。

1.5.1 全国管理库PPP项目情况和阶段分布

截至2020年末，管理库项目累计9 924个，同比增加484个，增长5.1%；累计投资额15.2万亿元，同比增加0.8万亿元，增长5.6%，覆盖31个省份及新疆生产建设兵团、19个行业领域；落地项目累计7 091个，投资额11.4万亿元，落地率71.5%，比2019年末上升4.4个百分点；开工项目累计4 270个，投资额6.6万亿元，开工率60.2%，比2019年末上升1.6个百分点；管理库准备、采购、执行阶段项目数分别为860个、1 973个、7 091个，投资额分别为1.1万亿元、2.7万亿元、11.4万亿元（如图1-2所示），目前无移交阶段项目。

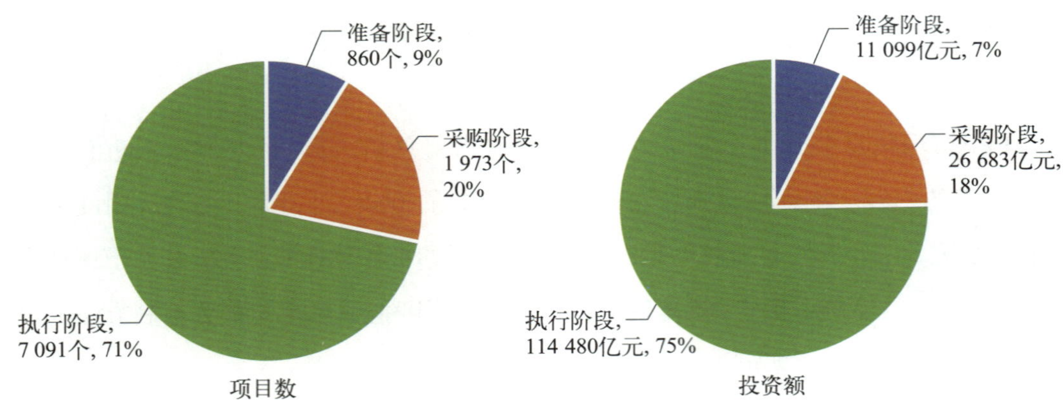

图1-2 2020年末管理库各阶段项目情况

2020年，PPP市场由过去的重数量和速度向重质量转变。全年新入管理库项目998个，同比减少436个，下降30.4%；新入库项目投资额1.6万亿元，同比减少0.6万亿元，下降27.3%。由于管理库内存量项目结构调整导致投资额变化，因而新入库项目投资额减去退库项目投资额与净入库项目投资额不一致。

全年净入库项目（即2020年末比2019年末新增在库项目）484个，同比减少302个，下降61.6%。

1.5.2 管理库项目地区分布情况

2020年各地新入库项目数排名前5位的是广西106个、贵州102个、云南85个、河南82个、江西78个；新入库项目投资额排名前5位的是云南2 809亿元、贵州1 027亿元、山西985亿元、四川931亿元、河南925亿元。2020年新入库项目数、投资额地区分布如图1-3所示。

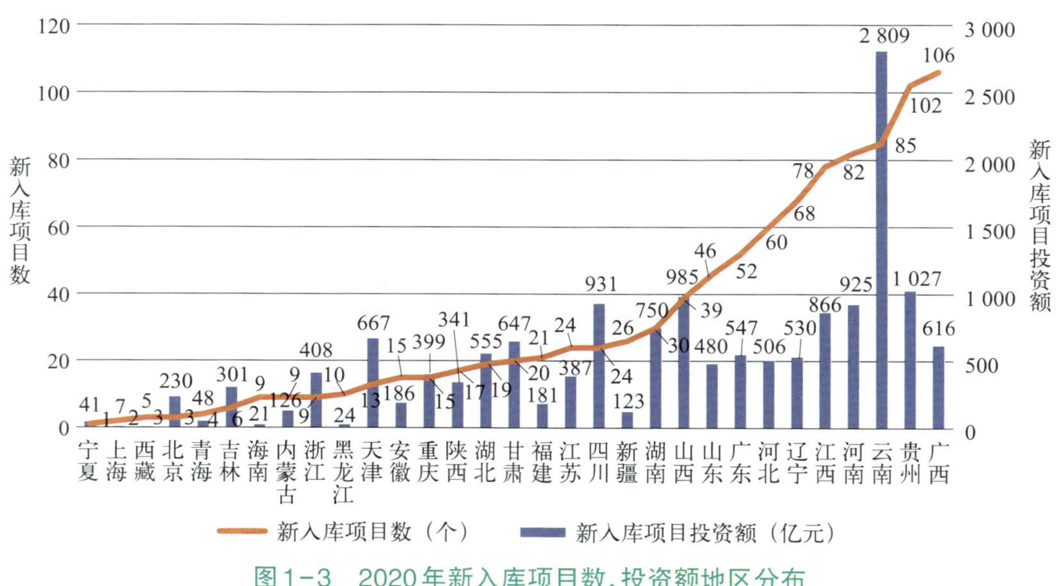

图1-3 2020年新入库项目数、投资额地区分布

截至2020年末，按累计项目数排序，管理库前5位是河南805个、山东（含青岛）755个、四川569个、广东566个、贵州549个，合计占入库项目总数的32.7%。按累计投资额排序，管理库前5位是云南1.3万亿元、贵州1.2万亿元、四川1.1万亿元、河南1.0万亿元、浙江9 839亿元，合计占入库项目总投资额的37.0%。截至2020年末，管理库各地项目数、投资额情况分别如图1-4和图1-5所示。

1.5.3 管理库项目行业分布情况

2020年管理库新入库项目数前5位是市政工程393个、交通运输107个、生态建设和环境保护66个、林业66个、教育66个；新入库项目投资额前5位是交

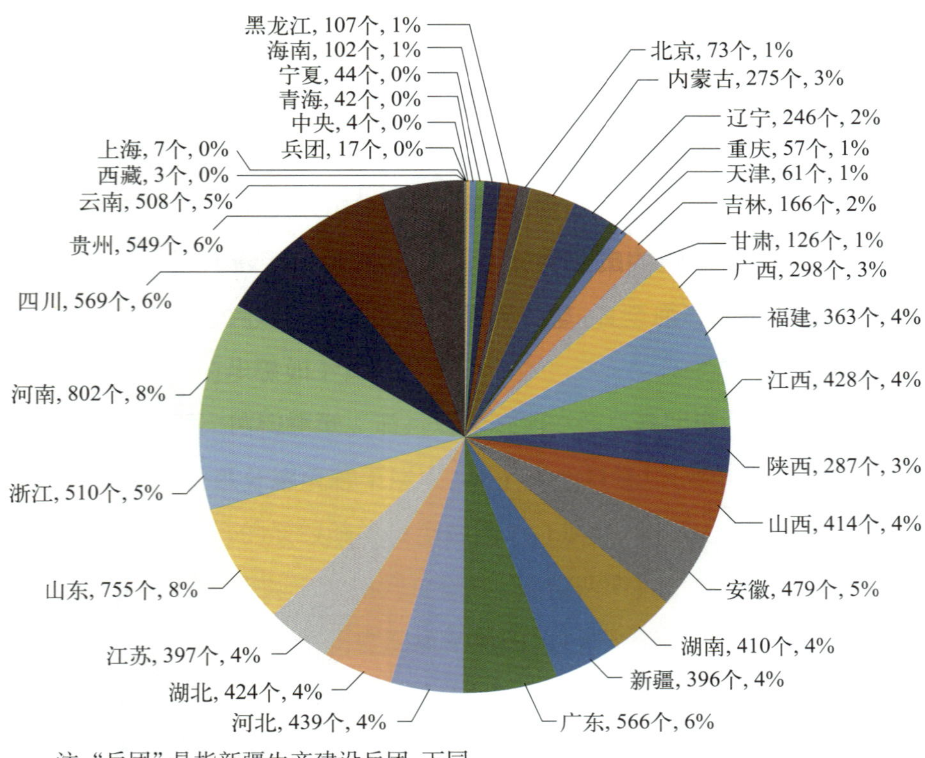

注:"兵团" 是指新疆生产建设兵团,下同。

图1-4　截至2020年末各地管理库项目数

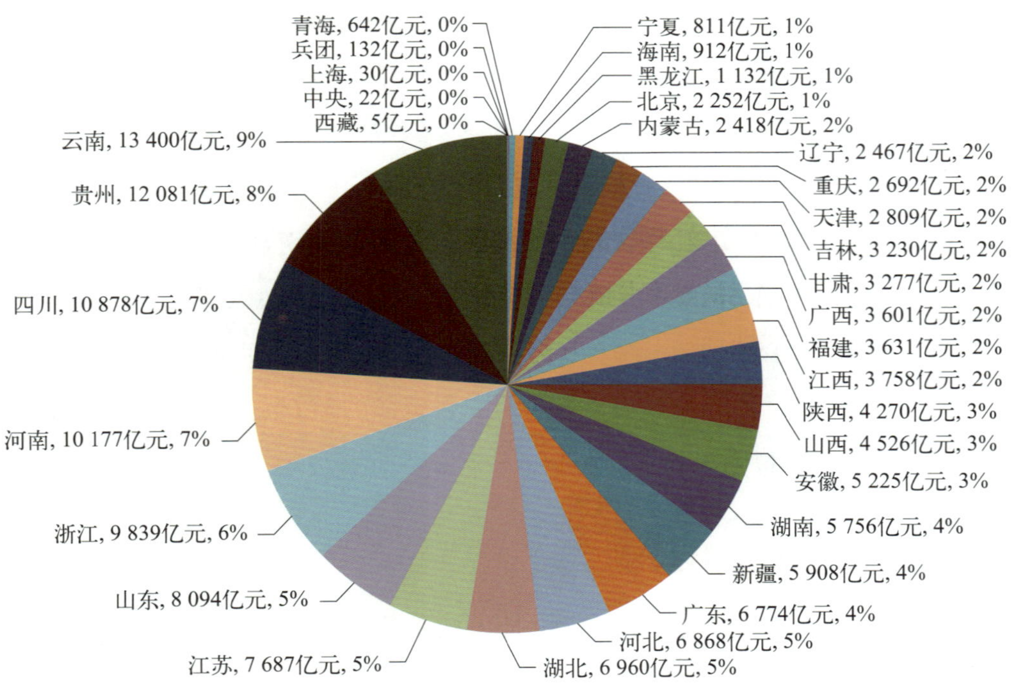

图1-5　截至2020年末各地管理库项目投资额

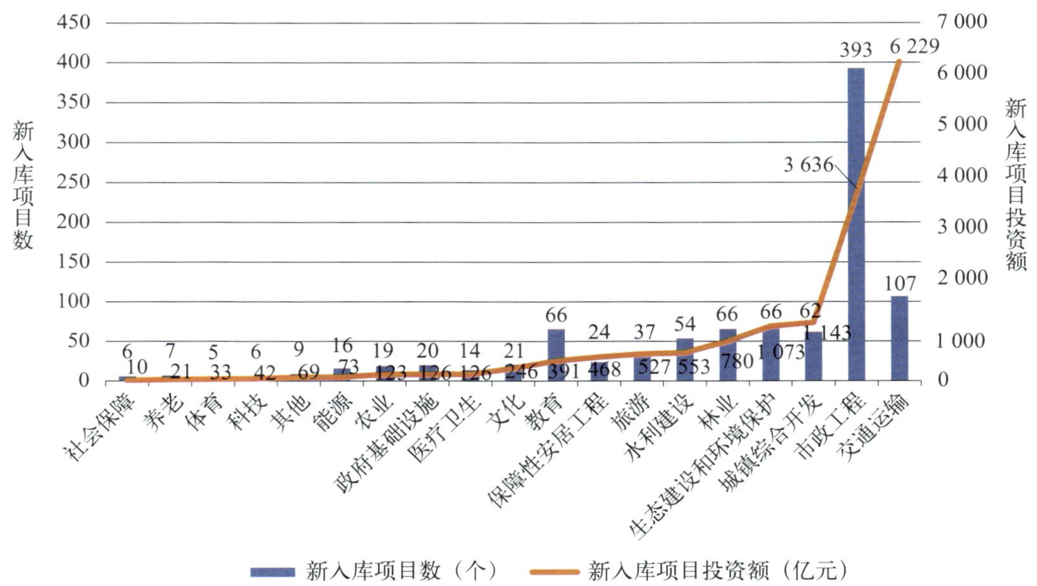

图1-6　2020年新入库项目数、投资额行业分布

通运输6 229亿元、市政工程3 636亿元、城镇综合开发1 143亿元、生态建设和环境保护1 073亿元、林业780亿元。2020年新入库项目数、投资额行业分布如图1-6所示。

截至2020年末，管理库各行业累计PPP项目数、投资额如图1-7和图1-8所示。其中，项目数前5位是市政工程4 051个、交通运输1 361个、生态建设和环境保护943

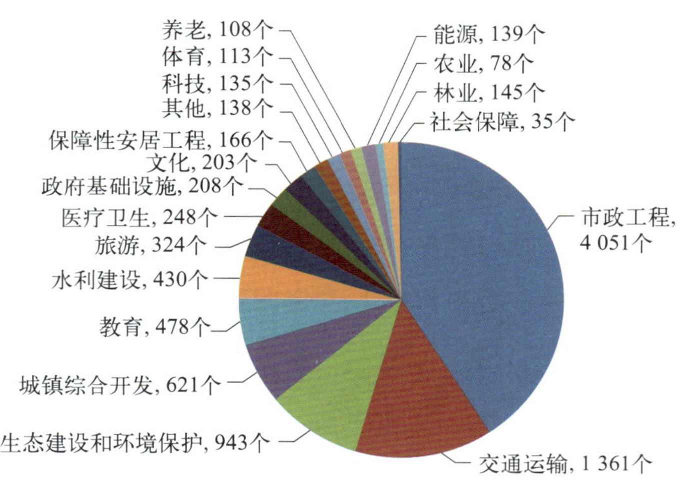

图1-7　截至2020年末管理库项目数行业分布

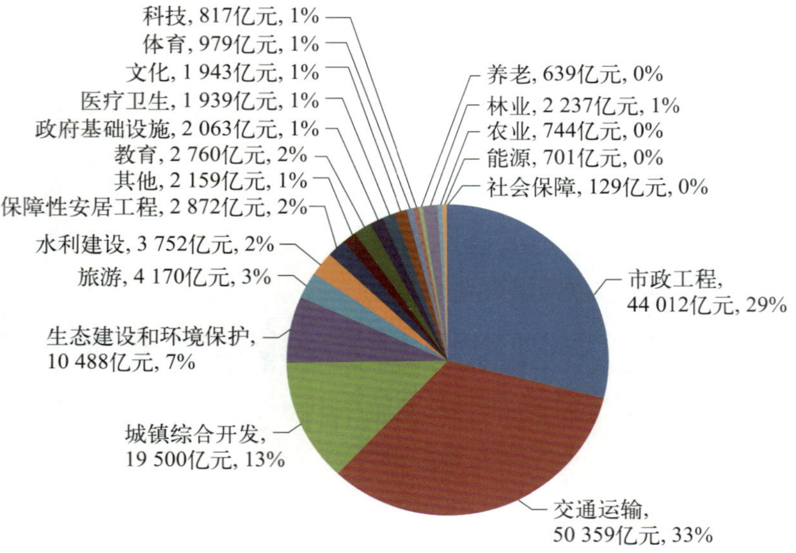

图1-8　截至2020年末管理库项目投资额行业分布

个、城镇综合开发621个、教育478个，合计占管理库项目总数的75.1%；项目投资额前5位是交通运输5.0万亿元、市政工程4.4万亿元、城镇综合开发2.0万亿元、生态建设和环境保护1.0万亿元、旅游4 170亿元，合计占管理库总投资额的84.4%。

1.5.4　管理库项目按回报机制分布情况

按照三种回报机制统计，2020年使用者付费类项目新入库40个，投资额1 716亿元，占净入库项目投资额的11.0%；可行性缺口补助（即政府市场混合付费）类项目新入库739个，投资额12 622亿元，占净入库项目投资额的80.5%；政府付费类项目净入库219个，投资额净减1 333亿元，占净入库项目投资额的8.5%。

截至2020年末，累计使用者付费类项目607个，投资额1.4万亿元，分别占管理库的6.1%和9.3%；累计可行性缺口补助类项目5 806个，投资额10.4万亿元，分别占管理库的58.5%和68.5%；累计政府付费类项目3 511个，投资额3.4万亿元，分别占管理库的35.4%和22.2%（如图1-9所示）。

1.5.5　管理库项目按运作方式分布情况

2020年管理库新入库项目数前3位是BOT743个、TOT110个以及其他72个，投

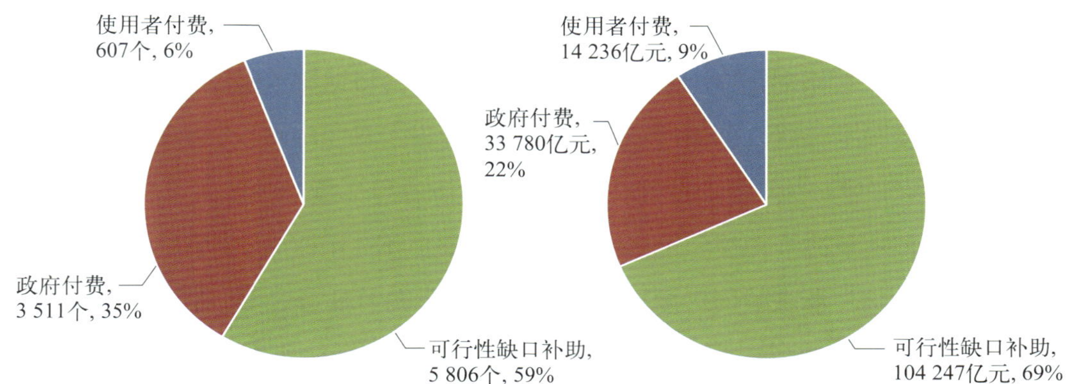

图1-9　2020年末管理库项目数和投资额按回报机制分布

资额前3位是BOT12 607亿元、其他1 130亿元以及TOT924亿元。2020年新入库项目数、投资额按运作方式分布如图1-10所示。

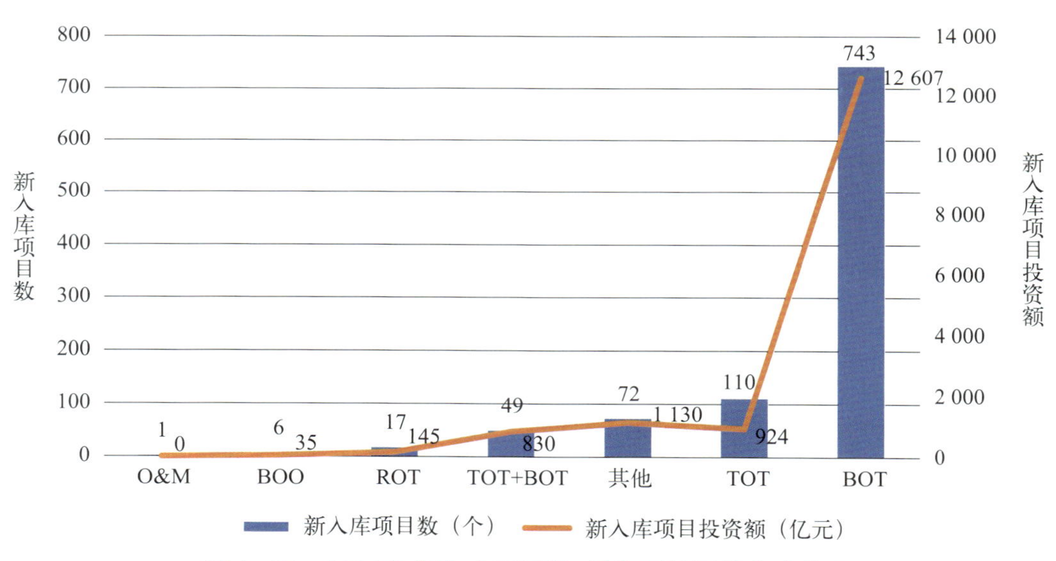

图1-10　2020年新入库项目数、投资额按运作方式分布

按照累计项目数排序，管理库前3位是BOT7 789个、其他971个以及TOT+BOT391个，合计占项目库项目数的92.2%。按累计投资额排序，管理库前3位是BOT1.2万亿元、其他2.0万亿元以及TOT+BOT3 891亿元。截至2020年末管理库各运作方式项目数、投资额情况如图1-11所示。

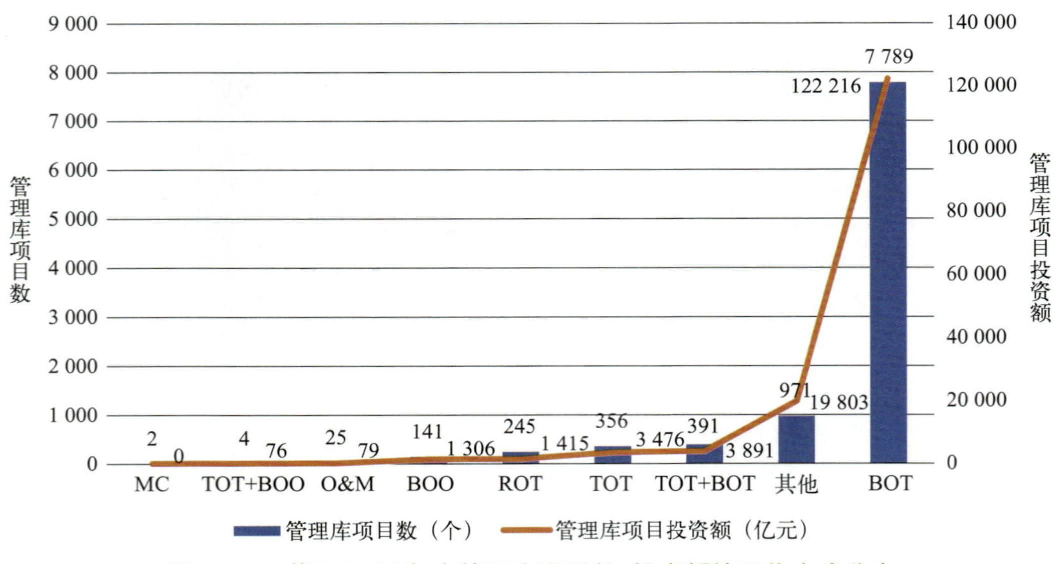

图 1-11　截至 2020 年末管理库项目数、投资额按运作方式分布

1.5.6　绿色低碳项目占比情况

绿色低碳项目占比逐步上升。2020年项目库新增项目中绿色低碳项目646个，项目投资额为6 777亿元，分别占比64.7%与43.2%，其中已落地项目数118个，落地率为18.3%。截至2020年末，项目库中绿色低碳项目累计5 762个，占比为58.1%，累计投资金额5.5万亿元，占比为36.3%，其中已经落地3 954个，落地率为68.6%。

2

指标体系与计算方法

2.1 指标体系构建

2.1.1 指标体系基本原则

指标体系是否科学、合理，直接关系到指数编制的质量和结果评估的可靠性。为此，设定的指标体系必须客观合理地、尽可能全面地反映影响PPP信息透明度的所有因素，同时也要考虑到数据的可获得性、可靠性等。要建立一套既科学又可执行的PPP市场透明度评价指标体系，必须遵照一定的原则。因此，课题组首先明确了PPP透明度评价指标体系构建中应该坚持的几个原则，主要包括层次性原则、共通性原则、连续性原则等。

（1）层次性原则。层次性指的是指标体系自身的多重性。由于PPP信息内容涵盖的多层次性，指标体系也必须由多层次结构组成，才能反映出各层次的特征。同时，各个要素相互联系构成一个有机整体，能从项目的不同阶段、不同层次反映PPP市场透明度的总体情况。具体而言，参考PPP相关信息公开管理办法的精神，PPP市场透明度的指标体系可以分为总指数、分阶段二级指标和底层具体指标三个层次，由此透明度指数可以分为总指数，以及识别阶段、准备阶段、采购阶段、执行阶段和移交阶段五个阶段的分指数等。当然，考虑到不同项目可能处于不同的阶段，因而并不是每一个项目的透明度指数都完整囊括这五个阶段。

（2）共通性原则。课题组评价的是每一个PPP项目的信息公开透明度，由于项目会存在一些特有的信息，因而基于可比性的考虑，课题组主要选取那些适用于全体项目样本的指标。那些不是对所有项目均适用的指标，如“设计文件及批复文件”“项目采购阶段调整、更新的政府方授权文件”“增减资情况”等，课题组暂时没有将其纳入指标体系，但会在报告末尾对完善该类指标信息披露工作的管理办法提供一些政策建议。

（3）连续性原则。本次编制的指数是课题组第四次评估PPP市场的透明度，因而指标体系不仅要反映2020年我国PPP项目信息披露的实际情况，而且要考虑到其与前面三年的衔接，保持指数的连续性，当然也要考虑到未来可能的变更。换言之，指标体系应具备较强的动态适应性。课题组希望可以通过长期追踪的方式，对我国PPP市场的信息公开状况进行持续性评估。

（4）突出性原则。指标的选择要尽量全面，但同时也应该区别主次和轻重，要突出重点。对于某些特别重要的指标，要尽量多地选择相关字段。同时，课题组通过专家问卷调查的方式，对比较重要的指标设置高分，对不太重要的信息设置低分。例如物有所值评价方面、财政承受能力论证方面，可以赋予比那些基本项目信息等更重要的分数值。

（5）公正性原则。作为一个政策效果评估的报告，PPP市场透明度报告发布后，预期会对不同的地区和项目产生一定的影响。因此，透明度指数报告必须坚持公平、公正的原则，做到一视同仁，坚持成绩和问题都点到、都说透。既要如实展示不同地区、不同类型的PPP项目信息公开的客观状况，同时也要尽可能讲清楚导致各地区和行业等PPP市场透明度指数结果出现差异的各类原因，特别是那些客观、外生的原因，要尽量做到公正公允。

（6）时点性原则。本次评估的是截止到2020年12月31日财政部PPP综合信息平台管理库里所有的项目信息披露情况，属于存量概念，即评估的对象是截至这个时点所有PPP项目历史累加的信息披露情况。囿于数据的可获得性，课题组的评估没有涉及这些信息披露的具体时间等动态特征，例如，部分指标作为适时公开指标，理论上课题组除了可以评估其是否披露外，还可以评估其披露的及时性，这也是信息披露工作的重要评价方面，然而课题组无法获得相关指标披露具体时点等细节信息，因而这方面的信息就暂时无法纳入课题组的指标体系。

2.1.2 指标体系设计依据

（1）设计依据。评估PPP市场的信息公开现状，首要的依据就是相关政策文件。2017年1月23日，财政部正式发布《政府和社会资本合作（PPP）综合信息平台信息公开管理暂行办法》（即1号文），这是主管部门对PPP项目信息披露工作的主要操作指南。各地的PPP项目信息披露工作均是按照该文件执行的。因此,1号文的政策细则便是课题组设计PPP市场透明度指标体系时最主要的依据。课题组设计的指标体系主要来自该1号文的要求,1号文中没有要求的信息,原则上就不进入课题组的指标体系,这样处理是为了使指标体系对不同地区而言是公平公正的。

(2)数据来源。根据主管部门财政部政府和社会资本合作中心的规定,各地的PPP项目均要在财政部政府和社会资本合作中心网站首页开设的PPP综合信息平台系统中进行入库和公布。考虑到数据来源的一致性,课题组选择该PPP综合信息平台系统作为主要数据来源。因此,本报告中指标设置的主要依据是1号文,数据来源则主要为财政部PPP综合信息平台系统。当然,由于1号文正式实施的时间尚不足够长,因而还存在一些需要完善的地方,比如很多字段在1号文中是要求披露的,但目前在PPP官方信息网站上并没有展示,从而无法纳入指标体系中,只能在未来PPP官方信息网站上披露的信息增加后再进一步完善相关指标体系。最后,由于财政部PPP综合信息平台上披露的个别字段的说法略有调整,因而在这次评估中也对相关指标进行了同步更新。

(3)评估对象。财政部办公厅于2017年11月10日发布《关于规范政府和社会资本合作(PPP)综合信息平台项目库管理的通知》,要求在全国PPP综合信息平台项目库基础上构建储备库和管理库。该文认为:“储备库是指识别阶段项目,是地方政府部门有意愿采用PPP模式的备选项目,但尚未完成物有所值评价和财政承受能力论证的审核。管理库是指准备、采购、执行和移交阶段项目。”结合PPP主管部门的政策意见,课题组将分析对象限定在至少已经进入准备阶段的项目,即已经进入管理库中的项目。此外,课题组也剔除了个别在PPP综合信息平台中无法查询到的项目。最终纳入课题组分析对象的样本共计9 662个,与2019年相比有一定的增加。

(4)获取方式。课题组以政府和社会资本合作中心网站可获取数据为基础①,同时参考2017年1号文中的要求来筛选及获取指标,并对其进行归类。经过课题组的整理,指标体系共包含68个指标字段,课题组对其进行了逐个提取,包括网站直接阅读提取和下载PDF文件阅读提取等方式。

---

① 财政部PPP中心也向课题组直接提供了部分数据。课题组对此表示感谢。

在68个字段中，部分指标的信息需要阅读相应PDF文件后方可提取，然而课题组在人工阅读后发现，其中存在“伪造”的样本：一些项目显示某个指标上传了PDF附件，但实际上只是一个空白文件或虚假文件，这是因为依据系统规定，该PDF文件是必填项，如不上传，整个项目就无法上网入库，也无法进行下一步操作，因此，为了整个项目信息的入库工作，一些项目选择了上传一个虚假的或空白的PDF文件。为了甄别并在未来减少这些“虚假上传”的行为，保障评估工作的科学和公平，课题组对所有项目的所有PDF文件进行了细致的人工核实，并对这些“虚假上传”行为进行“惩罚”。具体而言，对于PDF文件指标，课题组设置的得分细则为：上传文件且为真，可以赋值为1；没有上传文件，赋值为0；上传文件但为假文件，则赋值为−1。此外，还有部分文件字段上传不够全面，对于这种情形，课题组将其赋值为0.5。

2.1.3 指标体系具体构建

根据1号文的要求，PPP项目的有些信息应该即时公开，而有些信息则可以适时公开。其中，即时公开的指标很容易处理，但适时公开指标则比较棘手，原因是课题组需要界定什么时候公开算是“适时”，而课题组无法获得项目进入某个阶段的具体时间或该信息何时就应该被披露等信息。不过，按照1号文的规定，多数适时公开都是指“进入执行阶段的6个月内公开”，因此，为了克服这一难题，课题组延续前面三年的做法，决定选择2020年6月底进入执行阶段的项目作为适时公开的分析对象，这样对于在2020年6月底之前已经进入执行阶段的项目，如果截至2020年12月31日仍未公开对应的信息，课题组就可以判定该项目没有“适时”公开相应信息，换句话说，适时公开的工作做得不到位。

这样处理后，即时公开信息对应的研究样本和适时公开信息对应的研究样本就存在差异了。具体而言，截至2020年12月底进入管理库的总样本有9 662个，这些样本都可以作为即时公开透明度的评估样本；但在2020年6月底以前进入执行阶段的样本只有5 801个，这些样本将作为适时公开透明度的评估样本。对于单个项目而言，有些项目同时包含了即时公开和适时公开的信息，有些项目则仅包含即时公开的信息，无法放在一个框架下来评估。因此，对于单个项目的信息透明度而言，PPP信息透明度指数就包含两个独立的指标，一个是即时公开透明度指数，另一个是适时公开透明度指数。不过考虑到最终主要在地区和行业领域等类别层面上对PPP市场透明度进行评估分析，因此，在总指数计算上，课题组将通过层次分析法对即时公开透明度指数和适时公开透明度指数进行赋权，在省份、行业等层面上合成一个PPP市场透明度的总指数。

即时公开透明度指数和适时公开透明度指数下面均包括分阶段指数和具体指标两个层次。PPP项目一般分为五个阶段：识别阶段、准备阶段、采购阶段、执行阶段和移交阶段，但我国目前还没有进入移交阶段的PPP项目，因此，无论是即时公开透明度指数还是适时公开透明度指数，都暂不包含这一阶段。此外，由于对适时公开的指标，执行阶段也缺少合适的指标字段，因而适时公开透明度指数也不包含执行阶段的信息。由此，最终即时公开透明度指数包含识别阶段、准备阶段、采购阶段和执行阶段四个阶段，适时公开透明度指数则包含识别阶段、准备阶段和采购阶段三个阶段。

最终的指标体系层级如图2-1所示，即时公开透明度指数和适时公开透明度指数的具体指标体系则分别如表2-1和表2-2所示。

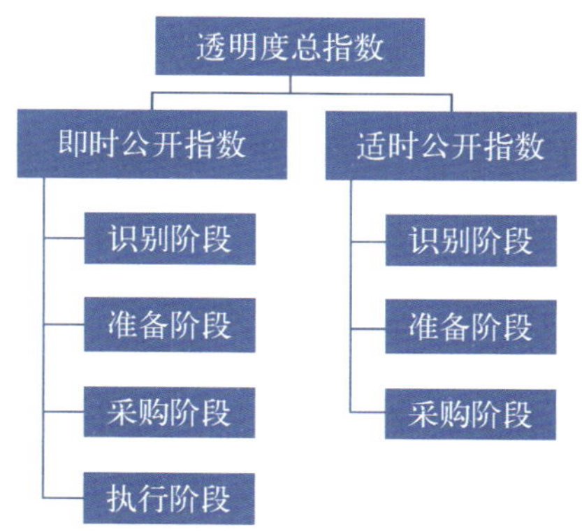

图2-1 PPP透明度指标体系层级

表2-1 PPP即时公开信息透明度指数指标体系

一级指标	具 体 指 标	备注
识别阶段	项目总投资	
	拟合作期限	
	二级行业	

（续表）

一级指标	具 体 指 标	备注
识别阶段	项目运作方式	
	回报机制	
	项目发起时间	
	发起类型	
	发起人名称	
	项目概况	
	项目联系人	
	项目联系电话	
	财政联系人	
	财政联系电话	
	项目用地总面积	
	计划开发年度	
	采购社会资本方式的选择	
	实施方案描述	
	项目合作范围（识别）	
	物有所值定性评价指标及权重、评分标准、评分结果	
	物有所值评价通过与否的评价结论（含财政部门对报告的审核意见）	
	本项目以及年度全部已实施和拟实施的PPP项目财政支出责任数额及年度预算安排情况，以及每一年度全部PPP项目从预算中安排的支出责任占一般公共预算支出比例情况	
	通过财政承受能力论证与否的结论	
准备阶段	拟引入社会资本投资额	
	政府拟出资额	
	审核通过实施方案的政府名称	
	本级政府对实施方案审核通过时间	
	本级人民政府对实施机构即PPP项目合同的政府方签约主体的授权文件	
	政府对实施方案的审核通过文件	

（续表）

一级指标	具 体 指 标	备注
采购阶段	项目资格预审公告（含资格预审申请文件）	
	预中标及成交结果公告；中标、成交结果公告及中标通知书	
	项目本级行业主管部门对拟签署PPP合同的审核意见	
	项目本级财政部门对拟签署PPP合同的审核意见	
	项目本级法制部门对拟签署PPP合同的审核意见	
	项目本级人民政府是否批准了拟签署的PPP合同	
	批准日期	
	项目本级人民政府对PPP项目合同中约定的政府跨年度财政支出责任纳入中期财政规划的审核意见	
	审核日期	
执行阶段	项目公司名称	
	项目公司成立时间	
	项目公司注册资金	
	项目公司经济性质	
	股东认缴	
	本级人民政府对政府方出资代表的授权	

表2-2　PPP适时公开信息透明度指数指标体系

一级指标	具 体 指 标	备注
识别阶段	物有所值评价报告及批复附件	
	财政承受能力论证报告及批复附件	
	新建或改扩建项目建议书及批复文件	
	可行性研究报告	
	设计文件及批复文件	
	存量公共资产或权益的资产评估报告	
准备阶段	物有所值评价完成时间	
	财政承受能力论证完成时间	
	审核通过的项目实施方案及修正案	

（续表）

一级指标	具 体 指 标	备注
采购阶段	资格预审：公告时间	
	资格预审：预审时间	
	项目采购：公告时间	
	采购结果：响应文件评审时间	
	采购结果：结果确认谈判时间	
	采购结果：政府审核时间	
	采购结果：合同签署时间	
	采购结果：合同公布时间	
	采购结果：合同公布媒体	
	合同签订的项目投资额	
	采购文件	
	资格预审专家评审结论性意见及资格预审专家名单	
	响应文件专家评审结论性意见及评审专家名单	
	确认谈判工作组成员名单	
	已签署的PPP项目合同	
	本项目政府支出责任确认文件或更新调整文件，以及同级人大（或人大常委会）将本项目财政支出责任纳入跨年度预算的批复文件	

2.1.4 其他核心问题说明

本报告主要评估是否进行了信息披露，而不是信息披露内容的“质量”。本报告评估的主要内容是PPP项目的信息披露工作，包括这些信息披露的完整程度、重要程度等的区分，但除了明显造假外，课题组的评估不涉及其披露的具体内容的“质量”和“优劣”。具体而言，对于一项指标，一个项目公开披露了其相关信息，在课题组的评估中就是得分的，但该信息中反映的具体工作可能做得很好，也可能做得很差，这暂时不在课题组的评估范围内。例如，对于财政承受能力论证报告的PDF文件，作为一个非常重要的信息，课题组通过人工核查的方法，一一核实其披露情况，同时专家打分中也可能对其赋予较高的分值，这些都是评估中要考虑的因素。至于财政承受能力论证报告做得是否规范、科学，论证是否充分，结论是否可靠等内容，则不在课题组的评估范围内。因为从逻辑上讲，即便这份财政承受能力论证报告不太规范，或者质量不高，但只要有关责任方选择了真实公开披露该报告，那在信息披露工作上就是得分的。当然，未来课题组会考虑超越"信息透明度评估"的范畴，对这些重点报告中所反映的某地或某领域PPP工作的规范性进行重点的专题评估。

2.2 指数计算方法

2.2.1 计算方法简介

在多指标综合评价中，权重确定直接影响评价的结果。确定权重的方法有很多，根据计算权重时原始数据的来源不同，大体上可分为主观赋权法和客观赋权法两大类。主观赋权法主要是由专家根据经验主观判断而得到，如Delphi法、层次分析法（The Analytic Hierarchy Process，AHP）、专家打分法等，这类方法能纳入权威专家对不同指标之间的相对重要程度的考量，但客观性稍差。客观赋权法主要是依据各指标的具体数值计算而得到，它不依赖于人的主观判断，因而客观性较强，但不一定能科学反映不同指标之间的相对重要程度，也不一定能满足决策者的主观要求。客观赋权法这类方法的代表有主成分分析法和变异系数法等。主观赋权法和客观赋权法各有优劣，本项目最终选择的是主观赋权法。具体而言，在计算各准则层指标对上层目标的权重时，课题组使用层次分析法；而在计算各具体指标对上一层准则层的权重时，课题组则选择了专家打分法。①

2.2.2 层次分析法

层次分析法是一种系统分析与决策的综合评价方法，它可以较合理地解决定性

① 课题组在计算各具体指标对上一层准则层的权重时，还使用了变异系数法，结果发现变异系数法与专家打分法得出的结果非常一致。最终选择专家打分法是因为这一方法更能够体现包括行业主管部门、高校学者、社会资本方在内的社会各界对不同指标重要性的看法与态度，而不是仅仅依赖于不同指标之间的统计特征，更有利于各个地区发现PPP信息披露工作中存在的问题并有针对性地改进。

问题定量化的处理过程。层次分析法的主要特点是通过建立层次结构，把人们的判断转化为若干因素两两之间重要性的比较，从而把难以量化的定性判断转化为可操作的定量判断。

在所构建的层次分析模型中，通过调查判断，形成判定矩阵。当检验判定矩阵通过一致性检验时，则可以接受判定矩阵，并计算得出各指标的权重值；若该一致性检验未通过，则意味着判定矩阵的元素值需要调整，直至通过一致性检验为止。具体地，层次分析法的实施步骤如下：

第一步，建立层次结构模型。通过对影响PPP信息透明度各因素的深入分析，将有关各因素按从属关系分解成若干层次，最上层为目标层，中间层为准则层，具体的指标在最下层。本报告的层级结构模型如图2-1所示。

第二步，构建判定矩阵。构建判定矩阵，比较两两具体指标之间的相对重要性。根据本项目构建的PPP项目透明度层级示意图，共涉及两个分类指数，因而涉及三个判定矩阵，分别是总指数判定矩阵（判定即时公开透明度指数和适时公开透明度指数在合成PPP市场透明度总指数时的相对重要性）、即时公开透明度指数判定矩阵（判定识别阶段、准备阶段、采购阶段和执行阶段的分指数在合成即时公开透明度指数时的相对重要性）和适时公开透明度指数判定矩阵（判定识别阶段、准备阶段和采购阶段的分指数在合成适时公开透明度指数时的相对重要性）。

一般地，假设比较n个因素$c_1, c_2, \cdots, c_n$对上一层因素的影响，判定矩阵要求每次两两比较两个因素对上一层因素的相对重要性，这一相对重要性通常用数值1～9来体现，以构成判定矩阵的每个元素赋值c_{ij}（数值的含义如表2-3所示，一般由具备丰富经验的专家来选择）。全部比较结果构成“成对比较矩阵”，也称为“正互反矩阵”。

表2-3 判定矩阵标度含义

标度c_{ij}	定　义	含　义
1	同等重要	c_i和c_j的影响相同
3	稍微重要	c_i比c_j的影响稍强
5	较强重要	c_i比c_j的影响强
7	强烈重要	c_i比c_j的影响明显地强

（续表）

标度c_{ij}	定 义	含 义
9	极端重要	c_i比c_j的影响绝对地强
2,4,6,8	两相邻判断的中间值	c_i与c_j的影响之比在上述两个相邻等级之间
1/2，…，1/9	倒数	c_i与c_j的影响之比为上面α_{ij}的互反数

$$C=\begin{pmatrix} c_{11} & c_{12} & \cdots & c_{1n} \\ c_{21} & c_{22} & \cdots & c_{2n} \\ \vdots & \vdots & \vdots & \vdots \\ c_{n1} & c_{n2} & \cdots & c_{nn} \end{pmatrix}$$

$C=(c_{ij})_{n\times n}, c_{ij}>0, c_{ji}=\dfrac{1}{c_{ij}}, c_{ii}=1$。

若正互反矩阵C满足$c_{ij}\times c_{jk}=c_{ik}$，则称$C$为完全一致性矩阵。

第三步，计算判定矩阵的最大特征值及其特征向量。在运用判定矩阵确定各指标权重时，实际上就是求解判定矩阵的特征向量。通过解正互反矩阵的最大特征值，可求得相应的特征向量，经归一化后即为权重向量。

$$CW=\lambda_{\max}W$$

第四步，一致性检验。首先，计算该n阶判定矩阵的一致性指标值CI。

$$CI=\frac{\lambda_{\max}-n}{n-1}$$

其次，计算平均随机一致性指标RI。从1～9及其倒数中随机抽取数字构成n阶正互反矩阵，计算其最大特征值；重复1 000次，得到1 000个随机正互反矩阵的最大特征值，再计算1 000个最大特征值的均值；计算平均随机一致性指标RI。

$$RI=\frac{k-n}{n-1}$$

最后，计算一致性比率CR，并验证是否一致。

$$CR = \frac{CI}{RI}$$

当$CR < 0.1$时，一般认为矩阵A的不一致程度在容许范围之内，可以用其特征向量作为权向量，否则需对判定矩阵进行修正（重复第二步和第三步），直至CR小于0.1为止。

第五步，计算权重向量。将通过一致性检验的判定矩阵最大特征值所对应的特征向量进行归一化即可得到该层各因素对上层因素的权重大小。

根据这一方法，课题组邀请了包括高校学者代表（3位）、政府主管部门代表（3位）、社会资本方代表（3位）以及中介咨询机构代表（2位）在内的共11位业内权威专家进行三个判定矩阵的填写，并随后通过前文所述的层次分析法计算出各阶段的具体权重，最后求得不同专家所赋权重的平均数。附件一给出了专家判定矩阵调查表。表2-4则给出了根据专家判定矩阵计算出的权重表。其中，在即时公开透明度指数方面，识别阶段、准备阶段、采购阶段和执行阶段的分指数在合成即时公开透明度指数时的权重分别为0.19、0.19、0.4和0.22；在适时公开透明度指数方面，识别阶段、准备阶段和采购阶段的分指数在合成适时公开透明度指数时的权重分别为0.25、0.30和0.45；而在将适时公开透明度指数和即时公开透明度指数加总合成PPP市场透明度总指数时，根据专家填写的判定矩阵计算出两者的权重分别是0.61和0.39。

表2-4 透明度指数专家判定矩阵权重表

即时公开透明度指数		适时公开透明度指数		总指数权重	
阶 段	权 重	阶 段	权 重	分指数	权 重
识别阶段	0.19	识别阶段	0.25	适时公开	0.39
准备阶段	0.19	准备阶段	0.30	即时公开	0.61
采购阶段	0.4	采购阶段	0.45	—	—
执行阶段	0.22	—	—	—	—

2.2.3 具体指标权重计算方法

以上AHP层次分析法确定了中间各层级相对其上一层级的权重大小，还需要确定最下层（即各具体指标）对其上一层的权重大小，对此，课题组使用了专家打分法。

具体而言，根据上文所讨论的内容，特别是其中的“突出性原则”，课题组将通过专家打分的方法，对其中的具体指标进行打分。经过专家打分后，不同的具体指标就相当于包含了一定的权重。课题组将不同的具体指标划分为“一般”“重要”和“特别重要”三种程度，分别用1分、2分和3分来表示，然后交由专家对不同的指标进行赋分。数值越高，代表该具体指标相对越重要。课题组同样邀请了包括高校学者代表、政府主管部门代表、社会资本方代表以及中介咨询机构代表在内的共11位专家进行打分。表2-5和表2-6给出了专家打分的具体结果。需要进一步说明的是，上述不同指标的具体得分都是在某阶段内相互对比的，而不是直接进行全部指标间的对比。为清晰展示这一点，我们在表2-5和表2-6中列出了得分所对应的在本阶段内的具体权重。

表2-5 即时公开透明度指数具体指标专家打分结果

所属阶段	具体指标	得分	权重
识别阶段	项目总投资	2.455	5.52
	拟合作期限	2.273	5.11
	二级行业	1.091	2.45
	项目运作方式	2.182	4.91
	回报机制	2.909	6.54
	项目发起时间	1.636	3.68
	发起类型	1.455	3.27
	发起人名称	1.182	2.66
	项目概况	2.000	4.50
	项目联系人	1.455	3.27
	项目联系电话	1.455	3.27
	财政联系人	1.455	3.27
	财政联系电话	1.455	3.27
	项目用地总面积	2.000	4.50

（续表）

所属阶段	具 体 指 标	得分	权重
识别阶段	计划开发年度	2.000	4.50
	采购社会资本方式的选择	2.455	5.52
	实施方案描述	2.364	5.32
	项目合作范围（识别）	2.182	4.91
	物有所值定性评价指标及权重、评分标准、评分结果	2.545	5.72
	物有所值评价通过与否的评价结论（含财政部门对报告的审核意见）	2.636	5.93
	本项目以及年度全部已实施和拟实施的PPP项目财政支出责任数额及年度预算安排情况，以及每一年度全部PPP项目从预算中安排的支出责任占一般公共预算支出比例情况	2.818	6.34
	通过财政承受能力论证与否的结论	2.455	5.52
准备阶段	拟引入社会资本投资额	2.182	18.2
	政府拟出资额	2.273	18.9
	审核通过实施方案的政府名称	1.727	14.4
	本级政府对实施方案审核通过时间	1.727	14.4
	本级人民政府对实施机构即PPP项目合同的政府方签约主体的授权文件	2.000	16.7
	政府对实施方案的审核通过文件	2.091	17.4
采购阶段	项目资格预审公告（含资格预审申请文件）	2.364	11.2
	预中标及成交结果公告；中标、成交结果公告及中标通知书	2.545	12.1
	项目本级行业主管部门对拟签署PPP合同的审核意见	1.909	9.1
	项目本级财政部门对拟签署PPP合同的审核意见	2.000	9.5
	项目本级法制部门对拟签署PPP合同的审核意见	1.909	9.1
	项目本级人民政府是否批准了拟签署的PPP合同	2.455	11.6
	批准日期	2.455	11.6
	项目本级人民政府对PPP项目合同中约定的政府跨年度财政支出责任纳入中期财政规划的审核意见	2.727	12.9
	审核日期	2.727	12.9
执行阶段	项目公司名称	1.636	15.6
	项目公司成立时间	1.545	14.8

（续表）

所属阶段	具 体 指 标	得分	权重
执行阶段	项目公司注册资金	1.818	17.4
	项目公司经济性质	1.455	13.9
	股东认缴	2.000	19.1
	本级人民政府对政府方出资代表的授权	2.000	19.1

表2-6 适时公开透明度指数具体指标专家打分结果

一级指标	具 体 指 标	得分	权重
识别阶段	物有所值评价报告及批复附件	3.000	18.0
	财政承受能力论证报告及批复附件	3.000	18.0
	新建或改扩建项目建议书及批复文件	2.333	14.0
	可行性研究报告	2.667	16.0
	设计文件及批复文件	2.677	16.1
	存量公共资产或权益的资产评估报告	3.000	18.0
准备阶段	物有所值评价完成时间	1.556	33.3
	财政承受能力论证完成时间	1.556	33.3
	审核通过的项目实施方案及修正案	1.556	33.3
采购阶段	资格预审：公告时间	1.778	5.5
	资格预审：预审时间	1.667	5.2
	项目采购：公告时间	1.889	5.9
	采购结果：响应文件评审时间	1.556	4.8
	采购结果：结果确认谈判时间	1.889	5.9
	采购结果：政府审核时间	1.778	5.5
	采购结果：合同签署时间	1.778	5.5
	采购结果：合同公布时间	1.889	5.9
	采购结果：合同公布媒体	1.444	4.5
	合同签订的项目投资额	2.556	8.0

（续表）

一级指标	具 体 指 标	得分	权重
采购阶段	采购文件	2.889	9.0
	资格预审专家评审结论性意见及资格预审专家名单	2.111	6.6
	响应文件专家评审结论性意见及评审专家名单	2.111	6.6
	确认谈判工作组成员名单	1.222	3.8
	PPP 项目合同附件	2.556	8.0
	本级政府支出责任确认文件	3.000	9.3

2.2.4 指数合成计算过程

在多指标体系综合评价中，合成是指通过一定的算式将多个指标对事物不同方面的评价值综合在一起，以得到一个整体性的评价。可用于合成的数学方法很多，常见的合成模型有加权算术平均合成模型、加权几何平均合成模型、加权算术平均和加权几何平均联合使用的混合合成模型。三种模型有各自的特点和适用场合，并没有优劣之分。在综合比较了三种合成方法之后，课题组选用了加权算术平均合成模型。加权算术平均合成模型的公式如下：

$$d = \sum_{i=1}^{n} w_i d_i$$

其中，d 为综合指数，w_i 为各评价指标归一化后的权重，d_i 为单个指标的评价得分，n 为评价指标的个数。具体指数合成时，是由下往上逐层汇总而成，先计算各层分组指数，然后由各层分组指数加权汇总得到综合指数（逐层级的计算过程详见第 4 章）。

具体而言，课题组首先通过网站读取方式获取各个具体指标的披露情况并赋值（共四种可能的取值，分别是：1 代表公开且无明显造假行为，0 代表没有公开，0.5 代表部分公开，−1 代表“虚假”公开）。之后根据专家打分法再将这些具体指标的得分加总，计算出某个阶段（比如适时公开的识别阶段等）的得分率（百分制）。随后，在此基础上再根据用层次分析法得出的权重，将不同阶段的分指数合成为即时公开透明度指数或适时公开透明度指数。最后，对即时公开透明度指数和适时公开透明度指数按照层次分析法得出的权重进行加权，计算出PPP市场透明度总指数。

根据课题组的指标体系设计和指数计算方法，理论上某项目的透明度总指数（或者分阶段指数）的满分可以达到100分，表示课题组设计的指标均得到了正确、完整的公开。最低分可以少于0分，即出现负分，表示该项目公布的信息中存在较多的虚假信息。0分则表示课题组设计的指标在该项目中均没有得到公开，也可能表示该项目公开了一些指标但同时也虚假公开了另外一些指标，导致成绩被"抹杀"了，经过课题组"惩罚"后，近似等于所有指标均没有公开，当然这一情况也很不容易出现，特别是对于很多指标合成后的总指数。

需要强调的是，在计算总指数时，由于有些项目没有完整的五个业务阶段，因此，为保证指数的稳定性，课题组通过权重归一化使得相对权重保持一致。例如，在即时公开透明度指数的计算中，识别、准备、采购和执行四个阶段的权重分别为0.19、0.19、0.40和0.22，但某个项目只有前三个阶段，那么这三个阶段的权重就分别为：

识别阶段=0.19/（0.19+0.19+0.40）=0.244

准备阶段=0.19/（0.19+0.19+0.40）=0.244

采购阶段=0.40/（0.19+0.19+0.40）=0.512

3

指数基本结果与总体分析

3.1 样本数据基本情况

3.1.1 样本概况

根据前文的介绍，课题组将PPP市场透明度指数编制分为即时公开透明度指数和适时公开透明度指数两部分。其中，即时公开透明度指数涉及9 962个项目样本，较2019年增加了564个；适时公开透明度指数则涉及5 801个项目，较2019年增加了639个。此外，在2020年的9 962个总样本中，处于准备阶段、采购阶段和执行阶段的项目分别有795个、1 889个和6 978个。从图3-1中可以看出，相对于2019年而言，2020年的项目样本中进入执行阶段和采购阶段的样本占比略微上升，处于准备阶段的样本占比则有所下降。

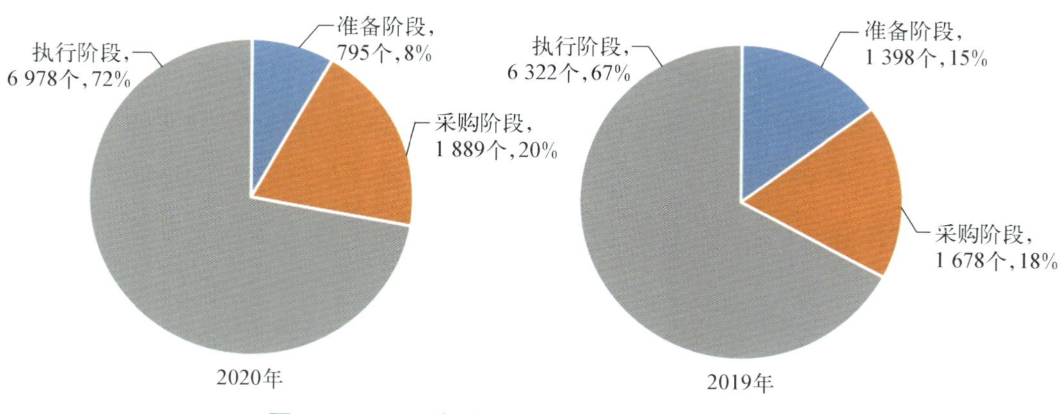

图3-1　2019年和2020年项目样本阶段分布

在下文，我们将发现2020年PPP市场透明度总指数与2019年相比变动很小。

3.1.2 指标构建

在第2章有关指标体系的介绍中，我们已经知道，本指数共包含68个指标字段，基本来自政府和社会资本合作中心网站，对于其中的31个指标字段，课题组需要从政府和社会资本合作中心网站上进行人工读取，主要目的是核实其真实性。在这些指标的构建中，对37个直接从网站或政府和社会资本合作中心获取的数据，课题组直接对其进行0和1的赋值，即某项目公布了该项指标，就赋1分，没有公布这些指标，就赋0分。而对于从政府和社会资本合作中心网站人工采集的指标，课题组对其打分更加细化：完整公布该指标信息，赋1分；部分公布，为0.5分；没有公布，为0分；显示公开了该信息（如有PDF附件）但为假文件或错误文件，则设为−1分，以示惩戒。

对部分公开和错误公开的样本，这里需要再稍作解释。所谓部分公布，主要是指该指标信息实际上包含了多个信息，但只公布了其中的一部分。例如，对于“物有所值定性评价指标及权重、评分标准、评分结果”，如果只公布了评分标准，或者只公布了评分结果，就只给0.5分。再如，对于物有所值评价报告、财政承受能力论证报告，文件要求是公布“物有所值评价报告及本级行业主管部门会同财政部门的审核通过意见”以及“财政承受能力论证报告及本级财政部门的审核通过意见”等，有些项目只公布其中的物有所值评价报告或财政承受能力论证报告，没有公布批复文件，或者情况相反，对这类情况，课题组也给0.5分。而赋值为-1分的所谓错误公开，主要情形为上传的PDF附件是空白文档、错误文档，以及信息的张冠李戴等情形。不过，对于极少一部分附件，虽然没有实质内容，但对为什么没有这些内容进行了合理化解释，例如，项目在政策要求之前就已经运行，根据不溯及既往的原则，课题组不认定这种解释文件为错误公开，以免产生“误伤”。

这里以适时公开的“物有所值评价报告及本级行业主管部门会同财政部门的审核通过意见”为例，来说明课题组手工数据采集的基本情况。如图3−2所示，在5 801个适时公开评估样本中，完整公开“物有所值评价报告及本级行业主管部门会同财政部门的审核通过意见”的样本有4 829个，部分公开的有941个，没有公开的有15个，公开但文件为假文件、错误文件的样本有16个。与2019年相比，该指标完整公开率从81%上升到2020年的83%，虚假公开比率从0.54%上升到1%，未公开比率从11%大幅下降至0%。

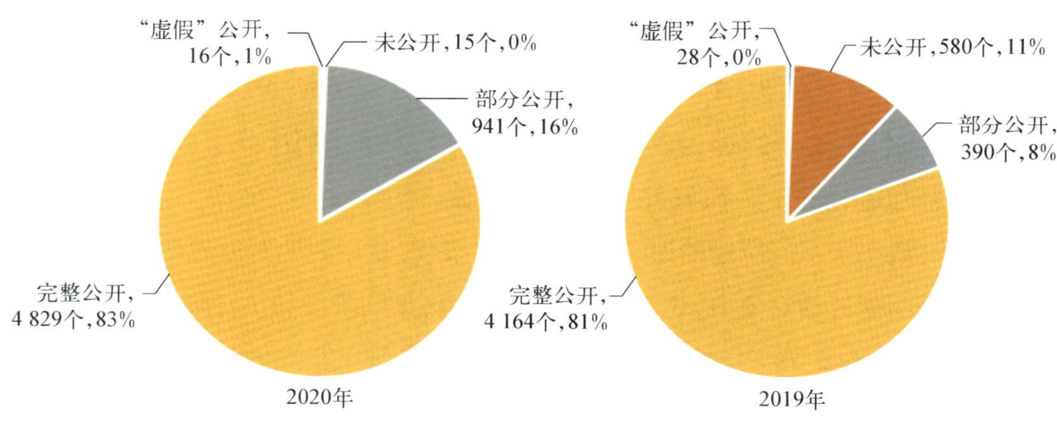

图3-2 物有所值评价报告及附件披露情况

最后，这些具体指标的公开程度得分再乘以上一章关于具体指标相对重要程度的专家评分，即可得到该指标的具体分数，进而可以逐级计算得到全国或某地区的PPP市场透明度指数。

3.2 全国总指数计算

3.2.1 指数合成

计算得到各指标的具体得分后，就可以计算出某个PPP项目在某阶段的得分率（标准化为100），这也就是透明度指数在该阶段的分指数。我们首先以适时公开透明度指数中的识别阶段为例进行说明，这个阶段包含6个信息，分别为"物有所值评价报告及本级行业主管部门会同财政部门的审核通过意见""财政承受能力论证报告及本级财政部门的审核通过意见""新建或改扩建项目建议书及批复文件""可行性研究报告或资金申请报告或申请核准项目的报告，及相关主管部门对上述报告的批复、批准或核准等文件；存量公共资产的资产评估报告""设计文件及批复文件"和"存量公共资产或权益的资产评估报告及存量资产或权益转让时所可能涉及到的各类方案等"。这6个指标在专家评分过程中的得分分别为3分、3分、2.333分、2.667分、2.667分和3分，这样，在适时公开的识别阶段总分就是16.667分。假如某个项目在识别阶段6个指标的信息公开中分别被判定为1（完全公开）、1（完全公开）、0.5（部分公开）、0.5（部分公开）、0（未公开）和−1（“虚假”公开），那么该项目在识别阶段的得分率就为［1×3+1×3+0.5×2.333+0.5×2.667+0×2.667+（−1）×3］/16.667×100=33。这个33即为该项目在适时公开阶段的透明度分指数。同理，可得到即时公开和适时公开各个阶段的透明度分指数。

表3-1给出了不同阶段的即时公开透明度指数，从中我们可以看出，在9 962个即时公开透明度评估对象中，识别阶段、准备阶段、采购阶段和执行阶段的平均指数分别为95.58、90.41、78.85和764.85。相对而言，在识别阶段和准备阶段，PPP项目信息披露较为理想，采购阶段和执行阶段的信息公开则差一些。从管理机制而言，识别阶段和准备阶段的信息大多是PPP项目入库时就必须提交的相关信息，由于入库时主管部门审查较严，因而指数普遍较高，但进入采购阶段和执行阶段后的项目，信息是否按照要求及时上传到PPP综合信息平台，并不妨碍项目工作往前推进，信息公开的监管工作缺乏强硬抓手，从而导致采购阶段和执行阶段的指数较低。此外，与2019年比较，识别阶段、准备阶段和采购阶段的指数均有上升，但执行阶段的指数则有下降。

表3-1　不同阶段的即时公开透明度指数

阶　段	2020年			2019年		
	样本量	均　值	标准差	样本量	均　值	标准差
识别阶段	9 662	95.58	3.30	9 398	89.71	4.38
准备阶段	9 662	90.41	16.61	9 398	84.48	25.39
采购阶段	8 866	78.85	23.24	8 000	73.61	21.19
执行阶段	6 978	64.85	32.15	6 322	71.17	28.86

表3-2给出了即时公开各个阶段透明度指数的具体分布，从中可以看出一些信息公开较好的项目在某些阶段指数可以达到100，但一些信息公开工作不到位的项目在某阶段的指数可能出现负值。我们在前文已经多次介绍过，这是因为部分项目上传的PDF文件附件中有假文件、错误文件等，而被课题组进行了“扣分”惩罚。我们关注这些“异常”项目，对其进行特别处理，是希望这样能够敦促相关责任部门尽

快改进这些方面的工作，补齐短板，推动PPP项目规范化管理。不过，相对而言，我们更关注大多数项目的信息公开情况，因为大多数项目的信息透明度指数结果才能代表整个PPP市场的信息透明程度。因此，我们在表3-2中也给出了不同阶段透明度分指数的25%和75%两个分位数对应的具体数值。对比2020年和2019年即时公开各阶段透明度指数分布可以看出：2020年的即时公开识别阶段信息公开工作要优于2019年，2020年即时公开识别阶段的25分位数和75分位数分别为 94.27和100，两项数值分别高于2019年的88.64和92.21；在那些指数较高的项目上，这两年的即时公开准备阶段信息公开工作没什么差异，因为这两年的75分位数和最大值完全相同；但从采购阶段看，在那些指数较低的项目上，2020年的即时公开信息工作稍优于2019年，2020年即时公开采购阶段的25分位数为76.71，2019年的这一数值为74.14；最后我们考察执行阶段，2020年即时公开执行阶段的25分位数和75分位数分别为 53.91和90.43，两项数值分别低于2019年的61.74和100，这表明在那些指数较低的项目上，2020年的即时公开执行阶段信息公开工作相对比较糟糕，不如2019年。总体来看，细致考察指数分布得到的结论与表3-1一致，在即时公开方面，2020年识别阶段和准备阶段的信息公开工作比2019年要好一些，不过采购阶段和执行阶段则稍劣于2019年。

表3-2 即时公开各阶段透明度指数的分布

阶 段	2020年				2019年			
	最小值	25分位	75分位	最大值	最小值	25分位	75分位	最大值
识别阶段	66.26	94.27	100	100	58.44	88.64	92.21	97.56
准备阶段	−17.425	83.33	100	100	−34.09	66.67	100	100
采购阶段	0	76.71	88.36	100	0	74.14	87.07	100
执行阶段	0	53.91	90.43	100	0	61.74	100	100

表3-3给出了不同阶段的适时公开透明度指数，从中我们可以看出，在5 801个适时公开透明度评估对象中，识别阶段、准备阶段、采购阶段的平均指数分别为50.50、97.83和74.80。在不同阶段的比较上，相对而言，识别阶段较差，而准备阶段的

信息公开工作较为理想，我们判断这主要是因为在识别阶段的适时公开信息中，需要公开的主要信息包括物有所值评价报告、财政承受能力论证报告等几个核心文件，对于这些文件，一些项目的信息公开工作做得不太理想。对比2019年的各阶段适时公开透明度指数可以发现，准备阶段这两年的平均指数差别不大，采购阶段2020年平均指数略高于2019年，识别阶段2020年平均指数比2019年高5.87。

表3-3　不同阶段的适时公开透明度指数

阶　段	2020年			2019年		
	样本量	均　值	标准差	样本量	均　值	标准差
识别阶段	5 801	50.50	13.71	5 162	44.63	20.03
准备阶段	5 801	97.83	6.86	5 162	95.81	11.66
采购阶段	5 801	74.80	11.01	5 162	70.37	16.18

表3-4给出了适时公开各阶段透明度指数的具体分布，包括最小值、最大值、上四分位数和下四分位数。从中我们可以看到，在适时公开的信息中，准备阶段和采购阶段的大部分项目的信息公开工作都较好，其中，至少有75%的项目的适时公开准备阶段透明度分指数为100。而识别阶段则较差，25%的项目的适时公开识别阶段透明度指数不足43.97。因此，如果想提高PPP项目适时公开信息的整体透明度，可以将焦点集中于物有所值评价报告、财政承受能力论证报告等几个核心报告的规范、完整披露上，相信补齐短板后能让适时公开透明度指数大幅上升。与2019年适时公开各阶段透明度指数对比，2020年识别阶段、准备阶段和采购阶段指数都要略高于2019年。

表3-4　适时公开各阶段透明度指数的分布

阶　段	2020年				2019年			
	最小值	25分位	75分位	最大值	最小值	25分位	75分位	最大值
识别阶段	−51.97	43.97	54.97	100.00	−63.96	43.97	52.97	100
准备阶段	0.00	100	100	100.00	0	100	100	100
采购阶段	0.00	70.42	84.78	94.12	−9.68	62.29	85.12	90.66

3.2.2 总指数结果

在得到各阶段的透明度分指数后，我们就可以按照第2章介绍的用层次分析法得到的各阶段分指数的权重来合成即时公开透明度指数和适时公开透明度指数。表3-5即为即时公开透明度指数和适时公开透明度指数的总体情况。从中可以看出，即时公开透明度指数和适时公开透明度指数平均数值分别为80.37和74.67。与2019年相比，2020年的这两项指标基本保持平稳，数值上略有提高，不过幅度都不大。

表3-5 即时公开和适时公开透明度指数

指　　数	2020年			2019年		
	样本量	均　值	标准差	样本量	均　值	标准差
即时公开透明度指数	9 962	80.37	8.57	9 398	79.14	13.95
适时公开透明度指数	5 801	74.67	3.02	5 162	71.57	13.90

最后，在得到即时公开透明度指数和适时公开透明度指数之后，在全国平均意义上，我们还可以按照用层次分析法计算得到的将即时公开透明度指数和适时公开透明度指数合成总指数时的权重，合成全国PPP市场透明度总指数。结论是：截至2020年12月底，全国PPP市场透明度总指数为78.15（80.37×0.61+74.67×0.39），略高于2019年的76.19。图3-3显示了全国PPP市场

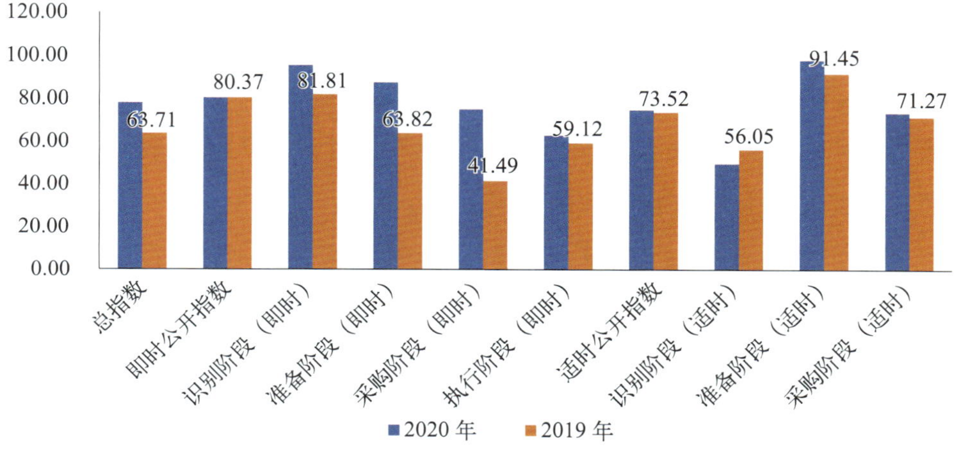

图3-3 全国PPP市场透明度总指数及各阶段指数

透明度总指数、即时公开透明度指数、适时公开透明度指数，以及各阶段透明度分指数的平均结果分布。与前文表3-1到表3-4显示的结果一致，图3-3再一次表明，2020年指数较2019年的变化主要体现为识别阶段、准备阶段和采购阶段分指数的提高以及执行阶段分指数的下降。

3.3 全国总指数的异质性分析

根据上文的分析，全国PPP市场透明度指数实际上是由全国约9 600个PPP项目的透明度指数平均而得到的。正如在上一节我们所看到的，全国PPP项目透明度平均结果可能掩盖了不同项目的异质性。因此，为了对全国的PPP市场透明度有更深入和直观的展示，在本节，我们主要从不同行业、不同类型等角度，对全国PPP市场透明度进行一些总体层面的分析。在后面的两章里，我们还将从省份和城市层面对各地PPP市场透明度进行更详细的讨论。

3.3.1 不同行业的PPP市场透明度指数

我们首先来看不同行业的PPP市场透明度指数。从图3-4中我们可以发现，不同行业的PPP市场透明度指数虽然存在一定的差异，但差异数值并不大。例如，分行业透明度总指数最高的为科技行业79.8，最低的是保障性安居工程行业76.5，最高和最低仅相差3.3。观察不同行业的即时公开透明度指数和适时公开透明度指数，以及不同阶段的分指数，也有类似发现。因此，总体而言，不同行业PPP项目在信息公开上没有呈现出明显的异质性。这表明不同行业的PPP项目在信息披露工作上并没有特别大的不同，或者说现存的PPP项目信息公开的制度规范具有一定的行业普适性。由于不同行业领域的PPP项目往往由不同的行业主管部门来负责具体的运行管理和监督，因而上述结果也说明不同行业主管部门在PPP项目信息公开的管理上并没有很明显的勤懒之分。此外，从图3-4中还可以观察到，除了社会保障，其余行业2020年的PPP市场透明度指数相比2019年均有所提高。

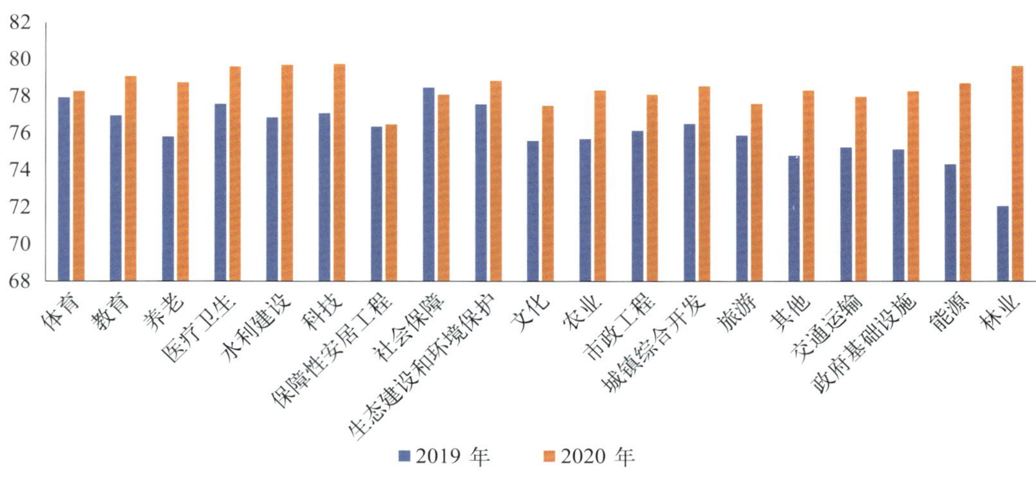

图 3-4 分行业 PPP 市场透明度总指数

3.3.2 示范项目和非示范项目的透明度指数

现在我们来分析示范项目和非示范项目在信息公开方面的差异。如图 3-5 所示，2020 年的示范项目和非示范项目的透明度指数相差不大①，示范项目的总体信息公开程度要略高于非示范项目。总结我们近三年的评估结果，示范项目的透明度指

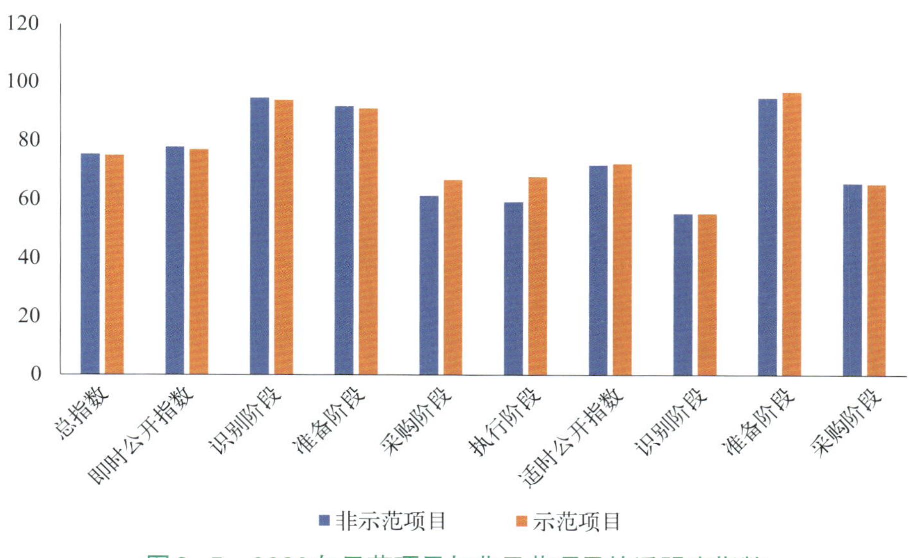

图 3-5 2020 年示范项目与非示范项目的透明度指数

① 2018 年的评估显示了类似的结果，即示范项目的透明度指数与非示范项目的透明度指数差别很小。

数从2018年的74.9提高到2019年的77.19，再提高到2020年的78.90，增长幅度并不大；同样，非示范项目的透明度指数从2018年的75.3增长到2019年的76.01，2020年的这一数值为78.23，增长幅度也不大。这些结果说明，“是否示范项目”这一变量随着时间的推移，越来越不能解释项目间透明度指数的差异。

4

省级指数的排名与分析

4.1 省级透明度总指数结果分析

4.1.1 省级指数总体排名

上一章介绍了全国层面的2020年PPP市场透明度指数的基本情况，本章主要介绍分省份的分析结果。为了得到各省份PPP市场透明度指数，课题组首先基于各个项目的透明度指数计算了各省份即时公开透明度指数和适时公开透明度指数，计算方法是先算出各省份所有项目的即时公开透明度指数和适时公开透明度指数的算术平均，然后按照第2章计算出来的权重合成得出各省份PPP市场透明度指数(即时公开权重为0.61，适时公开权重为0.39)。表4-1给出了2020年32个省级单位(省、直辖市、自治区、新疆生产建设兵团，下同)PPP项目的数量及透明度总指数的具体结果。从中我们可以得到以下几个结论：

第一，总体来看，2020年全国PPP市场透明度总指数省级平均为78.02[①]，与2019年(73.68)相比略有上升，可能的原因是更多新项目进入。而且78.02高于10年来上海财经大学公共政策研究中心发布的历年中国财政透明度评估结果的平均分(2017年各省份财政透明度平均分仅为48.3分)，这显示在相关部门的监管下，PPP市场的信息公开工作要领先于其他财政领域。

第二，省级层面的PPP市场透明度指数基本保持在良好水平，绝大多数省份的透明度指数在70～85之间分布。但与2019年相比，各省份PPP市场透明度指数开始出现一定的离散趋势。2019年各省份PPP市场透明度指数集中在70～80，而2020年则有少数省份的PPP市场透明度指数高于82或低于70，这表明随着PPP项目的持续推进，各省份PPP市场透明度指数开始逐渐分化。具体排名而言，透明度排名第一

① 这里是各个省份透明度总指数的简单算术平均，所以与前文全国总指数的数值略有不同。

的是云南（84.98），排名第二的是山东（83.72），排名第三的是河北（82.99），排名第四的是湖南（82.69），排名第五的是江苏（82.63）。而北京、宁夏、上海、海南、西藏则表现相对较差，它们占据了这份榜单的最后5名。对比2019年的排行榜可以发现，PPP项目信息透明度工作进步最大的省份是青海（79.22），其在全国的排名较上一年上升了12位，在2020年榜单中列第十四位。PPP市场透明度指数排名下降最多的省份是广西，其指数从2019年的77.03下降到了2020年的76.40，虽然只下降了不足1，但由于省份之间指数差距本就很小，因而该省份在2020年全国PPP市场透明度指数排名中仅列第二十七位，相较上一年排名下降了14位。天津、湖南、四川、云南和江苏等省份排名相较上一年均有较大幅度的上升，而广西、甘肃和宁夏等省份排名相较上一年均下降明显。

表4-1　2020年省级PPP市场透明度总指数与排名

省份	2020年项目数量	2020年透明度指数	2020年排名	较上一年排名变化	2019年项目数量	2019年透明度指数
云南	495	84.98	1	+4	481	80.17
山东	434	83.72	2	+2	765	80.20
河北	734	82.99	3	−1	390	81.29
湖南	160	82.69	4	+6	418	77.64
江苏	386	82.63	5	+4	398	77.69
吉林	376	81.82	6	−3	170	80.52
新疆	389	81.71	7	+4	381	77.48
陕西	278	81.25	8	−1	280	77.94
内蒙古	123	80.61	9	−3	283	78.07
甘肃	786	80.52	10	−9	124	81.97
河南	42	79.91	11	+3	752	76.17
安徽	474	79.65	12	−4	474	77.84
广东	551	79.30	13	−1	519	77.20
青海	262	79.22	14	+12	38	70.81
四川	552	78.99	15	+5	557	73.05

（续表）

省份	2020年项目数量	2020年透明度指数	2020年排名	较上一年排名变化	2019年项目数量	2019年透明度指数
山西	103	78.47	16	0	396	74.15
辽宁	406	78.22	17	−2	184	75.80
湖北	419	78.22	18	+3	417	72.96
黑龙江	293	78.17	19	+4	107	72.09
浙江	359	77.60	20	−3	513	73.86
天津	55	77.45	21	+7	49	68.28
福建	241	77.35	22	−4	351	73.80
贵州	507	77.17	23	−4	512	73.76
兵团	418	77.05	24	+3	18	69.28
江西	529	76.91	25	0	355	71.52
重庆	16	76.56	26	−4	43	72.23
广西	57	76.40	27	−14	204	77.03
北京	69	74.73	28	+1	70	67.49
宁夏	43	73.83	29	−5	47	71.57
上海	7	72.40	30	+1	5	60.77
海南	95	69.76	31	−1	96	62.89
西藏	3	56.45	32	0	1	52.22

注：① 本报告表格所涉及的项目数量总体指的是即时公开透明度指数所涉及的9 962个PPP项目，适时公开透明度指数所涉及的5 801个PPP项目是它的一个子集；② “+”表示排名上升，“−”表示排名下降，下同。

4.1.2 即时公开和适时公开省级排名

图4−1和图4−2分别给出了各省份2019年和2020年PPP项目即时公开透明度指数和适时公开透明度指数的分布图。从中我们可以发现：

第一，各省份即时公开透明度指数基本要高于适时公开透明度指数，这一发现与第3章的描述是一致的，再次表明全国各省份PPP项目对适时指标的信息披露工作做得不如即时公开理想。

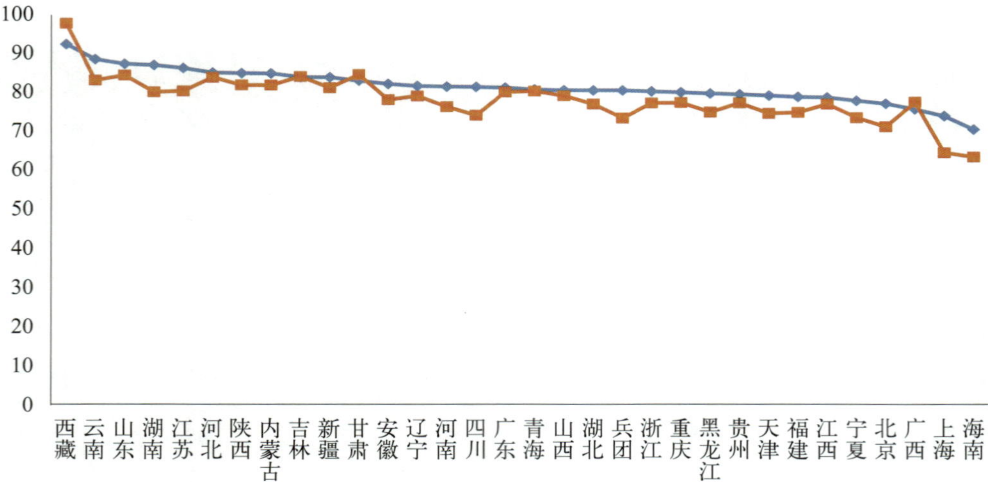

图 4-1　2019 年和 2020 年各省份 PPP 即时公开透明度指数

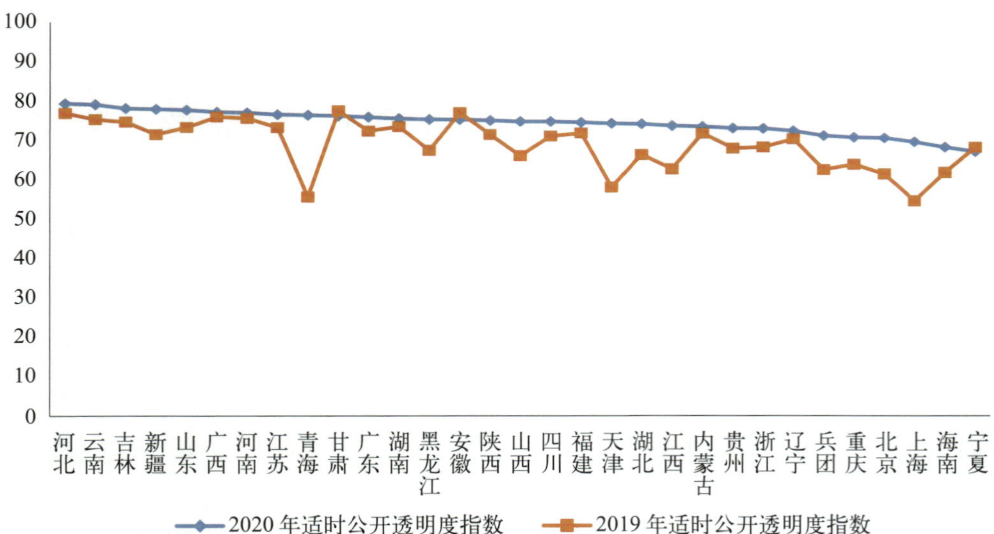

注：其中，西藏由于没有项目涉及适时公布的情况，故无法计算适时公开透明度指数，不参与相关排名。

图 4-2　2019 年和 2020 年各省份 PPP 适时公开透明度指数

第二，各省级行政区的透明度总指数、适时公开透明度指数与即时公开透明度指数的省份排名总体是一致的，但也不是完全相同。由于即时公开指数的权重为 0.61，而适时公开指数的权重为 0.39，不出意外，那些在即时公开透明度方面做得较好的省份会在总指数上获得一个较好的排名，比如除西藏外即时公开前 5 名的省份实际上就是总指数榜单上的前5名。尽管如此，即时公开透明度指数和适时公开透明度指数的省份排名之间还存在一定的差异。即时公开透明度指数排名第四位的湖南，适时公开透明度指数排名第十二位，说明湖南在相关信息即时公开方面的工作开展确实较好，但是在适时公开方面的工作较差。而即时公开透明度指数排名最末的上海，适时公开透明度指数排在倒数第二位，说明上海需要同时加强即时公开和适时公开两方面的工作。两份榜单的差异进一步表明各地区在PPP项目信息公开方面各有优劣，需要取长补短，才能提升整体的透明度，推动PPP项目信息更好地公开。

通过2020年和2019年数据对比可以发现，各省份即时公开透明度指数和适时公开透明度指数的跨期变动没有呈现出显性的规律，表现为有增有减。从即时公开透明度指数变化情况看，有28个省份的指数上升，4个省份的指数下降。即时公开透明度指数上升幅度最大的是上海，从2019年的64.60上升至2020年的74.05，其次是四川、海南和新疆生产建设兵团；而即时公开透明度指数下降幅度最大的是西藏，从2019年的97.89下降至2020年的92.53。从适时公开透明度指数变化情况看，有28个省份的指数上升，3个省份的指数下降。适时公开透明度指数上升幅度最大的是青海，从2019年的55.71上升到2020年的76.60，适时公开透明度指数上升幅度最小的是广西，从2019年的76.12上升到2020年的77.38，仅上涨1.26；适时公开透明度指数下降幅度最大的是安徽，从2019年的77.22下降到2020年的75.49。总体看，多数省份适时公开透明度指数呈现上升趋势，表明它们在PPP项目信息适时公开方面的管理工作不断加强。

4.1.3 透明度指数与项目数量关系

在指数编制过程中，有部分专家以及地方财政部门代表人员曾建议我们将各地区管理的PPP数量因素考虑在内，原因是部分省份需要管理的PPP数量较多，可能增大了其监管和督促信息公开的难度，从而拉低了PPP市场透明度指数。因此，为了具体考察各地管理的PPP项目数量与该地区PPP市场透明度指数的对应关系，我们使用省份的PPP市场透明度总指数和项目数量作散点图并进行线性拟合，结果如图4-3所示。结果表明，省份需要监管的PPP项目数量与该省份PPP市场透明度指数不仅没有明显的负向关系，反而呈现出一定的正相关关系。从统计学意义上讲，“由

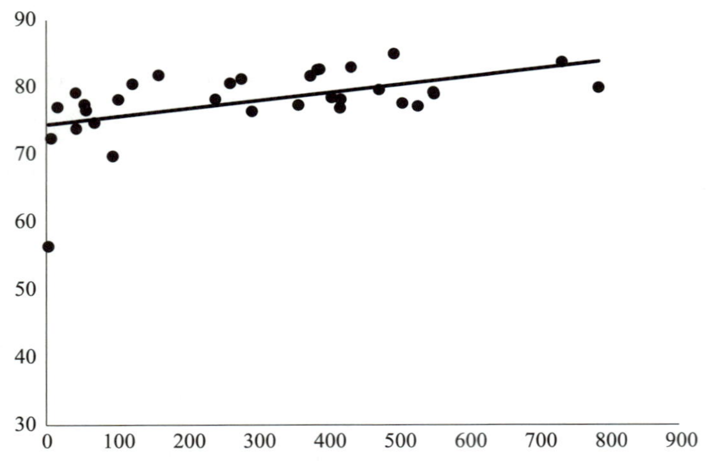

图 4-3　省份 PPP 项目数量与省份 PPP 市场透明度总指数的散点图

于管理了太多的PPP项目，所以造成该地区PPP市场透明度指数较低”的猜测似乎并不成立。

人们另一个可能的疑虑在于，部分省份的PPP项目数量过少，统计学意义不大，是否还有必要参与全国排名。课题组的做法是将所有省级单位全部纳入排名榜，没有在排名时人为删除项目数过少的省级单位，以便全面客观地反映当前各省份PPP信息披露工作的现状。这是因为项目数量多少的界限不好界定，不同的读者存在不同标准，如果读者认为某些省级单位项目过少，忽略这一省份的排名信息并不影响对其他省份PPP市场透明度指数相对排名的解读。此外，一个地区项目数量为什么与PPP市场透明度指数呈现正相关，是一个非常有趣也值得讨论的话题，一个可能的原因是，PPP项目数量多的地区，主管部门安排了更多的管理人员或专门的负责人。

4.2　分阶段省级透明度结果分析

4.2.1　即时公开

接下来我们分析各个省份在即时公开和适时公开各个阶段的信息披露工作成绩。首先，表4-2给出了即时公开和适时公开PPP市场透明度指数省份排名，并且展示了2020年排名相较上一年的变化。在即时公开方面，西藏、云南、山东、湖南和江苏位列排名前5位，而宁夏、北京、广西、上海和海南位列排名最后5位。即时公开透明度指数省份排名上升最多的是西藏，由2019年即时公开排名的第三十二名上升到2020年的第一名；排名下降最多的是广西，由2019年的第十六名下降了14个名次，2020年位列第三十名。在适时公开方面，河北、湖南、新疆、贵州和新疆生产建设兵团位列排名前5位，而湖北、浙江、四川、甘肃、内蒙古排名最末。适时公开透明度指数省份排名上升最多的是青海，由2019年的第三十名跃升至2019年的第八名；排名下降最多的是青海，2020年排名相较上一年下降了29个名次，位列第三十名。

表4-2 即时公开和适时公开透明度指数省份排名

排名	2020年即时公开透明度指数	较2019年变化	2020年适时公开透明度指数	较2019年变化
1	西藏	+31	河北	2
2	云南	+3	湖南	6
3	山东	−1	新疆	12
4	湖南	+8	贵州	16
5	江苏	+5	兵团	21
6	河北	−2	黑龙江	15
7	陕西	−1	山西	16
8	内蒙古	−1	青海	22
9	吉林	−6	云南	−3
10	新疆	−2	山东	−1
11	甘肃	−10	陕西	3
12	安徽	+3	安徽	−10
13	辽宁	+1	海南	14
14	河南	+8	河南	−9
15	四川	+11	广西	−11
16	广东	−5	吉林	−9
17	青海	−8	江西	8
18	山西	−5	上海	13

（续表）

排名	2020年即时公开透明度指数	较2019年变化	2020年适时公开透明度指数	较2019年变化
19	湖北	+1	福建	−7
20	兵团	+8	江苏	−10
21	浙江	−2	宁夏	−2
22	重庆	−5	重庆	2
23	黑龙江	0	辽宁	−6
24	贵州	−6	广东	−13
25	天津	0	北京	3
26	福建	−2	天津	3
27	江西	−6	湖北	−5
28	宁夏	−1	浙江	−10
29	北京	0	四川	−13
30	广西	−14	甘肃	−29
31	上海	−1	内蒙古	−18
32	海南	−1		

表4−3给出了2020年度PPP项目即时公开透明度指数以及即时公开所涉及的各个阶段的透明度分指数省份排名。

表4−3 2020年即时公开透明度指数及各个阶段透明度分指数省份排名

排　名	即时公开透明度指数	识别阶段	准备阶段	采购阶段	执行阶段
1	西藏	西藏	西藏	江苏	云南
2	云南	云南	兵团	湖南	内蒙古
3	山东	湖南	新疆	甘肃	山东
4	湖南	上海	云南	山东	湖南
5	江苏	甘肃	河北	新疆	江苏
6	河北	山东	甘肃	云南	河北
7	陕西	新疆	山东	陕西	吉林

（续表）

排　名	即时公开透明度指数	识别阶段	准备阶段	采购阶段	执行阶段
8	内蒙古	青海	山西	广东	兵团
9	吉林	北京	广西	内蒙古	四川
10	新疆	陕西	吉林	北京	宁夏
11	甘肃	江苏	湖北	福建	陕西
12	安徽	河北	河南	安徽	安徽
13	辽宁	广西	内蒙古	青海	浙江
14	河南	天津	重庆	江西	河南
15	四川	吉林	江西	河北	重庆
16	广东	辽宁	江苏	四川	贵州
17	青海	黑龙江	辽宁	浙江	湖北
18	山西	重庆	湖南	吉林	广东
19	湖北	广东	陕西	宁夏	黑龙江
20	兵团	四川	青海	黑龙江	上海
21	浙江	山西	贵州	天津	福建
22	重庆	江西	黑龙江	河南	海南
23	黑龙江	河南	天津	湖北	新疆
24	贵州	安徽	安徽	贵州	山西
25	天津	浙江	广东	重庆	辽宁
26	福建	兵团	浙江	山西	北京
27	江西	湖北	四川	辽宁	甘肃
28	宁夏	内蒙古	福建	海南	广西
29	北京	宁夏	北京	兵团	青海
30	广西	福建	宁夏	上海	天津
31	上海	贵州	上海	广西	江西
32	海南	海南	海南	西藏	西藏

云南、山东、吉林和河北在各阶段均表现优异且各阶段也相对稳健，并无明显短板。云南在识别阶段、准备阶段、采购阶段和执行阶段均表现不错，使其在即时公开

透明度指数排名中位列第二。河北在识别阶段、准备阶段和执行阶段均表现不错，但其在采购阶段排名为第十五名，导致其在及时公开透明度指数排名中只能位列第六，如将来能在采购阶段更好地做好信息披露工作，排名仍有上升的空间。新疆在识别阶段、准备阶段和采购阶段表现较好，但在执行阶段表现较差，从而拉低了其在即时公开透明度指数中的排名。

宁夏、北京、广西、上海和海南占据了即时公开透明度省级排名的最后5名。其中，上海在识别阶段的排名位列第四，但在其他阶段信息披露工作方面的糟糕表现拉低了其即时公开透明度指数排名。西藏在识别阶段和准备阶段的排名均位列第一，这使其在即时公开透明度指数排名中位列首位。其余三省份则在各个阶段的信息披露工作均表现不佳。

山东在各个阶段的排名都没有十分突出，但最终占据即时公开透明度指数第三名，而识别阶段、采购阶段和执行阶段分别排名第三、第二和第四的湖南几乎在各个阶段的PPP信息透明度指数都要高于山东，但在即时公开透明度指数排名上落后于山东，这反映了各省份PPP项目的阶段分布对课题组研究的最终结果的确存在着一定程度的影响。如果一个省份处于准备阶段的PPP项目占比较高，且这一阶段的工作做得较为出色，那么该省份很容易获得高分，因为按照第3章所述的算法，原本采购阶段和执行阶段的权重被“归并”到准备阶段和识别阶段中去了。相反，如果一个省份处于准备阶段的PPP项目并不多，那么该省份一旦在采购阶段和执行阶段中的工作略有不足，就可能对最终的透明度总指数产生不利影响。为了更清晰地反映这一问题，表4-4列出了各省份PPP项目按阶段的分布，经过对比很容易发现湖南处于准备阶段的项目占比要明显高于山东。当然，需要强调的是，我们这里指出项目分阶段的分布差异，只是为了解读少数省份排名结果及可能的原因，并不是说为了提高PPP市场透明度指数而应该刻意去放缓PPP项目进度。

表4-4　2020年各省份分阶段PPP项目数量

省　份	项目总数量	准备阶段	采购阶段	执行阶段
安徽	474	22	26	426
北京	69	1	5	63

（续表）

省　份	项目总数量	准备阶段	采购阶段	执行阶段
福建	359	19	30	310
甘肃	123	1	20	102
广东	551	29	80	442
广西	293	22	107	164
贵州	529	87	124	318
海南	95	6	13	76
河北	434	25	88	321
河南	786	97	215	474
黑龙江	103	6	22	75
湖北	419	38	100	281
湖南	389	47	68	274
吉林	160	15	27	118
江苏	386	20	66	300
江西	418	28	48	342
辽宁	241	53	85	103
内蒙古	262	16	47	199
宁夏	43	1	6	36
青海	42	2	13	27
山东	734	50	122	562
山西	406	64	147	195
陕西	278	30	57	191
上海	7	2	2	3
四川	552	19	130	403
天津	55	9	14	32
西藏	3	2	1	
新疆	376	13	43	320
兵团	16	2	4	10

（续表）

省　份	项目总数量	准备阶段	采购阶段	执行阶段
云南	495	42	110	343
浙江	507	22	50	435
重庆	57	5	19	33

4.2.2 适时公开

表4-5给出了2020年度PPP项目适时公开透明度指数以及适时公开所涉及的各个阶段的透明度分指数前十省份榜单。同样可以发现，河北和云南在各个阶段表现抢眼，特别是河北在识别阶段和采购阶段排名均列第二。广西依靠其在识别阶段的优秀表现，在适时公开透明度指数排名中位列第三。由于采购阶段的信息披露工作重要性最高（根据专家判定矩阵的计算结果，采购阶段权重为0.45），河北和云南凭借在采购阶段较高的指数占据了适时公开透明度指数排名的第一位和第二位。

表4-5　2020年适时公开透明度指数及各个阶段透明度分指数省份排名

排　名	适时公开透明度指数	识别阶段	准备阶段	采购阶段
1	河北	青海	上海	云南
2	云南	河北	吉林	河北
3	吉林	广西	重庆	吉林
4	新疆	云南	青海	新疆
5	山东	甘肃	河北	河南
6	广西	新疆	山东	山东
7	河南	山东	天津	江苏
8	江苏	江西	辽宁	甘肃
9	青海	安徽	云南	湖南
10	甘肃	吉林	广东	广西
11	广东	广东	黑龙江	黑龙江
12	湖南	天津	广西	广东

（续表）

排名	适时公开透明度指数	识别阶段	准备阶段	采购阶段
13	黑龙江	陕西	福建	四川
14	安徽	江苏	安徽	内蒙古
15	陕西	河南	湖北	山西
16	山西	福建	山西	陕西
17	四川	湖南	河南	安徽
18	福建	浙江	江苏	福建
19	天津	贵州	浙江	湖北
20	湖北	湖北	新疆	青海
21	江西	山西	江西	天津
22	内蒙古	黑龙江	四川	贵州
23	贵州	四川	湖南	江西
24	浙江	内蒙古	陕西	浙江
25	辽宁	兵团	北京	辽宁
26	兵团	辽宁	贵州	北京
27	重庆	重庆	甘肃	兵团
28	北京	上海	海南	海南
29	上海	宁夏	内蒙古	重庆
30	海南	北京	兵团	上海
31	宁夏	海南	宁夏	宁夏

这份榜单的后5名则被重庆、北京、上海、海南和宁夏占据。对比表4-3可以发现，其中北京、上海、宁夏和海南在即时公开信息披露方面的工作表现也不佳（参看前文分析），即时公开透明度指数也排在末尾，说明这些省份PPP项目信息公开的披露工作亟待加强。

我们使用折线图能更清楚地反映省级单位在适时公开或即时公开各个阶段的具体指数结果。图4-4展示了各个省级单位在即时公开各个阶段的指数结果，对比可以发现：识别阶段和准备阶段信息披露最充分，而采购阶段和执行阶段的指数普遍较低。这一结果基本符合预期：识别阶段和准备阶段的很多信息决定了PPP项目能

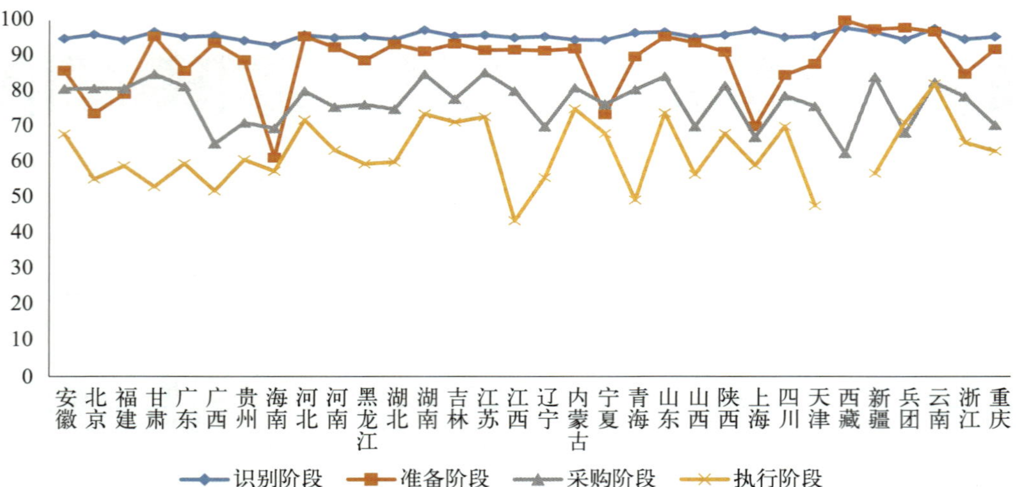

图4-4　2020年各省份即时公开透明度指数各阶段分布

否顺利通过审核，往往更受监管部门和社会参与方的重视，因而指数普遍较高。

图4-5则展示了各个省级单位在适时公开各个阶段的指数结果。与即时公开的情况有所不同，适时公开在识别阶段的信息披露明显不如准备阶段与采购阶段充分。这主要是因为识别阶段涉及两个重要的PDF文件，即“两评”（物有所值评价和财政承受能力论证），课题组对这两份PDF文件进行了颇为严格的审核，很多项目没有披露或者存在“虚假”披露，导致各省份这一阶段的指数普遍相对较低。

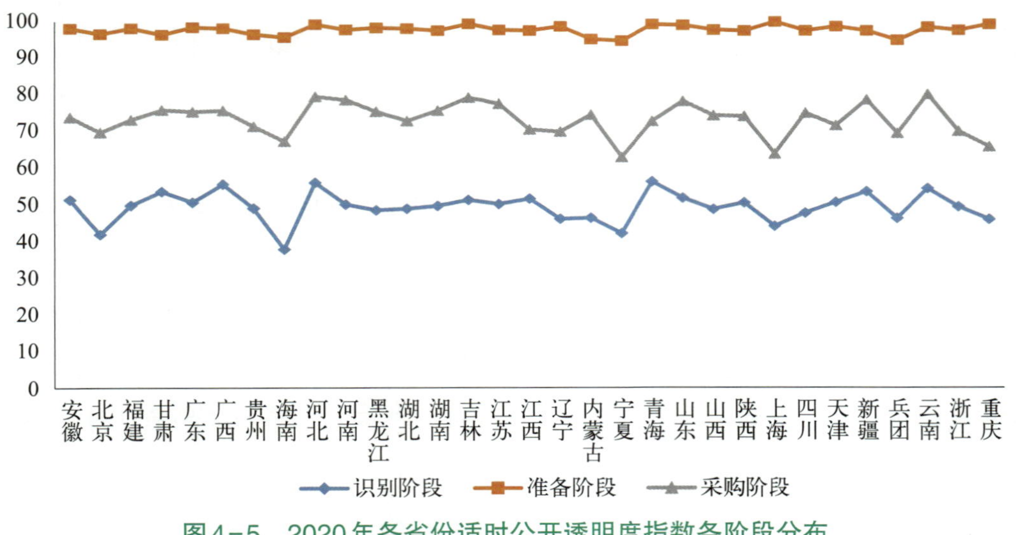

图4-5　2020年各省份适时公开透明度指数各阶段分布

4.3 “两评一案”省级结果分析

所谓“两评一案”，是指“物有所值评价报告及本级行业主管部门会同财政部门的审核通过意见”“财政承受能力论证报告及本级财政部门的审核通过意见”以及“实施方案附件”。“两评一案”在整个PPP项目的识别阶段和准备阶段处于非常重要的地位，也是目前我国PPP项目规范运行必不可少的重要步骤，在很大程度上将决定该PPP项目能否顺利实施。因此，我们在本小节对这几份重点报告的各省份披露情况进行简单总结。

由于“两评一案”涵盖的信息量非常丰富，往往通过长达几十页甚至上百页的PDF文件形式呈现在网站上，供社会各方进行查阅，因此，这三份PDF文件是课题组人工阅读和检查的重点对象。表4-6给出了这三个PDF文件得分的省级单位排序情况。从中可以发现，这三个PDF文件得分排名与适时公开透明度指数排名具有较高的一致性，比如河北占据了“物有所值评价报告及本级行业主管部门会同财政部门的审核通过意见”指标的第一名和“财政承受能力论证报告及本级财政部门的审核通过意见”指标的第二名，正因为其得益于这两项指标的优秀表现，河北在适时公开透明度指数排名中位列第一。此外，上海在适时公开透明度指数排名中列在最后一位，主要就是其在这三份文件上的得分排名较差导致的，这表明上海在“两评一案”上的信息披露工作亟待加强。重庆虽然占据了“实施方案附件”项目排名第二，但是“物有所值评价报告及本级行业主管部门会同财政部门的审核通过意见”和“财政承受能力论证报告及本级财政部门的审核通过意见”两项排名较差，因而其适时公开透明度指数排名只到第二十七位。吉林的“两评一案”指标均表现优秀，各项目排名都在前4位，因而其适时公开透明度指数位列第三。山东、广西和河南在“两评一案”中的工作各有优劣，因而分别在适时公开透明度指数排名中位列第五名、第六名和第七名。

表4-6 “两评一案”省级透明度排名

排　名	适时公开透明度指数	物有所值评价	财政承受能力论证	实施方案
1	河北	河北	青海	上海
2	云南	青海	河北	吉林

（续表）

排　名	适时公开透明度指数	物有所值评价	财政承受能力论证	实施方案
3	吉林	云南	天津	重庆
4	新疆	吉林	吉林	青海
5	山东	天津	云南	河北
6	广西	广西	福建	山东
7	河南	江西	广东	天津
8	江苏	广东	广西	辽宁
9	青海	福建	江西	云南
10	甘肃	山东	河南	广东
11	广东	河南	四川	福建
12	湖南	陕西	山东	黑龙江
13	黑龙江	新疆	山西	广西
14	安徽	山西	甘肃	安徽
15	陕西	甘肃	新疆	湖北
16	山西	贵州	重庆	浙江
17	四川	江苏	陕西	山西
18	福建	湖北	湖北	河南
19	天津	浙江	江苏	四川
20	湖北	黑龙江	浙江	江苏
21	江西	安徽	安徽	新疆
22	内蒙古	湖南	贵州	江西
23	贵州	重庆	黑龙江	湖南
24	浙江	四川	湖南	陕西
25	辽宁	辽宁	内蒙古	北京
26	兵团	内蒙古	兵团	海南
27	重庆	兵团	北京	贵州
28	北京	上海	上海	甘肃

（续表）

排　名	适时公开透明度指数	物有所值评价	财政承受能力论证	实施方案
29	上海	宁夏	辽宁	内蒙古
30	海南	北京	宁夏	兵团
31	宁夏	海南	海南	宁夏

未来课题组会考虑做一些专题评估，不仅评估这些关键性指标或核心PDF文件是否披露，还将评估这些报告具体内容的质量，以进一步推动PPP项目更加规范。

5

城市指数的排名与分析

5.1 城市PPP项目分布情况概述

在前面第3章、第4章对全国层面和省级层面的PPP市场透明度指数对比分析的基础上，本章将对中国PPP项目数量相对较多的部分城市的PPP市场透明度情况展开一些分析。在中国338个地级市（自治州、地区、盟等，以下统一都视作“市”）中，已经有328个城市引入了PPP模式（见表5-1），PPP模式推动范围之广，可见一斑。特别是广东、山东、河南、新疆、安徽、云南、辽宁、湖南、广西、江苏、湖北、内蒙古、河北、山西、浙江、江西、陕西、吉林、四川、福建、贵州、宁夏22个省份已经实现了PPP项目地级市的全覆盖。

表5-1 各省份引入PPP模式的城市个数

省 份	引入PPP模式的城市个数	城市总数	省 份	引入PPP模式的城市个数	城市总数
云南	16	16	江西	11	11
内蒙古	12	12	河北	11	11
吉林	9	9	河南	17	17
四川	21	21	浙江	11	11
宁夏	5	5	海南	2	3
安徽	16	16	湖北	13	13
山东	17	17	湖南	14	14
山西	11	11	甘肃	13	14
广东	21	21	福建	9	9
广西	14	14	贵州	9	9

（续表）

省 份	引入PPP模式的城市个数	城市总数	省 份	引入PPP模式的城市个数	城市总数
新疆	14	14	辽宁	14	14
陕西	10	10	青海	6	8
江苏	13	13	黑龙江	12	13
西藏	1	7			

这些开展PPP项目的城市中，有些拥有较为成熟的PPP市场，有些则刚刚起步。为了使得相关评估分析更具有稳健性、科学性，课题组在本次报告中选取了PPP项目数量较多的城市作为分析对象。为了方便画图，课题组选择了截至2020年12月31日在PPP综合信息平台中项目数量超过50个的46个地级以上城市作为城市层面PPP市场透明度指数具体分析的样本，其中项目数量超过30个的地级以上城市层面的PPP市场透明度指数的结果如附件四所示。这46个具体城市包括：山东济宁、新疆阿克苏、山东日照、云南玉溪、云南红河、河北承德、云南昆明、山东潍坊、河南南阳、河南新乡、山东菏泽、河北唐山、广东东莞、江苏徐州、新疆乌鲁木齐、贵州毕节、江苏南京、陕西西安、河南平顶山、山东济南、河南洛阳、山东临沂、内蒙古赤峰、四川成都、安徽阜阳、浙江杭州、福建泉州、河南郑州、湖北武汉、浙江丽水、新疆巴音、浙江温州、福建宁德、贵州遵义、山西临汾、河南信阳、四川宜宾、河南驻马店、福建漳州、山东青岛、江西宜春、江西赣州、浙江台州、福建福州、贵州黔南、贵州黔东南。

5.2 重点城市指数的基本情况

5.2.1 总指数城市排名

这46个PPP市场发展较为成熟的城市，其2020年PPP市场透明度总指数排名如表5-2所示。排在首位的是山东济宁，指数为82.81，比全国平均水平高6.86；紧随其后的是新疆阿克苏和山东日照，总指数分别达到84.59和83.94。此外，总指数在80

以上的城市还有云南玉溪、云南红河、河北承德、云南昆明、山东潍坊、河南南阳、河南新乡、山东菏泽、河北唐山、广东东莞、江苏徐州、新疆乌鲁木齐、贵州毕节，这些都是PPP信息公开工作开展得相对较好的城市。

表5-2 2020年部分城市PPP市场透明度总指数

排名	城市	2020年项目数量	2020年总指数	较2019年总指数差异	2019年总指数
1	山东济宁	177	87.22	+5.60	81.62
2	新疆阿克苏	54	85.96	+4.55	81.41
3	山东日照	56	85.78	−0.35	86.13
4	云南玉溪	53	85.72	−0.74	86.46
5	云南红河	60	85.19	+3.13	82.06
6	河北承德	62	85.09	+7.03	78.06
7	云南昆明	97	84.98	+3.57	81.41
8	山东潍坊	58	84.96	+3.17	81.79
9	河南南阳	112	83.41	+9.83	73.58
10	河南新乡	74	83.16	+2.31	80.85
11	山东菏泽	62	82.91	+1.33	81.58
12	河北唐山	55	82.48	+1.16	81.32
13	广东东莞	51	82.41	+7.23	75.18
14	江苏徐州	69	82.35	+2.92	79.43
15	新疆乌鲁木齐	57	82.26	−3.98	86.24
16	贵州毕节	82	81.94	+4.58	77.36
17	江苏南京	66	81.62	+1.53	80.09
18	陕西西安	68	81.61	+3.55	78.06
19	河南平顶山	70	81.50	−0.98	82.48
20	山东济南	66	81.33	+1.46	79.87
21	河南洛阳	108	81.00	+6.01	74.99

（续表）

排　名	城　市	2020 年项目数量	2020 年总指数	较 2019 年总指数差异	2019 年总指数
22	山东临沂	61	80.56	+4.70	75.86
23	内蒙古赤峰	68	80.54	+3.45	77.09
24	四川成都	68	80.47	+2.08	78.39
25	安徽阜阳	59	80.24	+3.63	76.61
26	浙江杭州	61	80.06	+0.18	79.88
27	福建泉州	62	79.56	+3.71	75.85
28	河南郑州	58	79.25	+2.82	76.43
29	湖北武汉	52	79.21	+5.67	73.54
30	浙江丽水	135	78.65	+8.24	70.41
31	新疆巴音	81	78.56	+2.59	75.97
32	浙江温州	70	78.29	+1.20	77.09
33	福建宁德	55	78.06	+3.16	74.9
34	贵州遵义	56	78.06	+4.39	73.67
35	山西临汾	86	78.00	+0.50	77.5
36	河南信阳	59	77.90	+0.65	77.25
37	四川宜宾	51	77.78	+5.35	72.43
38	河南驻马店	55	77.50	+4.60	72.9
39	福建漳州	63	77.45	+3.18	74.27
40	山东青岛	81	76.94	−3.34	80.28
41	天津市辖	93	76.53	+6.19	70.34
42	江西宜春	59	76.47	+5.54	70.93
43	江西赣州	62	76.35	+4.27	72.08
44	浙江台州	54	75.88	+2.59	73.29
45	福建福州	53	74.30	+3.02	71.28
46	贵州黔南	56	73.47	−3.44	76.91

通过和2019年PPP市场透明度指数进行对比可以发现，大部分地级以上城市2020年指数较2019年有所增长，尤其是河南南阳，其2020年指数较2019年上升了9.83，紧随其后的是浙江丽水，较2019年上升了8.24。不过，同时也可以发现，少数地级以上城市2020年指数较2019年有所降低，降幅较大的是新疆乌鲁木齐和贵州黔南，2020年总指数较2019年下降最多，分别下降了3.98和3.44。

5.2.2 与全国平均水平比较

此外，从46个城市的透明度总指数分布图来看，在大力推广PPP模式的过程中，大多数城市PPP市场透明度指数的差异并不是很明显，但也应该注意到部分城市的PPP市场透明度指数远低于其他城市。如图5-1所示，可将这46个城市的PPP市场透明度总指数的分布分成两个梯队：第一梯队城市的PPP市场透明度情况均领先于全国平均水平，即包括山东济宁到安徽阜阳在内的25个城市；第二梯队城市的PPP市场透明度情况则落后于全国平均水平，即包括浙江杭州到贵州黔东南在内的21个城市。由于这里的分析对象都是开展PPP项目数量相对较多的城市，因而业务不熟悉不应该成为第二梯队城市PPP市场透明度指数不高的“借口”，而是说明部分城市确实需要加强PPP信息公开相关工作力度，避免出现整个PPP市场只重视规模而忽视规范化管理的问题。

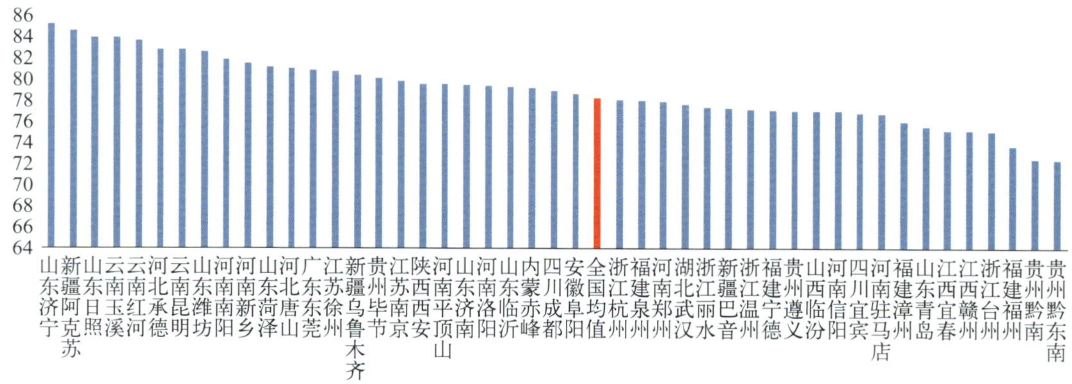

图5-1 2020年部分城市PPP市场透明度总指数分布

5.2.3 各城市即时公开和适时公开结果分析

图5-2和图5-3分别展示了这46个城市的即时公开透明度指数和适时公开透

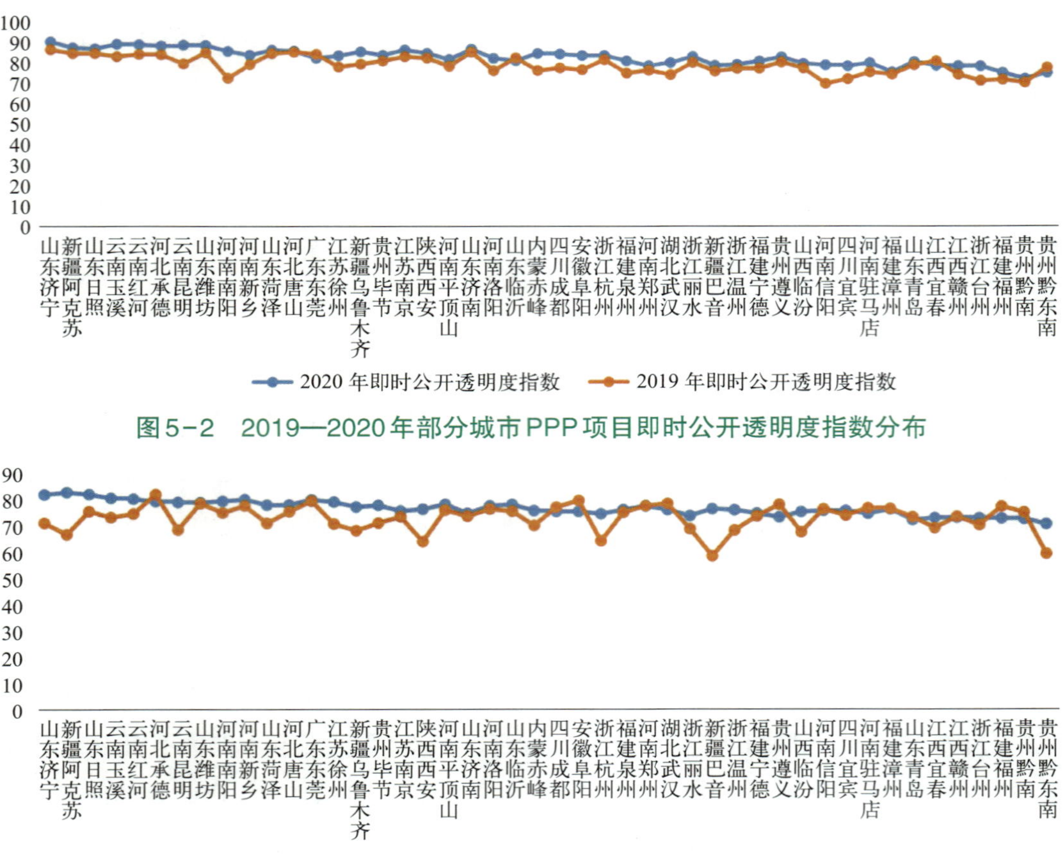

图5-2　2019—2020年部分城市PPP项目即时公开透明度指数分布

图5-3　2019—2020年部分城市PPP项目适时公开透明度指数分布

明度指数的结果分布。通过图5-2可以看出，2020年即时公开透明度指数的平均结果高于2019年，但差异不大：2020年即时公开透明度指数平均为82.89，2019年即时公开透明度指数平均为79.02。同时，通过图5-3可以观察到，2020年除了新疆巴音、贵州黔南和湖北武汉外，其他城市的适时公开透明度指数和2019年差异不大。此外，还可以发现从新疆乌鲁木齐到江西赣州在内的大部分城市2020年即时公开透明度指数和适时公开透明度指数都高于2019年，而贵州黔南的即时公开透明度指数和适时公开透明度指数都低于2019年，说明2020年PPP项目信息透明度工作做得好的城市在即时公开和适时公开方面做得都好，但是也有城市在即时公开和适时公开方面均在“走下坡路”。

在即时公开上，2020年较2019年进步幅度位居前三的城市为河南南阳、云南昆明和河南信阳，其中，河南南阳由2019年的86.14上升到2020年的72.83，云南昆明由2019年的79.86上升到2020年的89.18，河南信阳由2019年的70.07上升到2020年的79.20；退步最多的城市依次为贵州黔东、江西宜春和广东东莞。在适时公开上，2020年较2019年进步幅度位居前三的城市为新疆巴音、贵州黔南和湖北武汉；退步最多的城市依次为贵州遵义、福建福州和安徽阜阳。而且通过图5-4也可以发现，总体而言，2020年的即时公开透明度指数高于适时公开透明度指数，说明各城市在PPP项目信息适时公开方面的工作还有待进一步加强。

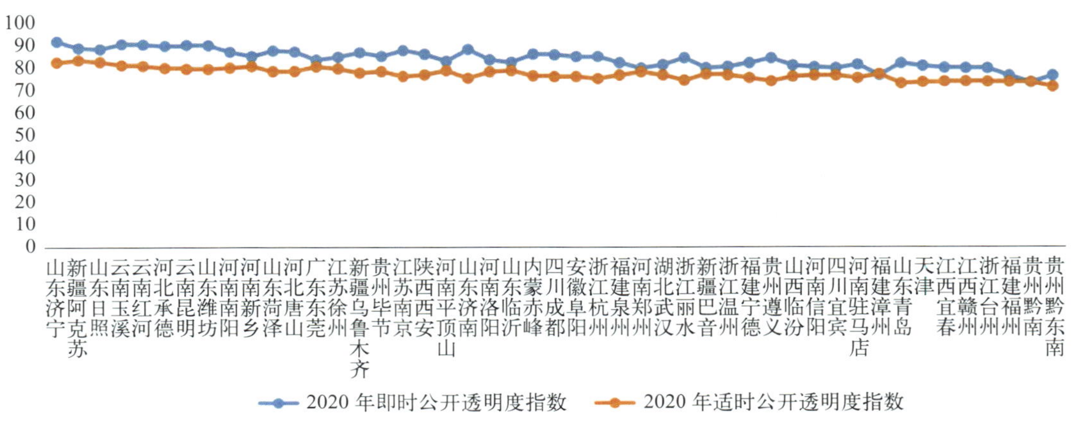

图5-4　2020年部分城市PPP项目即时公开和适时公开透明度指数分布

5.2.4　分阶段的各城市透明度结果分析

这些城市PPP项目不同阶段的分指数结果如图5-5和图5-6所示。图5-5展示了各个城市的即时公开透明度指数在识别阶段、准备阶段、采购阶段和执行阶段的情况对比，从中可以很明显地得出如下结论：在即时公开部分，各个城市的识别阶段和准备阶段信息公开工作做得比较好，指数普遍高于其他各阶段。出现这一结果的现实原因可能在于：识别阶段、准备阶段基本信息的完善有助于吸引社会资本方的参与，直接影响到PPP项目的招标结果，因而大多数项目的主管部门会较为重视识别阶段和准备阶段即时公开的信息填报，其平均指数分别达到95.50和90.71。而采购阶段和执行阶段的信息透明度指数平均分别为79.59和64.21，处在四个阶段公开情况的中下水平，且执行阶段、准备阶段的即时公开透明度指数的跳跃性很大。同时，也应该注意到，部分城市准备阶段的即时公开透明度指数是低于采购阶段和执行阶段的。

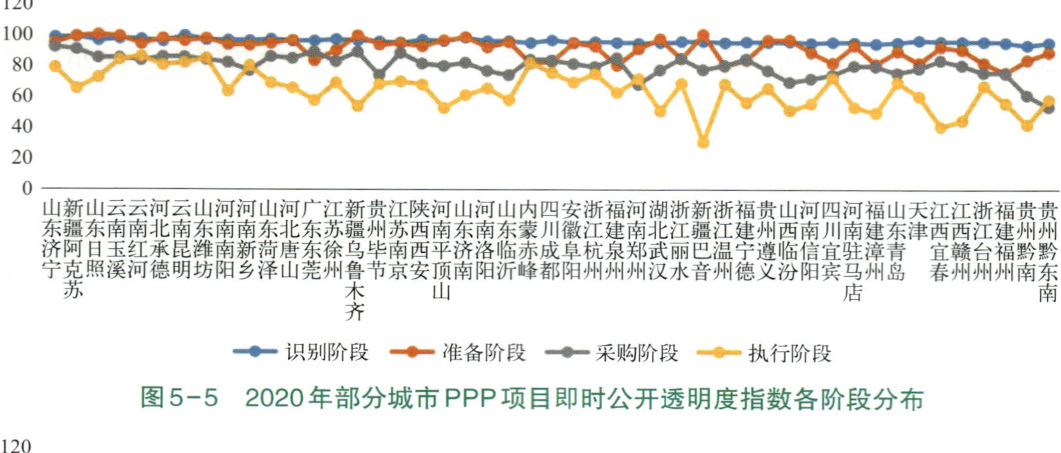

图5-5　2020年部分城市PPP项目即时公开透明度指数各阶段分布

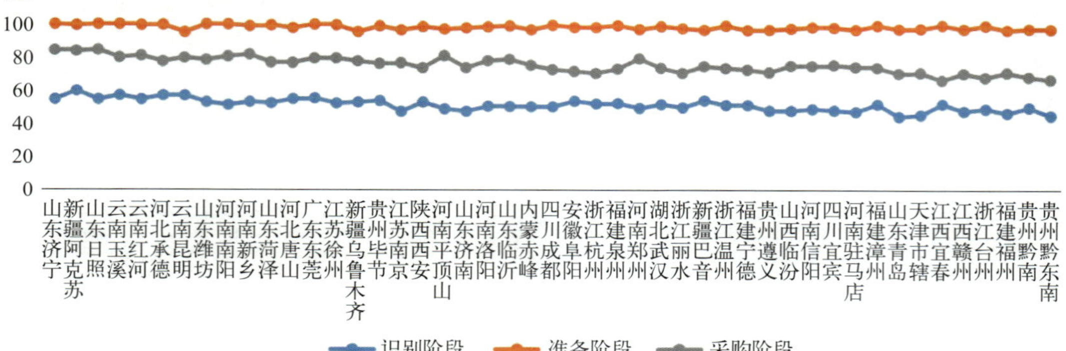

图5-6　2020年部分城市PPP项目适时公开透明度指数各阶段分布

对于适时公开透明度指数的情况（见图5-6），在适时公开部分所包含的识别阶段、准备阶段和采购阶段中，明显处于最低位的是各个城市的识别阶段信息公开情况，其平均指数为51.31，而适时公开的准备阶段的信息公开工作则做得较好，平均指数达到98.29。出现这种情况可能是因为适时公开的识别阶段包括物有所值评价报告、财政承受能力论证报告、可行性研究报告等重要的报告附件，这些报告信息的披露情况经过课题组的严格考察，发现存在问题的报告数量很多，甚至会出现“虚假”披露的情况。因此，物有所值评价报告、财政承受能力论证报告、可行性研究报告的不规范导致识别阶段的适时公开透明度指数在识别、准备、采购三阶段中排名最低。同时，这47个城市之间三个阶段的适时公开透明度指数没有发生很大的跳跃。

如此鲜明的对比也可以警示各个地方相关部门应该重视“两评”的工作质量和

信息公开工作，同时也提醒中央主管部门不能放松对“两评”的规范要求，由于问题普遍存在，所以有必要针对这些重点工作提出更详细、更具有可操作性的政策指引。

5.3 主要城市“两评一案”结果

本节将延续省级分析的内容，对重点城市“两评一案”的透明度结果进行分析。从表5-3可以看出，山东日照、山东济宁、云南玉溪和广东东莞在“两评一案”报告信息披露上的工作成绩值得肯定，特别是山东日照和山东济宁的物有所值评价报告和财政承受能力论证报告的排名均是第一位，在这两项的信息披露上均取得了满分的成绩，根据前文的定义，即没有信息披露不全，更没有“虚假”披露行为。新疆阿克苏虽然在三项指标上都没有进入前5名，但综合来看其三项指标的排名都靠前，这使其在适时公开透明度指数中排名第一。

表5-3 “两评一案”城市的结果排序

排名	适时指数	物有所值评价报告	财政承受能力论证报告	实施方案
1	新疆阿克苏	山东日照	山东日照	山东日照
2	山东日照	山东济宁	山东济宁	山东济宁
3	山东济宁	云南玉溪	云南玉溪	云南玉溪
4	云南玉溪	广东东莞	广东东莞	广东东莞
5	云南红河	江苏徐州	河南南阳	河南南阳
6	河南新乡	山东菏泽	山东潍坊	山东潍坊
7	广东东莞	河南南阳	江苏徐州	河北承德
8	河南南阳	福建泉州	贵州毕节	江苏徐州
9	河北承德	新疆阿克苏	山东菏泽	江西宜春
10	江苏徐州	福建漳州	福建泉州	四川成都
11	云南昆明	贵州黔南	新疆阿克苏	云南红河
12	山东潍坊	贵州毕节	福建漳州	山东菏泽

（续表）

排名	适时指数	物有所值评价报告	财政承受能力论证报告	实施方案
13	河南平顶山	四川成都	河北承德	福建泉州
14	山东临沂	云南红河	贵州黔南	新疆阿克苏
15	河北唐山	河南新乡	四川成都	福建漳州
16	山东菏泽	河北承德	河南洛阳	浙江台州
17	贵州毕节	江西宜春	云南红河	浙江温州
18	河南洛阳	河北唐山	安徽阜阳	贵州黔南
19	河南郑州	陕西西安	河南新乡	山东临沂
20	新疆乌鲁木齐	湖北武汉	山西临汾	贵州毕节
21	新疆巴音	河南洛阳	江西宜春	河南新乡
22	陕西西安	浙江温州	河北唐山	湖北武汉
23	福建漳州	安徽阜阳	新疆巴音	陕西西安
24	福建泉州	内蒙赤峰	陕西西安	河南洛阳
25	湖北武汉	云南昆明	湖北武汉	河南信阳
26	浙江温州	山东潍坊	河南信阳	浙江杭州
27	河南信阳	山东济南	内蒙古赤峰	安徽阜阳
28	内蒙赤峰	河南平顶山	浙江台州	四川宜宾
29	四川宜宾	河南信阳	云南昆明	山东济南
30	江苏南京	山西临汾	山东济南	福建宁德
31	安徽阜阳	山东临沂	福建宁德	河北唐山
32	四川成都	新疆巴音	四川宜宾	浙江丽水
33	山西临汾	浙江台州	浙江温州	山西临汾
34	山东济南	福建宁德	浙江杭州	山东青岛
35	福建宁德	贵州遵义	河南平顶山	江西赣州
36	河南驻马店	福建福州	福建福州	河南平顶山
37	浙江杭州	河南驻马店	江西赣州	贵州黔东南
38	浙江丽水	河南郑州	贵州遵义	河南郑州
39	贵州遵义	江苏南京	河南郑州	河南驻马店
40	江西赣州	江西赣州	山东临沂	贵州遵义

（续表）

排名	适时指数	物有所值评价报告	财政承受能力论证报告	实施方案
41	江西宜春	浙江杭州	河南驻马店	内蒙赤峰
42	浙江台州	四川宜宾	浙江丽水	新疆巴音
43	福建福州	浙江丽水	江苏南京	福建福州
44	贵州黔南	新疆乌鲁木齐	新疆乌鲁木齐	江苏南京
45	山东青岛	山东青岛	贵州黔东南	新疆乌鲁木齐
46	贵州黔东南	贵州黔东南	山东青岛	云南昆明

此外，江西宜春在物有所值评价报告和财政承受能力论证报告方面均排在靠前的位置，但是适时公开透明度指数却排名倒数，主要归因于实施方案方面做得很差。而新疆乌鲁木齐和云南昆明在物有所值评价报告和财政承受能力论证报告方面均排在垫底的位置，在实施方案方面做得还可以。

5.4 总指数与经济财政的相关性

本节以《2017中国城市统计年鉴》中统计的城市为研究对象，共289个地级以上城市，具体包括4个直辖市、15个副省会城市、17个省会城市和253个地级市。采用定量分析的方法，以这289个地级以上城市2020年PPP市场透明度总指数为基础，作2020年PPP市场透明度总指数与2017年财政收支缺口的散点图（见图5-7），其中横轴为2017年财政收支缺口的情况，纵轴为2020年PPP市场透明度总指数，并作2020年PPP市场透明度总指数与2019年GDP增长率的散点图（见图5-8），其中横轴为2019年GDP增长率，纵轴为2020年PPP市场透明度总指数。选定2017年289个城市层面的数据作为研究对象主要基于以下考虑：首先，这289个城市涵盖了全国90%的人口规模，基本可以代表全国的情况；其次，选定2017年财政收入、财政支出、人均GDP数据，可以避免内生性问题，而且从《2017中国城市统计年鉴》获得的数据也可以确保其权威性。

通过图5-7可以发现，2020年PPP市场透明度指数与2017年财政收支缺口存在正

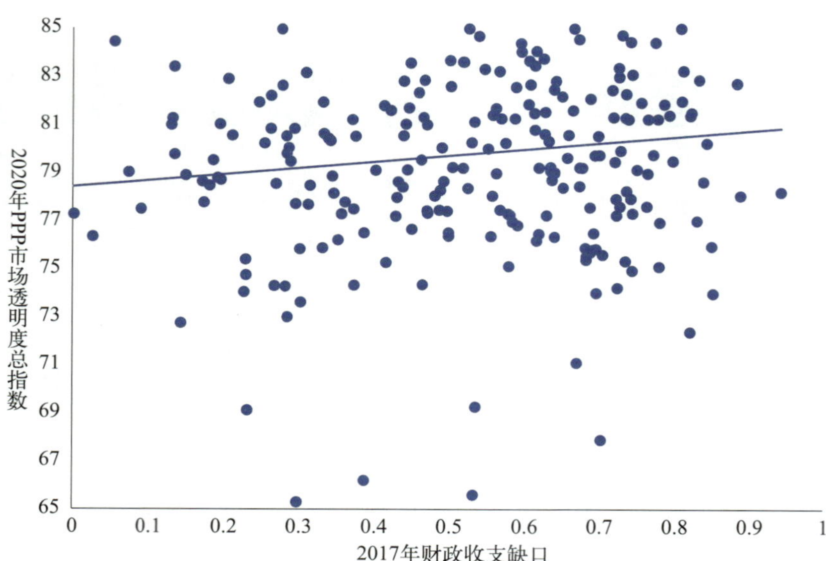

图 5-7 2020 年 PPP 市场透明度指数与 2017 年财政收支缺口相关性

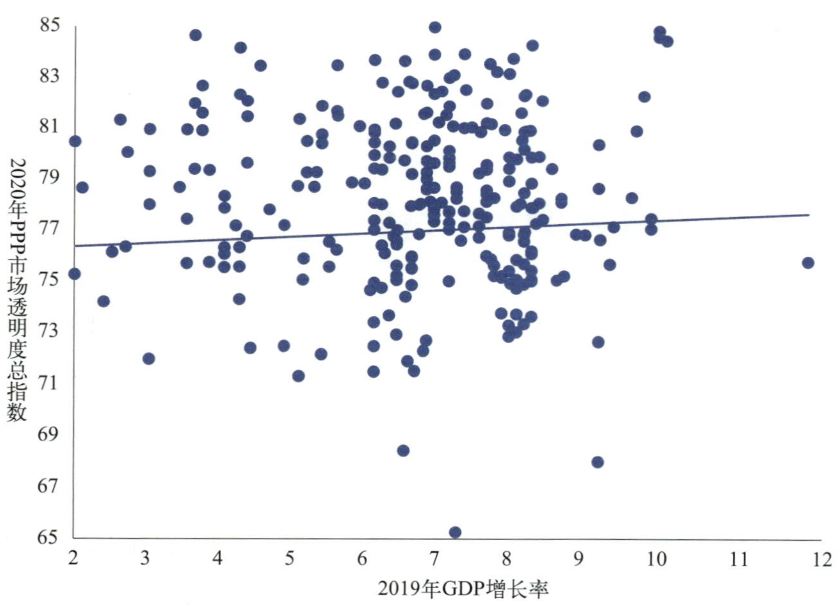

图 5-8 2020 年 PPP 市场透明度指数与 2019 年 GDP 增长率相关性

相关关系，财政收支缺口越大，2020 年 PPP 市场透明度指数越大。这可能是因为财政收支缺口越大的地区，更需要通过 PPP 来融资，也就更有压力将其做得更规范，以吸引社会资本方，从而透明度指数就更高。通过图 5-8 可以发现，2020 年 PPP 市场透明度指数与 2019 年 GDP 增长率负相关，即经济增长越慢的地区，PPP 市场透明度指数越高。

6

PPP中介机构信息公开现状评估

6.1 中介机构透明度评估意义

PPP项目反映了政府和社会资本方的长期合作关系，项目质量也需要接受长期考验，因而各方对PPP项目各类专业性咨询服务的需求和要求均远高于传统项目，聘请专业的中介咨询机构已成为国外政府实施PPP项目的通用做法。为了提高项目开发以及实施的质量和效率，我国财政部也在多个文件中提出，要在PPP项目中引进专业中介提供技术服务，以完善项目设计、优化项目方案。例如，2014年，《政府和社会资本合作模式操作指南（试行）》（财金〔2014〕113号）提出要积极发挥第三方专业机构的作用。2015年，财政部在《关于进一步做好政府和社会资本合作项目示范工作的通知》（财金〔2015〕57号）中进一步提出，要选择一批能力较强的专业中介机构，为示范项目实施提供技术支持。

具体来说，PPP项目中关联主体众多且关系复杂，在PPP项目的识别、准备、采购、执行和移交等过程中，往往会用到财务、法律、金融等多方面的专业知识，政府官员一般很难具备项目所需的全部技能。中介机构则不然，他们在各自的领域内具备核心竞争力，实践经验丰富，可以帮助政府设计物有所值评价报告和可行性研究报告，从而提高政府与社会资本方的谈判能力。

然而，在我国PPP项目“井喷式”发展的同时，相关咨询服务需求的激增带动了很多公司转行做PPP中介机构，导致我国PPP中介机构能力参差不齐，甚至有些PPP中介机构根本不具备相应的专业技能。为此，相关监管部门也非常重视PPP中介机构的监督管理，制定了《PPP咨询机构库管理暂行办法》（财金〔2017〕8号）等管理办法，对PPP中介机构提交的信息进行核查和公开，向全社会开放入库中介机构信息查询功能，主动接受服务对象和社会各界人士的监督，促进PPP项目咨询服务质量提升，推进我国PPP中介市场秩序的规范化。

为了考察我国PPP中介机构信息公开的现状，促进中介机构加大信息公开力度，从而更好地维护PPP市场可持续发展的良好市场环境，参考前文关于PPP项目信息透明度指数的编制，我们在本章也编制了一套PPP中介机构信息透明度指数，对PPP中介机构信息公开的现状进行了评估。[①]不过，考虑到PPP中介机构信息公开的指标体系、评估对象与PPP项目信息透明度指数之间存在巨大的差异，我们并没有将两者编入同一个指数体系中，而是单独对PPP中介机构的信息公开现状进行指数编制和分析。

6.2 指标体系构建与指数计算

在汇报PPP中介机构信息透明度指数的结果之前，我们首先简要介绍PPP中介机构信息公开评估的指标体系和指数计算方法。

6.2.1 指标体系设计的原则和依据

（1）指标体系设计的原则。由于中介机构信息内容涵盖的多层次性，指标体系也必须由多层次结构组成，才能反映出各层次的特征。因此，参考前文关于PPP项目信息透明度指数编制的方法，课题组对PPP中介机构信息透明度指数的编制和信息公开现状的评估也划分了几个不同的层级。具体而言，参考PPP相关信息公开管理办法的精神和PPP综合信息平台中的中介库现状，课题组将PPP中介机构信息透明度的指标体系分为总指数、二级指标（具体包括机构基本信息、机构承担的PPP项目信息以及机构网站信息）以及底层具体指标三个层次。

（2）指标体系设计依据与数据来源。根据主管部门财政部政府和社会资本合作中心的规定，PPP中介机构的信息均要在财政部政府和社会资本合作中心举办的PPP综合信息平台中“机构库信息公开”系统中进行公布。考虑到数据来源的一致性，课题组选择该数据库系统中的具体字段作为评估依据和主要数据来源，具体包括机构基本信息、机构承担的PPP项目信息两部分内容。此外，为了进一步丰富指标体

① 需要再次说明的是，这里评估的依然是中介机构的信息公开情况，并不是信息公开的内容质量，更不涉及PPP中介机构总体经营规范性或业务规模、市场占有率等的评估。

系，考虑到PPP中介机构并不太多，课题组还逐个检索登录中介机构的官方网站查阅相关公开信息，以评估其网站中是否披露与PPP有关的信息，从而构成中介机构网站信息这个二级指标。

（3）评估对象。结合PPP主管部门的政策意见以及考虑到实际可操作性，课题组将分析对象界定为在PPP综合信息平台中“机构库信息公开”系统中入库且在PPP综合信息平台中公示的中介机构，共计360家。

（4）数据采集。课题组以政府和社会资本合作中心网站可获取数据为基础[①]，同时登录各家中介机构官方网站获取指标，并对其进行归类。经过课题组的整理，指标体系共包含28[②]个指标字段，课题组对其进行了逐个提取，包括网站直接阅读提取和复制粘贴提取等方式。

6.2.2　PPP中介机构信息公开评估指标体系

根据上述原则和方法，PPP中介机构信息透明度指数最终的指标体系层级如图6-1所示，PPP中介机构信息公开评估指标体系包括总指数，机构基本信息、项目信息、机构网站信息三个二级分指数，以及再下一层级的具体指标。

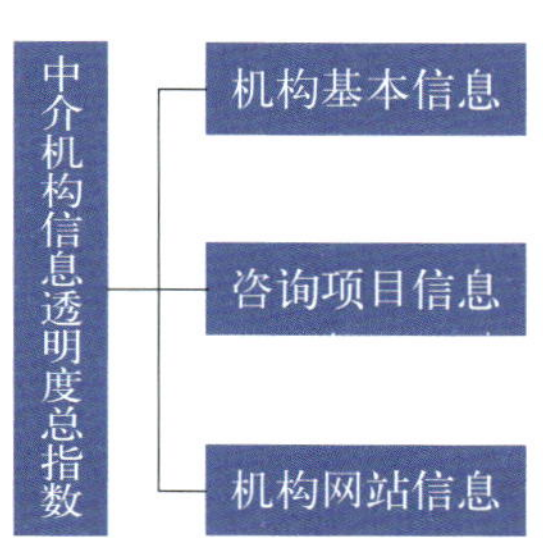

图6-1　PPP中介机构信息透明度指数层级图

PPP中介机构信息公开评估的具体指标如表6-1所示。在这些具体指标的评估得分上，课题组采取简单化原则。对于大部分指标，有信息公布，则得分为1，否则就得分为零。但对于个别信息含量较为丰富的指标，课题组也设计了0.5分这一中间得分的情形。具体而言，对于“机构网站”这个指标，如果在政府和社会资本合作中心

① 本章数据全部来自课题组的手工收集。
② 与2019年的评估相比，减少了“成立年份”这一指标。

网站上有公布网址，则得1分；如果通过百度等检索手段可以检索到公司网址，则得0.5分；既未在政府和社会资本合作中心网站上公布公司网址，也无法检索到，则得0分。此外，对于机构网站上的新闻，如果没有新闻，则得0分；有新闻但最近三条新闻时间间隔超过30天，则得0.5分；间隔时间不超过30天，则得1分。如此设计这些指标的得分，是为了有更好的区分度。

表6-1　PPP 中介机构信息透明度评价指标体系

二级指标	具体指标
机构基本信息	公司名称
	机构简介
	经营范围
	注册成立时间
	通讯地址
	邮政编码
	机构网站
	业绩统计
	委托方评价
	核心高管
	机构荣誉
	机构资质
	历史退库记录
咨询项目信息	项目名称
	项目阶段
	所属地区
	项目行业
	投资总额
	示范级别
	咨询服务业业绩类别
	咨询机构项目经理

（续表）

二级指标	具体指标
咨询项目信息	项目经理PPP从业经历
	咨询服务委托方名称
	咨询服务合同签字页
网站信息	网站高管介绍
	公司资质
	业务项目
	公司最近新闻

6.2.3 指数合成计算方法

在多指标综合评价中，权重确定直接影响评价的结果。考虑到与上一年评估结果的可比性，课题组对指数合成采取的办法与上一年一致。具体地，在具体指标合成为二级指标的过程中，课题组选择了变异系数法进行合成。该方法的基本思路是根据各个指标在所有评价对象上观测值的变异程度大小，对其进行赋权。也就是说，如果一项指标的变异系数较大，那么说明这个指标在衡量评估对象总体的差异方面具有较大的解释力，则对这个指标就应该赋予较大的权重。

具体地，利用变异系数法确定各指标权重，首先要计算各指标的变异系数，该值反映了各指标的绝对变异程度：

$$CV_i = \frac{S_i}{\bar{x}_i}, \ i = 1, 2, 3, \cdots, n$$

其中，S_i为各指标标准差，$\bar{x}_i$为各指标均值。然后，对各个指标变异系数进行归一化处理，计算各指标权重：

$$q_i = \frac{CV_i}{\sum_{i=1}^{n} CV_i}, \ i = 1, 2, 3, \cdots, n$$

最后，将二级指标再合成为总指数。此时，课题组则选择了最为简单的简单平均法：机构基本信息、咨询项目信息和机构网站信息的权重各占1/3。

6.3 中介机构信息透明度指数分析

6.3.1 指数基本特征

表6-2是PPP中介机构信息透明度指数的基本描述性统计，从中我们可以看出，358个中介机构的透明度指数平均为70.16。具体到三个二级分指数上，从表6-2中也可以看出，咨询的PPP项目信息的分指数比较高，达到89.62；在PPP综合信息平台中披露的中介机构基本信息次之，分指数平均为67；课题组从PPP中介机构官网上自行设计指标并采集的机构网站信息的分指数最低，仅为53.86。从时间前后对比看，2020年中介机构信息透明度指数比2019年略有下降；从分项指标看，三个分项的信息公开工作均有一定的下滑，主要反映为中介机构的网站公布情况及网站建设情况不理想；从政策角度看，与2019年类似，我们仍建议未来进一步加强机构网站信息公开工作。

表6-2 指数描述统计

变 量	2019年			2020年		
	观测值	均 值	标准差	观测值	均 值	标准差
总指数得分	357	75.20	17.25	358	70.16	20.83
机构基本信息	357	76.09	22.41	358	67.00	29.67
咨询项目信息	357	90.89	20.06	358	89.62	12.46
机构网站信息	357	58.63	39.00	358	53.86	39.11

图6-2则进一步给出了PPP中介机构透明度总指数和三个二级分指数的直方分布图，从中可以看出PPP中介机构的项目信息和机构基本信息大部分公布较好，而机构网站信息的公布则存在两极分化的现象，有一部分机构网站信息公开较好，但确实也有一些机构网站信息公开情况较差，这一结果也就导致表6-2中显示的网站信息公开分指数标准差较大。

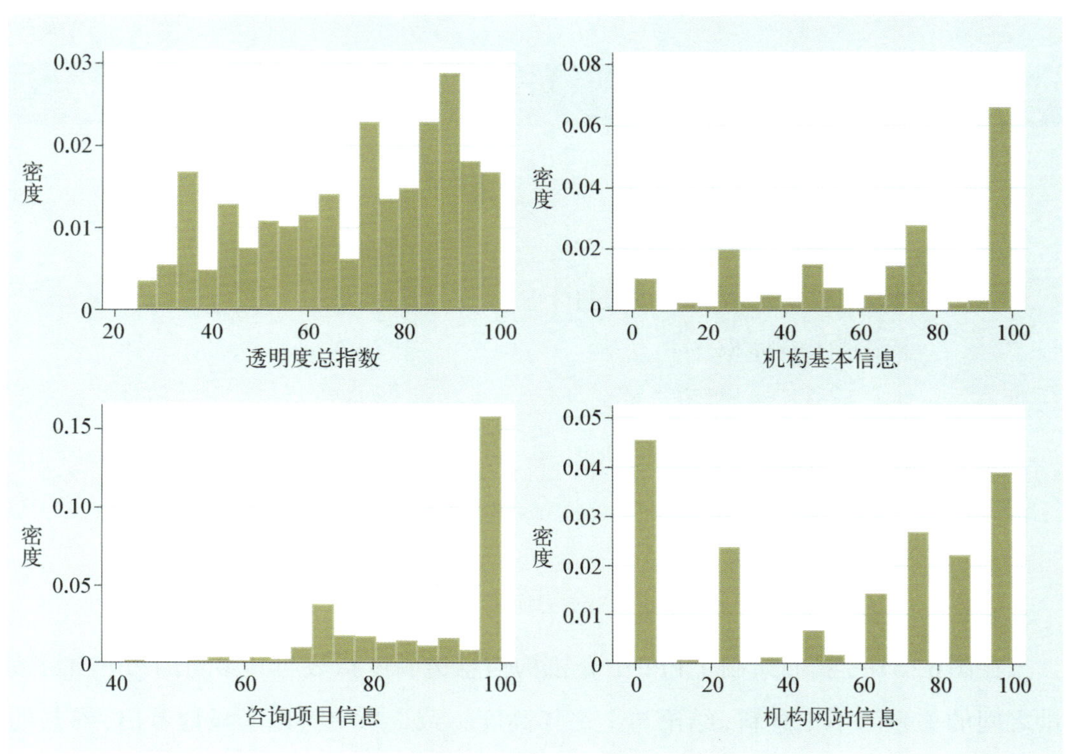

图6-2　PPP中介机构信息透明度总指数及分指数直方图

表6-3则给出了PPP中介机构透明度总指数排名前10位的中介机构具体名单。可以看出，前10位的公司信息公开均比较好，在课题组设计的28个中介机构信息公开指标中，接近满分。其中，河南永正项目管理有限公司、华春建设工程项目管理有限责任公司、中招国际招标有限公司三个公司排前三。与上一年对比看，最好的前10名变化并不大，换句话说，上一年度排前10名的机构大多数今年仍在前10名。河南永正项目管理有限公司、天和国咨控股集团有限公司和中核华纬工程设计研究有限公司进步较大，进入前10名。

表6-3　PPP中介机构信息透明度总指数前10名

排名	机　构　名　称	总 指 数	较上一年排名变化
1	河南永正项目管理有限公司	99.756	+15
2	华春建设工程项目管理有限责任公司	99.071	−1

（续表）

排名	机构名称	总指数	较上一年排名变化
3	中招国际招标有限公司	99.048	+3
4	天和国咨控股集团有限公司	99.045	+16
5	中工武大设计研究有限公司	99.041	+2
6	中核华纬工程设计研究有限公司	99.022	+15
7	瀚景项目管理有限公司	99.010	+9
8	北京大岳咨询有限责任公司	98.962	+11
9	安徽省招标集团股份有限公司	98.956	−7
10	上海济邦投资咨询有限公司	98.863	−1

6.3.2 PPP中介信息公开与业务量相关关系

在图6−3中，我们绘制了PPP中介机构信息透明度指数与其参与的PPP项目数量之间的关系。不出意料，结论与上一年高度一致。从中可以明显地看出，参与的PPP项目数量越多，PPP中介机构信息透明度指数就越高。从逻辑和实践上讲，参与PPP项目数量与中介机构信息公开存在相互促进的关系。一方面，参与项目数量越

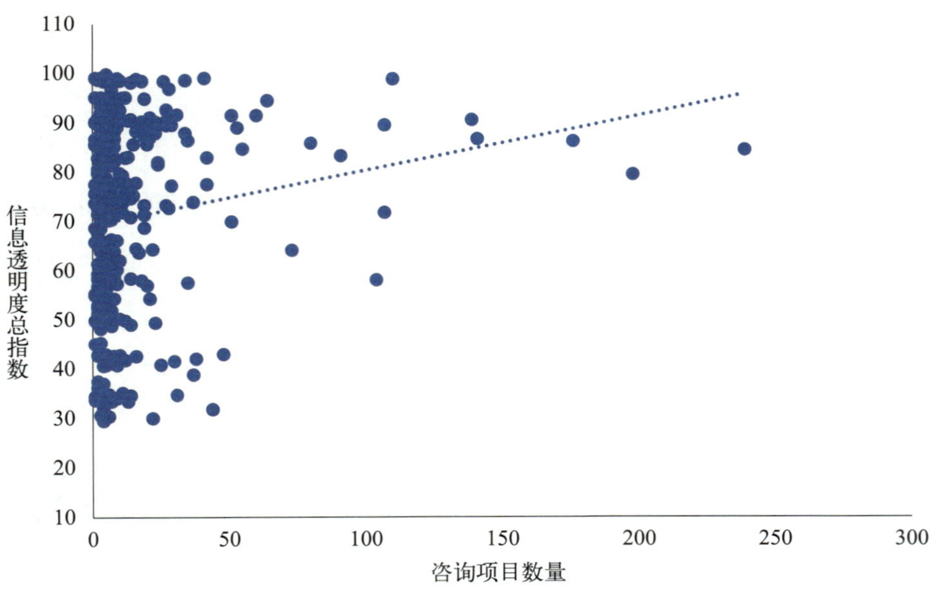

图6−3　PPP中介机构信息透明度总指数与咨询项目数量的关系

多，说明公司规模越大，管理越规范，从而更加重视自身的信息公开工作，信息透明度指数就越高；另一方面，中介机构信息公开工作做得越好，也就越能吸引更多的客户，从而参与更多的PPP项目。这两方面的原因共同作用，使得PPP中介机构信息透明度指数与中介机构参与的PPP项目数量之间呈现显著的正相关关系。

6.3.3 PPP中介信息公开与公司资历相关关系

如前文所述，PPP中介机构信息透明度与中介机构业务能力高度正相关，这里我们进一步分析中介机构信息透明度与中介机构资历的关系。从图6-4中可以看出，中介机构经营时间越久，其信息公开工作的确也就做得越好，中介机构“年龄”与中介机构信息透明度指数之间存在高度显著的正相关关系。这一发现与上一年的结果也非常类似。

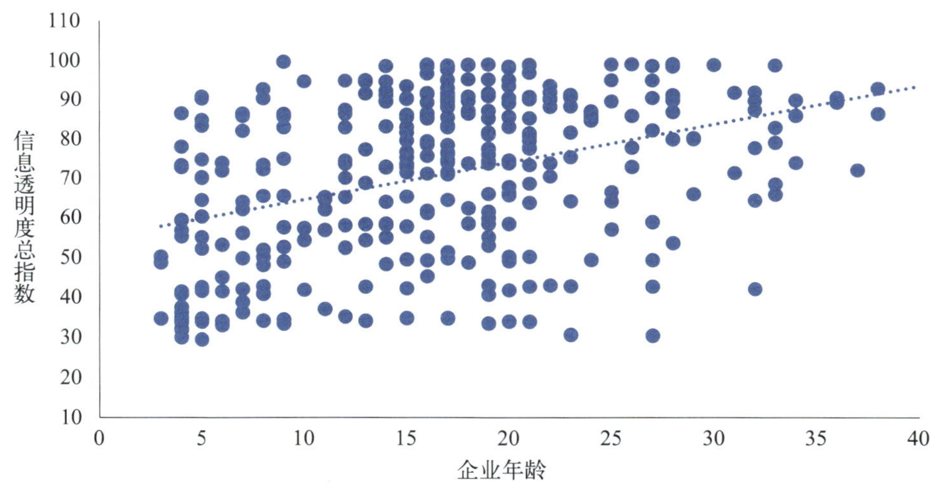

图6-4 PPP中介机构信息透明度总指数与企业年龄的关系

7

总结与展望

7.1 报告总结

PPP是Public-Private Partnerships的英文首字母缩写，译为政府和社会资本合作。当前，中国的PPP模式已经不仅仅是政府的一种市场化投融资手段，更是一次全面的、系统的公共服务供给市场化社会化改革举措，因而各界对PPP的发展都寄予厚望，希望PPP能起到引领财政体制机制改革、助力公共事业全面深化改革的作用。在这一背景下，PPP项目的规范化管理就显得尤为重要，其中PPP项目及时、完善的信息公开又是PPP项目规范化管理的基础。2017年以来，财政部连续发布的多份文件都涉及PPP项目的信息公开工作，特别是2017年初发布的《政府和社会资本合作（PPP）综合信息平台信息公开管理暂行办法》（财金〔2017〕1号），详细规定了PPP项目信息公开的各方面要求。进入2018年后，PPP项目的退库清理成为PPP管理的重心之一，2 000多个不符合管理规范的PPP项目被清理退库，同时也有不少新增项目加入PPP管理库中。进入2019年后，伴随着更多的PPP项目进入执行阶段，如何有效推动PPP项目适时公开信息的管理工作显得愈发重要。同时，公众对提高PPP项目信息质量的呼声也越来越高。2020年3月31日，财政部发布《政府与社会资本合作项目绩效管理操作指引》，全方位建立了完整的PPP绩效考核体系，明确了责任主体，将信息真实、公开、透明、质量纳入具体的考核细则。

在此背景下，上海财经大学PPP研究中心课题组继过去连续三年对PPP项目信息公开工作进行评估后，又对截至2020年12月31日的中国PPP项目的最新信息公开状况进行了详细的评估。具体而言，课题组对2020年底财政部PPP管理库的9 662个项目的信息公开工作进行了详细评估，编制了一套"2020中国PPP市场透明度指数"。该指数囊括68个指标字段，并分为即时公开透明度指数、适时公开透明度指数，以及识别阶段、准备阶段、采购阶段和执行阶段等各阶段的透明度分指数。课题组采用层次分析法和专家打分法相结合的方法对指数进行合成：对于分指数下面的具体指标，按照专家对其重要程度的判定，设置不同的分值；而在分指数合成总指数时，则采用同类指数编制过程中常用的层次分析法，以保证指数编制方法的可靠性。最终，通过对指数具体结果的统计分析，课题组得到以下几个主要发现：

第一，2020年全国PPP市场透明度总指数为78.15，较2019年略有提高。截至2020年12月31日，全国PPP市场透明度总指数为78.15（满分100，下同），与2019年的76.19相比上升了2左右。其中即时公开透明度指数为80.37，相比2019年（79.14）上升了1.2，而适时公开透明度指数为74.67，相比2019年（71.57）上升了3。进一步对PPP项目的异质性分析表明，PPP项目透明度指数没有明显的行业差异，示范项目和非示范项目的透明度指数也差别不大。

第二，省级层面的PPP市场透明度指数稳中有升，但不同省份的PPP市场透明度指数差异有所扩大。绝大多数省份的PPP市场透明度指数在70～85之间分布，但也有少数省份的PPP市场透明度指数高于82或低于70。云南（84.98）、山东（83.72）、河北（82.99）、湖南（82.69）和江苏（82.63）位列省份榜单的前5名。

第三，多数城市PPP市场透明度指数较2019年有所提高。课题组挑选了46个PPP项目数量较多（入管理库的项目超50个）的城市，对其PPP信息公开工作进行了分析。通过和2019年PPP市场透明度指数对比可以发现，部分地级以上城市2020年的指数较2019年是大幅上升的，尤其是新疆阿克苏，其2020年总指数较2019年上升了15.39，紧随其后的是广东东莞，较2019年上升了13.62。不过，同时也可以发现，很多地级以上城市2020年的PPP市场透明度指数较2019年有所降低，尤其是贵州黔南和海南海口，2020年的总指数较2019年下降最多，分别下降了13.10和12。

第四，PPP中介机构信息公开指数跨期差异不大，中介机构透明度指数与其资历、业务量正相关。课题组分析了PPP中介机构的信息公开现状，主要得到以下几个发现：中介机构信息透明度指数平均为70.16，而在二级指数中，中介机构参与的项目信息公开得分较高，但部分中介机构网站主动公开相关信息的工作不理想，与2019年相比意愿进一步降低。进一步的分析还发现，中介机构信息透明度指数与中介机构参与的PPP项目数量和中介机构存续年龄具有明显的正相关关系。

7.2 政策建议

根据本报告的分析，我们可以看到，与2019年相比，2020年中国PPP市场信息公开工作进一步稳中有进。信息公开工作的完善为PPP市场的规范发展提供了重要保障，也对财政体制机制的改革起到了牵引作用。当然，在调查研究中，我们也注意到了一些PPP市场信息公开方面存在的问题。因此，针对这些问题，我们提出以下几条政策建议，以期PPP信息公开工作能进一步完善，提高PPP市场的信息透明度，进而推动中国PPP项目的规范管理。

第一，完善“不适用”信息和临时性重大事项信息公开的操作规范。PPP项目涵盖了跨度很大的不同行业和领域，在合作方式、回报机制等方面也存在很大的区别，因此，有些信息可能对一些项目适用，对另外一些项目就不适用。在指数编制中，对这些不完全适用于所有项目的信息，课题组没有将其纳入指数编制的指标范围内，因为该信息如果是空白，则课题组不知道该信息是不适用于该项目，还是适用于该项目但没有公布这一信息。其实对于该类信息，如果不适用于某项目，则可以要求其特别注明“该信息不适用于本项目”或有类似表述。这样处理后，我们就可以辨别所有项目在该类信息上究竟是不适用，还是适用但未公开。此外，对于临时性重大事项信息公开的管理，也应该有类似的要求。例如，对于“重大违约及履约担保的提取情况、对公众投诉的处理情况”等临时性重大事项的信息公开，应该要求如果没有发生该类事项，应该特别注明“截至目前，本项目没有发生重大违约及履约担保的提取、公众投诉等需要披露的事项”或有其他类似表述。这一方法在上市公司、商业银行等机构的信息披露管理规范中是非常常见的。

第二，进一步完善即时公开、适时公开信息的分类管理。正如前文所述，将PPP项目的信息公开分为即时公开和适时公开是非常重要的举措。不过根据课题组的调查走访和专家座谈，我们发现对于什么信息应该即时公开、什么信息应该适时公开的分类标准，仍有进一步探讨改进的空间。例如，部分目前要求适时公开的信息其实可以进一步提高要求，改为即时公开；而另外一些资料整理工作较费时的即时公开的信息，也可以考虑改为适时公开。具体如何进一步完善这一分类管理的标准，我们建议主管部门广泛征求项目公司代表、中介咨询机构代表和学界代表的专业意见。

第三，加强PPP项目重点信息公开的监督检查力度。根据前文的分析，我们可以发现不同阶段的信息公开执行情况有较大差异。例如，在适时公开的信息中，识别阶段的物有所值评价报告、财政承受能力论证报告等公布情况相对于其他信息的公开情况不够理想，因而应该加强对这些信息的监督检查力度。通过随机抽查等方式，对这些报告的披露进展进行敦促。此外，对于执行阶段等信息，要完善制度的具体抓手，敦促有关责任主体主动公开、即时公开相关信息。例如，可以通过合同约定等方式，将项目公司在执行阶段的信息披露工作与政府付费等挂钩，推动PPP项目信息公开工作。最后，为了防止虚假上传的现象，可以考虑通过关键词识别的方式进行自动化甄别。比如上传附件中不包含某些关键词的，不得上传。

第四，进一步明确PPP信息公开的责任主体和分工。自2017年3月1日开始施行《政府和社会资本合作（PPP）综合信息平台信息公开管理暂行办法》以来，PPP信息公开工作取得的积极成效有目共睹，这个在我们近三年的评估结果中一目了然。当然正如前文的指数结果所展示的，在PPP的信息公开中也存在一些难题尚待解决。具体而言，PPP信息公开的责任主体不够明晰会给PPP信息披露带来一系列系统性的问题。根据财金〔2017〕1号文第四条有关规定，“地方各级财政部门会同同级政府有关部门推进、指导、协调、监督本行行政区域范围内的PPP项目信息公开工作，结合当地实际具体展开工作”。在具体实施过程中，财政部门需要协调水利局、交通局、体育局以及各方社会资本和第三方咨询机构收集汇总资料，而信息公开工作对财政部门以外的同级部门的约束力有限，往往会造成地方财政系统不能及时更新数据。这样的现象在财力较强的地方可能会得到缓解，因为信息公开进度不匹配，政府可以选择延迟付费的方式来惩罚相关部门。但这样的掣肘手段在财力单薄的地方难以实现，因为这些地方本身的条件可能就难以吸引到优质的社会资本，这样的做法无异于雪上加霜。因此，还需要进一步明确责任主体和建设配套的激励机制。

第五，加强对PPP中介机构信息公开力度的推动。PPP项目是一种长期合作关系，项目质量会长期经受考验，对项目问题解决方案和项目协议的要求远远高于传统项目，聘请咨询公司已成为国外政府实施PPP项目的惯例。因此，在PPP项目的规范运行与管理中，PPP中介机构发挥着重要作用。通过第6章的讨论，我们发现PPP中介机构的信息公开工作还有很多有待加强的地方。这主要体现在两方面：一方面，要加大PPP中介机构自身的信息公开力度，在PPP中介信息平台上增加更多字段信息的要求，例如，增加PPP中介机构人员数量、人员结构、主要团队等信息；另一方面，在PPP项目运行过程中，也要加大对相关中介机构参与度、尽职度、主要参与的项目类型、中介机构分类等信息的公开力度。此外，可以对中介机构参与的项目中后期被退库的比例等信息进行公示，以及对其在服务某级地方政府时是否同时服务了与该政府有合作关系的社会资本方等信息（避免商业伦理冲突）进行公示，从而对PPP中介机构形成一种压力，推动其参与PPP项目时更加谨慎。

7.3 未来展望

以上是我们报告的全部内容。总的来说，在2017—2019年指数编制和分析的基础上，我们通过编制指数的方式，对截至2020年底的中国PPP项目的信息公开情况进行了详细的分析。报告保持了指标体系和指数编制方法的连续性。然而，虽然精益求精，但我们相信在指标体系设置、指数编制方法和指数结果具体分析等方面，本报告依然存在很多不足之处，未来至少在以下几个方面可以进一步改进：

第一，指标体系可以进一步完善。正如报告中所阐述的，由于相关信息缺失等原因，PPP市场透明度指数被人为分成了即时公开指数和适时公开指数，而随着PPP综合信息平台的进一步完善，特别是如果各指标公布时间节点这样的信息也能准确得到记录的话，未来有望将即时公开和适时公开合而为一，从而使得PPP市场透明度指数的指标体系更加完善。除了评估相关信息是否披露外，还可以进一步评估披露的及时性等。此外，随着PPP事业的进一步深入发展，将会有越来越多的项目进入执行甚至移交阶段，而处于这些阶段的信息公开工作也会越来越重要，因而指标体系的重心也可以适当后移。

第二，信息质量可以纳入评估范围。正如前文提及过的，本报告仅评估PPP项目的信息公开工作，不评估这些信息所代表的具体工作的质量。例如，课题组仅仅评估了PPP物有所值评价报告、财政承受能力论证报告是否得到披露，而不对物有所值评价报告、财政承受能力论证报告具体内容的优劣、科学与否等作出判断。但我们知道这些信息都是非常重要的，因而未来这些重点报告的具体内容也可以考虑纳入专门的评估分析中，以考察各地区、各方在PPP规范化管理方面的工作业绩。

附件一　专家判定矩阵调查表

受亚洲开发银行的委托，上海财经大学PPP研究中心承担了《2020中国PPP市场透明度评估报告》的研究工作。报告将通过编制指数的方式，全面反映我国PPP市场透明度工作的成绩和不足。在指数编制过程中，不同具体指标之间包含的信息量和重要程度差异很大，因此，课题组想通过专家问卷调查的方式，确定PPP项目信息透明度各影响因素的相对权重（层次图如图3-1所示）。

为此，课题组根据层次分析法（AHP）的形式设计如下调查表。这种方法是在同一个层次对影响因素的重要性进行两两比较。衡量尺度划分为9个等级，其中9、7、5、3、1的数值分别对应绝对重要、十分重要、比较重要、稍微重要、同样重要，而8、6、4、2表示重要程度介于相邻的两个等级之间。

在下面的表格中，靠左边的等级单元格表示左列因素重要于右列因素，靠右边的等级单元格表示右列因素重要于左列因素。请根据您的看法，在相应的单元格画"√"即可。您的判断对我们科学严谨地编制PPP市场透明度指数至关重要。

真诚感谢您的帮助！

上海财经大学PPP研究中心课题组

2021年1月8日

下列各组两两比较要素，对于“透明度总指数”的相对重要性如何？																		
重要性比较																		
适时公开	9	8	7	6	5	4	3	2	1	2	3	4	5	6	7	8	9	即时公开

下列各组两两比较要素，对于“适时公开”的相对重要性如何？																		
重要性比较																		
识别阶段	9	8	7	6	5	4	3	2	1	2	3	4	5	6	7	8	9	准备阶段
识别阶段	9	8	7	6	5	4	3	2	1	2	3	4	5	6	7	8	9	采购阶段
准备阶段	9	8	7	6	5	4	3	2	1	2	3	4	5	6	7	8	9	采购阶段

下列各组两两比较要素，对于“即时公开”的相对重要性如何？																		
重要性比较																		
识别阶段	9	8	7	6	5	4	3	2	1	2	3	4	5	6	7	8	9	准备阶段
识别阶段	9	8	7	6	5	4	3	2	1	2	3	4	5	6	7	8	9	采购阶段
识别阶段	9	8	7	6	5	4	3	2	1	2	3	4	5	6	7	8	9	执行阶段
准备阶段	9	8	7	6	5	4	3	2	1	2	3	4	5	6	7	8	9	采购阶段
准备阶段	9	8	7	6	5	4	3	2	1	2	3	4	5	6	7	8	9	执行阶段
采购阶段	9	8	7	6	5	4	3	2	1	2	3	4	5	6	7	8	9	执行阶段

附件二　PPP综合信息平台信息公开管理暂行办法

关于印发《政府和社会资本合作（PPP）综合信息平台信息公开管理暂行办法》的通知

（财金〔2017〕1号）

各省、自治区、直辖市、计划单列市财政厅（局），新疆生产建设兵团财务局，财政部驻各省、自治区、直辖市、计划单列市财政监察专员办事处：

为进一步贯彻落实《国务院办公厅转发财政部 发展改革委 人民银行关于在公共服务领域推广运用政府和社会资本合作模式指导意见的通知》》（国办发〔2015〕42号）有关要求，加强和规范政府和社会资本合作（PPP）项目信息公开工作，促进PPP项目各参与方诚实守信、严格履约，保障公众知情权，推动PPP市场公平竞争、规范发展，我们研究起草了《政府和社会资本合作（PPP）综合信息平台信息公开管理暂行办法》，现印发你们，请遵照执行。

财政部

2017年1月23日

政府和社会资本合作（PPP）综合信息平台信息公开管理暂行办法

第一章　总　则

第一条　为加强和规范政府和社会资本合作（PPP）信息公开工作，促进PPP项目各参与方诚实守信、严格履约，保障公众知情权，推动PPP市场公平竞争、规范发展，依据《中华人民共和国预算法》、《中华人民共和国政府采购法》和《国务院办公厅转发财政部 发展改革委 人民银行关于在公共服务领域推广政府和社会资本合作模式指导意见的通知》(国办发〔2015〕42号)等有关规定，制定本办法。

第二条　中华人民共和国境内已纳入PPP综合信息平台的PPP项目信息公开，适用本办法。

第三条　PPP项目信息公开遵循客观、公正、及时、便利的原则。

第四条　地方各级财政部门(以下简称“财政部门”)会同同级政府有关部门推进、指导、协调、监督本行政区域范围内的PPP项目信息公开工作，结合当地实际具体开展以下工作：

(一) 收集、整理PPP项目信息；

(二) 在PPP综合信息平台录入、维护和更新PPP项目信息；

(三) 组织编制本级政府PPP项目信息公开年度工作报告；

(四) 根据法律法规规定和实际需要，在其他渠道同时公开PPP项目信息；

(五) 与PPP项目信息公开有关的其他工作。

政府有关部门、项目实施机构、社会资本或PPP项目公司等PPP项目参与主体应真实、完整、准确、及时地提供PPP项目信息。

第二章　信息公开的内容

第五条　项目识别阶段应当公开的PPP项目信息包括：

(一) 项目实施方案概要，包含：项目基本情况(含项目合作范围、合作期限、项目产出说明和绩效标准等基本信息)、风险分配框架、运作方式、交易结构(含投融资结构、回报机制、相关配套安排)、合同体系、监管架构、采购方式选择；

(二) 经财政部门和行业主管部门审核通过的物有所值评价报告，包含：定性评价的指标及权重、评分标准、评分结果；定量评价测算的主要指标、方法、过程和结果(含PSC值、PPP值)等(如有)；物有所值评价通过与否的结论；

(三) 经财政部门审核通过的财政承受能力论证报告，包含：本项目各年度财政支出责任数额及累计支出责任总额，本级政府本年度全部已实施和拟实施的PPP项目各年度财政支出责任数额总和及其占各年度一般公共预算支出比例情况；财政承受能力论证的测算依据、主要因素和指标等；财政承受能力论证通过与否的结论；

（四）其他基础资料，包括：新建或改扩建项目建议书及批复文件、可行性研究报告（含规划许可证、选址意见书、土地预审意见、环境影响评价报告等支撑性文件）及批复文件、设计文件及批复文件（如有）；存量公共资产建设、运营维护的历史资料以及第三方出具的资产评估报告，以及存量资产或权益转让时所可能涉及到的员工安置方案、债权债务处置方案、土地处置方案等（如有）。

第六条　项目准备阶段应当公开的PPP项目信息包括：

（一）政府方授权文件，包括对实施机构、PPP项目合同的政府方签约主体、政府方出资代表（如有）等的授权；

（二）经审核通过的项目实施方案（含同级人民政府对实施方案的批复文件），包含：项目基本情况（含项目合作范围、合作期限、项目产出说明和绩效标准等基本信息），风险分配框架，运作方式，交易结构（含投融资结构、回报机制、相关配套安排），合同体系及核心边界条件；监管架构；采购方式选择；

（三）按经审核通过的项目实施方案验证的物有所值评价报告（如有）；

（四）按经审核通过的项目实施方案验证的财政承受能力论证报告（如有）。

第七条　项目采购阶段的信息公开应遵照政府采购等相关规定执行，应当公开的PPP项目信息包括：

（一）项目资格预审公告（含资格预审申请文件）及补充公告（如有）；

（二）项目采购文件，包括竞争者须知、PPP项目合同草案、评审办法（含评审小组组成、评审专家人数及产生方式、评审细则等）；

（三）补遗文件（如有）；

（四）资格预审评审及响应文件评审结论性意见；

（五）资格预审专家、评审专家名单、确认谈判工作组成员名单；

（六）预中标、成交结果公告；

（七）中标、成交结果公告及中标通知书；

（八）项目采购阶段更新、调整的政府方授权文件（如有），包括对实施机构、PPP项目合同的政府方签约主体、政府方出资代表（如有）等的授权；

（九）同级人民政府同意签署PPP项目合同的批复文件，以及已签署的PPP项目合同，并列示主要产出说明及绩效指标、回报机制、调价机制等核心条款。

第八条　项目执行阶段应当公开的PPP项目信息包括：

（一）项目公司（如有）设立登记、股东认缴资本金及资本金实缴到位情况、增减资情况（如有）、项目公司资质情况（如有）；

（二）项目融资机构名称、项目融资金额、融资结构及融资交割情况；

（三）项目施工许可证、建设进度、质量及造价等与PPP项目合同有关约定的对照审查情况；

（四）社会资本或项目公司的运营情况（特别是出现重大经营或财务风险，可能严重影响到社会资本或项目公司正常运营的情况）及运营绩效达标情况；

（五）项目公司绩效监测报告、中期评估报告、项目重大变更或终止情况、项目定价及历次调价情况；

（六）项目公司财务报告，包括项目收费情况，项目获得的政府补贴情况，项目公司资产负债情况等内容；

（七）项目公司成本监审、PPP项目合同的变更或补充协议签订情况；

（八）重大违约及履约担保的提取情况，对公众投诉的处理情况等；

（九）本级政府或其职能部门作出的对项目可能产生重大影响的规定、决定等；

（十）项目或项目直接相关方（主要是PPP项目合同的签约各方）重大纠纷、诉讼或仲裁事项，但根据相关司法程序要求不得公开的除外；

（十一）本级PPP项目目录、本级PPP项目示范试点库及项目变化情况、本级人大批准的政府对PPP项目的财政预算、执行及决算情况等。

第九条　项目移交阶段应当公开的PPP项目信息包括：

（一）移交工作组的组成、移交程序、移交标准等移交方案；

（二）移交资产或设施或权益清单、移交资产或权益评估报告（如适用）、性能测试方案，以及移交项目资产或设施上各类担保或权益限制的解除情况；

（三）项目设施移交标准达标检测结果；

（四）项目后评价报告（含对项目产出、成本效益、监管成效、可持续性、PPP模式应用等进行绩效评价），以及项目后续运作方式。

第三章　信息公开的方式

第十条　PPP项目信息公开的方式包括即时公开和适时公开。

第十一条　即时公开是指财政部门会同有关部门和项目实施机构等依据PPP项目所处的不同阶段及对应的录入时间要求，在PPP综合信息平台录入本办法规定的相关信息时即自动公开。即时公开的内容及要求详见本办法附件。

第十二条　适时公开是指在录入本办法规定的相关信息时不自动公开，而是由财政部门会同有关部门选择在项目进入特定阶段或达成特定条件后再行公开。除本办法另有规定外，项目识别、准备、采购阶段的信息，由财政部门会同有关部门选择在项目进入执行阶段后6个月内的任一时点予以公开；项目执行阶段的信息，由财政部门会同相关部门选择在该信息对应事项确定或完成后次年的4月30日前的任一时点予以公开。前述期限届满后未选择公开的信息将转为自动公开。适时公开的内容及要求详见本办法附件。

第十三条　依照本办法公开的PPP项目信息可在财政部政府和社会资本合作中心官方网站（www.cpppc.org）上公开查询。其中PPP项目政府采购信息应当在省级以上人民政府财政部门指定的政府采购信息发布媒体上同步发布。

第四章　监督管理

第十四条　财政部对全国PPP项目信息公开情况进行评价和监督，省级财政部门负责对本省PPP项目信息公开工作进行监督管理。下级财政部门未按照本办法规定真实、完整、准确、及时录入应公开PPP项目信息的，上级财政部门应责令其限期改正；逾期拒不改正或情节严重的，予以通报批评。

第十五条　政府有关部门、项目实施机构、社会资本或PPP项目公司等PPP项目信息提供方应当对其所提供信息的真实性、完整性、准确性、及时性负责。一经发现所提供信息不真实、不完整、不准确、不及时的，PPP项目信息提供方应主动及时予以修正、补充或采取其他有效补救措施。如经财政部门或利益相关方提供相关材料证实PPP项目信息提供方未按照规定提供信息或存在其他不当情形的，财政部门可以责令其限期改正；无正当理由拒不改正的，财政部门可将该项目从项目库中清退。被清退的项目自清退之日起一年内不得重新纳入PPP综合信息平台。

第十六条 财政部门应会同政府有关部门在每年2月28日前完成上一年度本级政府实施的PPP项目信息公开年度工作报告，报送省级财政部门，并由省级财政部门在每年3月31日前汇总上报至财政部。报告内容应包括：

（一）即时和适时公开PPP项目信息的情况；

（二）PPP项目信息公开工作存在的主要问题及改进情况；

（三）其他需要报告的事项。

第十七条 财政部门工作人员在PPP项目信息公开监督管理工作中存在滥用职权、玩忽职守、徇私舞弊等违法违纪行为的，按照《公务员法》、《行政监察法》、《财政违法行为处罚处分条例》等国家有关规定追究相应责任；涉嫌犯罪的，移送司法机关处理。

第十八条 公民、法人或者其他组织可以通过PPP综合信息平台对PPP项目信息公开情况提供反馈意见，相关信息提供方应及时予以核实处理。

第五章 附 则

第十九条 PPP综合信息平台是指依据《关于规范政府和社会资本合作（PPP）综合信息平台运行的通知》（财金〔2015〕166号）由财政部建立的全国PPP综合信息管理和发布平台，包含项目库、机构库、资料库三部分。

第二十条 PPP项目信息公开涉及国家秘密、商业秘密、个人隐私、知识产权，可能会危及国家安全、公共安全、经济安全和社会稳定或损害公民、法人或其他组织的合法权益的，依照相关法律法规处理。

第二十一条 本办法自2017年3月1日起施行。

PPP项目信息公开要求

项目所处阶段	公 开 内 容	公开方式	公开的时点	信息提供方
项目识别	项目概况、项目合作范围、合作期限、项目运作方式、采购社会资本方式的选择	即时公开	实施方案编制完成之日起10个工作日内	项目发起方

（续表）

项目所处阶段	公　开　内　容	公开方式	公开的时点	信息提供方
项目识别	交易结构（含投融资结构、回报机制、相关配套安排）、项目产出说明和绩效标准、风险分配框架、合同体系、监管体系	适时公开	进入项目执行阶段后6个月内	项目发起方
	物有所值定性评价指标及权重、评分标准、评分结果	即时公开	报告定稿之日起10个工作日内	
	物有所值评价通过与否的评价结论（含财政部门会同行业部门对报告的审核意见）	即时公开	实施方案批复文件下发后10个工作日内	
	审核通过的物有所值评价报告（含财政部门对报告的批复文件）	适时公开	进入项目执行阶段后6个月内	
	本项目以及年度全部已实施和拟实施的PPP项目财政支出责任数额及年度预算安排情况，以及每一年度全部PPP项目从预算中安排的支出责任占一般公共预算支出比例情况	即时公开	实施方案批复文件下发后10个工作日内	
	财政承受能力论证的测算依据、主要因素和指标	即时公开	报告定稿之日起10个工作日内	
	通过财政承受能力论证与否的结论	即时公开	实施方案批复文件下发后10个工作日内	
	审核通过的财政承受能力论证报告（含财政部门对报告的批复文件）	适时公开	进入项目执行阶段后6个月内	
	新建或改扩建项目建议书及批复文件	适时公开	进入项目执行阶段后6个月内	实施机构
	可行性研究报告（含全套支撑性文件）及批复文件，设计文件及批复文件（如适用）	适时公开	进入项目执行阶段后6个月内	实施机构
	存量公共资产或权益的资产评估报告，以及存量资产或权益转让时所可能涉及到的各类方案等（如适用）	适时公开	进入项目执行阶段后6个月内	实施机构

（续表）

项目所处阶段	公　开　内　容	公开方式	公开的时点	信息提供方
项目准备	政府方授权文件，包括对实施机构、PPP项目合同的政府方签约主体、政府方出资代表（如适用）等的授权	即时公开	授权后10个工作日内	项目所在地本级政府
	项目概况、项目合作范围、合作期限、项目运作方式、采购社会资本方式的选择	即时公开	进入采购程序后10个工作日内	实施机构
	交易结构（含投融资结构、回报机制、相关配套安排）、项目产出说明和绩效标准、风险分配框架、核心边界条件、合同体系、监管体系	适时公开	进入项目执行阶段后6个月内	实施机构
	政府对实施方案的审核批复文件	即时公开	批复文件下发后10个工作日内	实施机构
	审核通过的项目实施方案及修正案	适时公开	进入项目执行阶段后6个月内	实施机构
项目采购	项目资格预审公告（含资格预审申请文件）	即时公开	资格预审公告发布后10个工作日内	实施机构
	项目采购文件、补遗文件（如有）	适时公开	进入项目执行阶段后6个月内	实施机构
	资格预审评审报告及响应文件评审报告中专家组评审结论性意见，附资格预审专家和评审专家名单	适时公开	进入项目执行阶段后6个月内	采购监管机构
	确认谈判工作组成员名单	适时公开	进入项目执行阶段后6个月内	实施机构
	预中标及成交结果公告；中标、成交结果公告及中标通知书	即时公开	依法律规定及采购文件约定	实施机构、采购监管机构
	已签署的PPP项目合同	适时公开	进入项目执行阶段后6个月内	实施机构
	PPP项目合同核心条款，应包括主要产出说明、绩效指标回报机制、调价机制	即时公开	项目合同经人民政府审核通过后10个工作日内	实施机构、项目公司

（续表）

项目所处阶段	公　开　内　容	公开方式	公开的时点	信息提供方
项目采购	本项目政府支出责任确认文件或更新调整文件（如适用），以及同级人大（或人大常委会）将本项目财政支出责任纳入跨年度预算的批复文件（如适用）	适时公开	进入项目执行阶段后6个月内	实施机构
	项目采购阶段调整、更新的政府方授权文件（如有）	即时公开	项目合同经人民政府审核通过后10个工作日内的附件依据相关法律规定公开	实施机构
项目执行	项目公司设立登记、股东认缴及实缴资本金情况、增减资（如适用）	即时公开	设立时及资本金到位后10个工作日内	项目公司
	融资额度、融资主要条件及融资交割情况	适时公开	对应事项确定或完成后次年的4月30日前	项目公司
	项目施工许可证、建设进度、质量及造价等与PPP项目合同的符合性审查情况	即时公开	依据PPP项目合同约定；如PPP项目合同未约定时，则在对应活动结束后次年的4月30日前予以公开	实施机构、项目公司
	社会资本或项目公司的年度运营情况及运营绩效达标情况	即时公开	依据PPP项目合同约定；如PPP项目合同未约定时，则在对应活动结束后次年的4月30日前予以公开	项目公司
	项目公司绩效监测报告、中期评估报告、项目重大变更或终止情况、项目定价及历次调价情况	即时公开	依据PPP项目合同约定；如PPP项目合同未约定时，则在对应活动结束后次年的4月30日前予以公开	实施机构
	项目公司成本监审、所有的PPP合同修订协议或补充协议	适时公开	对应活动结束后次年的4月30日前	实施机构项目公司
	项目公司财务报告相关内容，包括项目收费情况，项目获得的政府补贴情况，项目公司资产负债情况等	适时公开	对应活动结束后次年的4月30日前	项目公司
	重大违约及履约担保的提取情况，对公众投诉的处理情况等	即时公开	发生之日起10个工作日内	实施机构
	本级政府或其职能部门作出的对项目可能产生重大影响的规定、决定等	即时公开	规定及决定 下发后10个工作日	实施机构

（续表）

项目所处阶段	公 开 内 容	公开方式	公开的时点	信息提供方
项目执行	项目或项目直接相关方重大纠纷、涉诉或涉仲情况	即时公开	除本办法另有规定外，发生后10个工作日内	项目公司
	本级PPP项目目录、本级PPP项目示范试点库及项目变化情况、本级人大批准的政府对PPP项目的财政预算、执行及决算情况等	即时公开	依法律规定（如有）公开或每季度公开	
项目移交	移交工作组的组成、移交程序、移交标准等移交方案	即时公开	移交方案确定后10个工作日内	实施机构
	移交资产或设施或权益清单、移交资产或权益评估报告（如适用）、性能测试方案	即时公开	清单或报告定稿或测试完成后10个工作日内	实施机构
	移交项目资产或设施上各类担保或权益限制的解除情况（如适用）	即时公开	对应解除完成后10个工作日内	实施机构、项目公司
	项目设施移交标准达标检测结果	即时公开	达标检测结果出具后10个工作日内	实施机构
	项目后评价报告，以及项目后续运作方式	即时公开	后评估报告定稿或项目后续运作方式确定后10个工作日内	实施机构

附件三　PPP信息公开和规范管理制度目录

序号	发布时间	文件号	文　　件	发布者
1	2013.12.19	财政部74号令	《政府采购非招标采购方式管理办法》	财政部
2	2014.09.23	财金〔2014〕76号	《关于推广运用政府和社会资本合作模式有关问题的通知》	财政部
3	2014.11.29	财金〔2014〕113号	《关于印发政府和社会资本合作模式操作指南（试行）的通知》	财政部
4	2014.11.30	财金〔2014〕112号	《关于政府和社会资本合作示范项目实施有关问题的通知》	财政部
5	2014.12.30	财金〔2014〕156号	《关于规范政府和社会资本合作合同管理工作的通知》	财政部
6	2014.12.31	财金〔2014〕215号	《关于印发〈政府和社会合作项目政府采购管理办法〉的通知》	财政部
7	2014.12.31	财金〔2014〕214号	《关于印发〈政府采购竞争性磋商采购方式管理暂行办法〉的通知》	财政部
8	2015.02.13	财建〔2015〕29号	《关于推进市政公共领域开展政府和社会资本合作项目推介工作的通知》	财政部 住建部
9	2015.03.10	发改投资〔2015〕445号	《关于推进开发性金融支持政府和社会资本合作有关工作的通知》	国家发改委
10	2015.04.07	财金〔2015〕21号	《关于印发〈政府和社会合作项目财政承受能力论证指引〉的通知》	财政部
11	2015.05.19	国办发〔2015〕42号	《国务院办公厅转发财政部发展改革委人民银行关于在公共服务领域推广政府和社会资本合作模式指导意见的通知》	国务院办公厅

（续表）

序号	发布时间	文件号	文　件	发布者
12	2015.06.25	财金〔2015〕57号	《关于进一步做好政府和社会资本合作项目示范工作的通知》	财政部
13	2015.12.18	财金〔2015〕166号	《关于规范政府和社会资本合作（PPP）综合信息平台运行的通知》	财政部
14	2015.12.18	财金〔2015〕167号	《关于印发〈PPP物有所值评价指引（试行）〉的通知》	财政部
15	2016.01		《中华人民共和国政府和社会资本合作法（征求意见稿）》	财政部
16	2016.05.28	财金〔2016〕32号	《关于进一步共同做好政府和社会资本合作（PPP）有关工作的通知》	国家发改委、财政部
17	2016.10.20	财金〔2016〕92号	《关于印发〈政府和社会资本合作项目财政管理暂行办法〉的通知》	财政部
18	2016.12.21	发改投资〔2016〕2698号	《关于推进传统基础设施领域政府和社会资本合作（PPP）项目资产证券化相关工作的通知》	国家发改委
19	2016.12.30	财金〔2016〕144号	《财政部政府和社会资本合作（PPP）专家库管理办法》	财政部
20	2017.01.23	财金〔2017〕1号	《关于印发〈政府和社会资本合作（PPP）综合信息平台信息公开管理暂行办法〉的通知》	财政部
21	2017.03.22	财金〔2017〕8号	《关于印发〈政府和社会资本合作（PPP）咨询机构库管理暂行办法〉的通知》	财政部
22	2017.10.19		《政府和社会资本合作（PPP）项目资产支持证券挂牌条件确认指南和信息披露指南》	上海证券交易所
23	2017.11.10	财办金〔2017〕92号	《关于规范政府和社会资本合作（PPP）综合信息平台项目库管理的通知》	财政部
24	2019.03.07	财金〔2019〕10号	《财政部关于推进政府和社会资本合作规范发展的实施意见》	财政部
25	2020.03.16	财金〔2020〕13号	《政府和社会资本合作（PPP）项目绩效管理操作指引》	财政部

附件四　项目数大于30的城市PPP市场透明度排名

排名	城　　市	2020年项目数量	即时公开透明度指数	适时公开透明度指数	透明度总指数
1	云南大理	39	91.74	82.93	86.37
2	山东济宁	76	90.82	81.60	85.20
3	新疆博州	45	87.36	83.06	84.74
4	新疆阿克苏	56	87.88	82.48	84.59
5	山东东营	32	88.77	81.21	84.16
6	山东日照	54	87.40	81.72	83.94
7	云南玉溪	56	89.60	80.28	83.91
8	云南红河	53	89.39	79.97	83.64
9	山东烟台	38	89.37	79.72	83.49
10	安徽宣城	34	88.87	79.52	83.16
11	湖南益阳	31	91.03	78.05	83.11
12	河北邢台	40	84.56	82.01	83.00
13	河北承德	59	88.78	79.05	82.85
14	山东德州	38	88.86	78.93	82.80
15	云南昆明	62	89.18	78.70	82.79
16	河北石家庄	37	85.12	81.14	82.69
17	山东潍坊	93	89.03	78.59	82.66

（续表）

排名	城　市	2020年项目数量	即时公开透明度指数	适时公开透明度指数	透明度总指数
18	广西玉林	32	87.83	79.13	82.52
19	河北沧州	48	85.22	80.70	82.46
20	河北衡水	39	85.97	80.04	82.35
21	云南曲靖	44	88.21	78.47	82.27
22	河南南阳	81	86.14	79.13	81.87
23	河北保定	42	82.01	81.26	81.55
24	河南新乡	51	84.19	79.81	81.52
25	山东菏泽	63	86.68	77.65	81.17
26	河北唐山	55	86.23	77.70	81.03
27	河北邯郸	46	84.38	78.84	81.00
28	吉林长春	47	83.76	79.12	80.93
29	湖南长沙	43	87.33	76.80	80.91
30	湖南常德	38	88.49	75.97	80.85
31	广东东莞	135	82.67	79.68	80.85
32	江苏徐州	55	83.93	78.82	80.82
33	贵州黔西南	48	86.85	76.53	80.56
34	新疆乌鲁木齐	59	85.89	76.96	80.44
35	云南文山	35	87.24	75.98	80.37
36	贵州毕节	70	84.19	77.59	80.16
37	内蒙古呼伦贝尔	32	82.67	78.33	80.02
38	四川巴中	44	86.20	75.92	79.93
39	江苏南京	86	86.77	75.44	79.86
40	湖北宜昌	40	82.63	78.07	79.85
41	江苏宿迁	40	84.18	77.03	79.82
42	云南楚雄	37	85.70	75.97	79.76
43	陕西西安	81	85.14	76.10	79.62
44	广东江门	40	84.24	76.66	79.61

（续表）

排名	城　　市	2020 年项目数量	即时公开透明度指数	适时公开透明度指数	透明度总指数
45	河南平顶山	59	82.08	77.95	79.56
46	山东济南	56	87.19	74.56	79.48
47	河南洛阳	62	82.61	77.36	79.41
48	山西长治	42	82.85	77.19	79.40
49	江西九江	33	82.03	77.72	79.40
50	湖北荆门	33	84.53	76.06	79.36
51	山东临沂	68	81.46	77.87	79.27
52	内蒙古赤峰	52	85.03	75.54	79.24
53	贵州贵阳	49	82.15	77.36	79.22
54	山西大同	33	81.60	77.32	78.99
55	四川成都	58	84.70	75.21	78.91
56	山西吕梁	49	84.27	75.39	78.85
57	广西南宁	38	80.14	77.80	78.71
58	安徽阜阳	61	83.94	75.23	78.62
59	四川广元	34	81.13	76.92	78.56
60	贵州铜仁	32	79.94	77.51	78.46
61	江西萍乡	34	82.87	75.55	78.41
62	安徽亳州	34	82.45	75.60	78.27
63	四川乐山	32	80.28	76.96	78.26
64	浙江杭州	68	84.02	74.34	78.11
65	贵州六盘水	40	80.28	76.72	78.11
66	福建泉州	66	81.33	75.90	78.02
67	山西太原	37	82.58	75.04	77.98
68	河南濮阳	41	79.90	76.72	77.96
69	河南郑州	66	78.94	77.28	77.93
70	湖北武汉	70	80.43	75.86	77.64
71	河南周口	47	82.02	74.60	77.49

（续表）

排名	城　市	2020 年项目数量	即时公开透明度指数	适时公开透明度指数	透明度总指数
72	安徽滁州	36	81.23	75.02	77.44
73	湖南湘西	43	85.11	72.48	77.41
74	浙江丽水	61	83.38	73.58	77.40
75	浙江宁波	50	82.67	73.90	77.32
76	新疆巴音	51	78.99	76.20	77.28
77	浙江温州	82	79.52	75.78	77.24
78	辽宁沈阳	31	82.94	73.45	77.15
79	河南商丘	38	83.77	72.90	77.14
80	福建宁德	68	81.13	74.54	77.11
81	河南开封	37	77.74	76.70	77.11
82	贵州遵义	108	83.18	73.10	77.03
83	安徽安庆	48	79.74	75.25	77.00
84	山西临汾	57	79.96	75.09	76.99
85	河南信阳	55	79.20	75.55	76.98
86	湖南郴州	31	77.80	76.28	76.88
87	江苏淮安	39	84.99	71.60	76.82
88	安徽宿州	40	81.29	73.96	76.82
89	四川宜宾	62	78.77	75.53	76.79
90	河南驻马店	69	80.31	74.39	76.70
91	四川凉山	40	82.92	72.66	76.66
92	四川南充	37	85.43	70.86	76.54
93	山西运城	35	79.34	74.55	76.42
94	广东汕头	31	77.95	75.38	76.38
95	河南安阳	42	79.62	74.20	76.31
96	广东惠州	45	79.41	74.31	76.30
97	福建漳州	60	75.74	76.09	75.96
98	辽宁大连	48	79.77	73.44	75.91

（续表）

排名	城　　市	2020 年 项目数量	即时公开 透明度指数	适时公开 透明度指数	透明度总指数
99	安徽蚌埠	32	80.00	73.22	75.86
100	江西抚州	41	77.70	74.63	75.83
101	山西晋中	50	81.08	72.10	75.60
102	山西忻州	33	80.43	72.43	75.55
103	山东青岛	74	80.88	72.07	75.51
104	湖北咸宁	33	81.03	71.80	75.40
105	天津市辖	112	79.70	72.61	75.38
106	江西宜春	58	78.87	72.86	75.20
107	江西上饶	48	76.90	74.11	75.20
108	江西赣州	97	78.75	72.91	75.19
109	浙江台州	62	78.65	72.74	75.05
110	安徽六安	39	81.26	71.05	75.03
111	重庆县	43	77.69	73.11	74.89
112	湖北孝感	32	79.43	71.96	74.87
113	浙江湖州	45	81.08	70.64	74.71
114	广西柳州	35	78.12	71.65	74.17
115	福建福州	53	75.37	72.63	73.70
116	湖北襄阳	44	76.67	70.66	73.00
117	贵州黔南	54	72.43	72.46	72.45
118	贵州黔东南	56	75.38	70.47	72.39
119	浙江衢州	40	76.98	69.28	72.28
120	浙江金华	41	73.22	71.05	71.90
121	天津省本	177	73.65	68.53	70.53
122	海南海口	48	65.98	64.20	64.90

后　记

这份《2020中国PPP市场透明度报告》是由上海财经大学PPP研究中心课题组通力合作、共同撰写的。课题组核心成员包括上海财经大学公共经济与管理学院投资系方芳教授、宗庆庆副教授和石成博士生。课题组在2017—2019年连续三年PPP市场透明度指数编制的基础上，对截至2020年底的中国PPP市场的信息公开状况进行调查、分析和评估。评估过程中，课题组尽可能延续保持了指标体系和指数编制的稳定性，从而保证了2020年PPP市场透明度与前三年的评估结果可比，同时也对比分析了2020年PPP项目信息公开与前三年的情况变化。课题组希望能够通过准确、客观地反映中国PPP市场的信息公开状况，为中国PPP事业的健康持续发展尽绵薄之力。

本研究项目的顺利完成，得益于各方的大力支持与帮助。首先，上海财经大学公共经济与管理学院克服种种困难，为本课题的顺利开展提供了宝贵的经费资助。此外，财政部政府和社会资本合作中心为本课题的顺利开展给予了宝贵的数据支持，在此一并谢过。但需要再次说明的是，本报告是由课题组独立开展的，仅代表课题组的学术观点，并不代表上述机构的官方观点。

最后，陈纯、陈慧洁、陈宇莎、陈子浩、成莹、李少棠、李心怡、梁效、林煜辉、林子健、刘怡廷、戎佳祺、孙瑜诗、王婧涵、王俊淇、王开元、吴亚宁、武涵淇、曾薇、张志杰、赵晗、郑豪、徐铭昕等上海财经大学的研究生和本科生参与了本项目数据收集和整理等助研工作，在此一并致谢。

课题组再次对各方给予的支持和帮助表示最诚挚的谢意，同时也欢迎各界专家和从业者对课题组的工作提出宝贵意见和建议，以期未来编制的PPP市场透明度指数更加科学严谨。具体可与课题组成员联系：

宗庆庆老师（邮箱：zong.qingqing@mail.sufe.edu.cn）

PPP

2020

China PPP Market Transparency Report

PPP Research Center
Shanghai University of Finance and Economics

Shanghai University of Finance and Economics Press

2020

China PPP Market Transparency Report

Research Group

Fang Fang　　Zong Qingqing　　Shi Cheng

Abstract

PPPs is the acronym for Public-Private Partnerships. At present, China's PPP model is not only a means of market-oriented investment and financing by government, but also has become a comprehensive and systematic market and social reform on the provision of public infrastructure and services. Therefore, all stakeholders (both internal and external) have high expectations for the further development and implementation of PPP, hoping it could play a key role in leading the reform of public finance system and assisting the public sector in deepening reform. In this context, standardized arrangements for the management of PPP projects are particularly important. In particular, the timely and complete information disclosure of PPP projects is the basis for standardized management of PPP projects. From 2017, a number of documents issued by the Ministry of Finance have made provisions concerning the information disclosure of PPP projects. In particular, the *Interim Measures for Administration of Information Disclosure for Public-Private Partnership Integrated Information Platform* (Cai Jin [2017] No. 1) released in early 2017 specified all the requirements for information disclosure of PPP projects. When it came to 2018, the removal of PPP projects from management database became a key mission in PPP management. In specific, more than 2 000 PPP projects that failed to meet the management specifications were cleaned and removed from management database, while many new projects were added to the database as well. From the beginning of 2019, as more PPP projects come to the implementation stage, how to effectively promote the disclosure in due time of PPP projects becomes increasingly important. Meanwhile, the public has higher and higher requirements for the quality of PPP project information disclosed. On March 31, 2020, the Ministry of Finance released the *Guideline for*

PPP Project Performance Management, proposing a complete appraisal system for PPP performance. While clarifying who to take accountability, the document has also incorporated truthfulness, openness, transparency and quality into specific assessment rules.

Against this backdrop, the Research Group of Shanghai University of Finance and Economics, following the evaluation of the information disclosure of PPP projects in the past three years, carried out a detailed assessment on the latest status as of December 31, 2020. The Research Group assessed in detail the information disclosure work of 9 662 projects included into the management database as of the end of 2020, and compiled a set of "2020 China PPP Market Transparency Index", which incorporates 68 index fields and is divided into transparency index of immediate disclosure, transparency index of disclosure in due time, and transparency sub-indexes at each stage, i.e. identification, preparation, procurement, and implementation. Regarding the synthesis of indexes, the Research Group adopted an approach combining analytic hierarchy process (AHP) and expert scoring: for specific indexes under sub-indexes, different scores were set according to the importance determined by selected experts; and for the synthesis of sub-indexes, the Research Group adopted AHP, a method commonly used in the compilation of similar indexes, thus guaranteeing the reliability of the index preparation method. In the end, through the statistical analysis of final results, the Research Group obtained the following findings:

First, the overall national PPP market transparency index 2020 was 78.15, a slight improvement from 2019. As of December 31, 2020, the overall national PPP market transparency index recorded 78.15 (out of 100, the same below), an increase of about 2 points from 76.19 in 2019. In specific, the transparency index of immediate disclosure was 80.37, an increase of 1.2 points from last year (79.14), while the transparency index of disclosure in due time was 74.67, three points higher from last year (71.57). Further analysis on heterogeneity shows no obvious difference in the transparency scores between industries or between demonstration and non-demonstration projects.

Second, the overall PPP market information transparency index at the provincial level rose steadily, yet with a larger gap between different provinces. The transparency indexes of most provinces ranged from 70 to 85, but there are also a few provinces that presented a PPP transparency index higher than 82 or lower than 70. The top five provinces

are Yunnan (84.98), Shandong (83.72), Hebei (82.99), Hunan (82.69) and Jiangsu (82.63).

Third, most cities delivered PPP market transparency indexes higher than those in 2019. The Research Group selected 46 cities that managed a relatively large number of PPP projects (>50 projects in the management database) for more detailed analysis. Comparison with the indexes in 2019 shows that some cities above the prefecture level scored significantly higher in 2020 than in 2019. Among them, the largest increase was delivered by Aksu of Xinjiang, the 2020 overall score of which increased by 15.39 points compared to 2019; and followed by Dongguan of Guangdong, with increase of 13.62 points from 2019. However, it can also be found that the indexes of many cities above the prefecture level decreased in 2020 from 2019, especially Qiannan of Guizhou and Haikou of Hainan. They recorded the largest decline from 2019 by 13.10 and 12 points, respectively.

Fourth, PPP intermediaries showed minor cross-phase differences in information disclosure, with their transparency indexes positively related to qualifications and business volumes. Based on the assessment of information disclosure by PPP projects, we made a further analysis on the status quo of information disclosure by PPP intermediaries in this year's report. The main findings are as follows: the average transparency index of intermediaries was 70.16. In secondary indexes, projects engaged by intermediaries scored relatively high in terms of information disclosure, but some of them delivered less satisfactory performance in active information disclosure; further analysis also found that intermediaries' transparency indexes showed a clear positive correlation with the number of PPP projects they were engaged in and how long they had been operating.

During the preparation of this Report and the analysis behind it, the Research Group has also reached some policy recommendations for the further improvement of the information disclosure of PPP projects, such as to improve the management over the disclosure of "inapplicable" information and temporary major events, to further clarify the accountability and specific division of labor in information disclosure, etc. We hope to further enhance the information transparency in the PPP market by refining the system of PPP information disclosure and standardized management, thereby facilitating the better and more sustainable development of the entire PPP market.

Contents

1

Introduction

1.1 Basic Concept and Operating Procedure of PPP

1.1.1 PPP Definitions

Definitions of Public-Private Partnerships (PPPs) differ from international organizations and different governments, however they generally involve the use of private capital and in some cases, other forms of social capital in the investment and operation of infrastructure and public utility projects. The Asian Development Bank describes PPPs as a range of possible relationships among public and private sectors in the context of infrastructure and other services. The United Nations Development Programme, also refers to the partnership between government, for-profit companies and non-for-profit organizations regarding certain infrastructure and services projects. Typically, government does not transfer the project responsibility wholly to the private sector. Instead, the parties involved in the cooperation share responsibility and financing risks. The European Commission refers it to the partnership between public sector and private sector, with the aim of providing public projects or services traditionally provided by public sector. The World Bank also provides a definition of PPPs as long-term contracts between the private sector and a government entity regarding the provision of public infrastructure assets or services, in which the private sector bears material risks and management and delivery responsibility. The Chinese government has adopted a specific definition for the PPP model incorporating a long-term benefit and risk sharing partnership established by the government through franchising, reasonable pricing, financial subsidies and other agreed revenue sharing rules disclosed in advance, to introduce social capital to the investment and operation of public infrastructure projects such as urban utility, thus enhancing capacity of supplying public goods and services and improving supply efficiency. The main difference between the Chinese government definition and those by other international organizations and governments relates to the use of the word "social capital" in addition

to the word "private capital". In China, social capital covers private capital, foreign capital, state-owned enterprise capital, etc.

For the purposes of this Report, PPP refers to the provision of public products or services (usually infrastructure and public services) through a co-operative partnership between government and social capital. The government generally follows a competitive tendering model to select a social capital partner with optimal investment, financing, operation and management capabilities. The partnership is contracted so that the social capital partner provides public infrastructure and services and the government pays consideration to the social capital partner based on the performance and delivery evaluation of the contracted public infrastructure and/or services. Specifically, in this PPP model, the social capital partner can take charge of project design, construction, operation and maintenance of the infrastructure and the delivery of services as well as assuming commercial and financial risks, for a commensurate investment return (within a contract which clearly specifies the delivery obligations of the social capital partner). The government in turn supervises the quality and pricing of public services and infrastructure, protects the interests of consumers to ensure the maximization of public interests, and bears policy and legal risks. PPPs worldwide have evolved to cover most public infrastructure and/or service areas, including transportation, energy, water conservancy, water utilities and other economic infrastructure, as well as technology, environmental protection, education, culture, sports, health, tourism, social welfare and other social infrastructure.

1.1.2 PPP Operating Procedure

The *Guidelines for the Public-Private Partnerships Model* issued by the Ministry of Finance on November 2014 stipulate the operating standards for the life cycle of PPP projects, incorporating the stages of design, financing, construction, operation, maintenance, and termination & transfer. The operating procedure can be divided into five stages: identification, preparation, procurement, implementation and transfer of project. The separation of the five stages is a crucial intermediate step in the compilation of PPP market transparency indexes.

On this basis, in November 2017, the Ministry of Finance issued the *Circular on Regulating Project Database of the National PPP Integrated Information Platform* (Cai Ban Jin (2017) No. 92), which further optimizes the process management of PPP projects

Identification stage → Preparation stage → Procurement stage → Implementation stage → Transfer stage

Figure 1–1 Operating Procedure of PPP Projects

by implementing classification management, classifying the project database into Project Reserve List and Project Management Database according to the stage of the project. Projects in the Project Reserve List shall focus on project incubation and promotion; while those in the Project Management Database are subject to strict supervision and life cycle management. Compared with the five-stage division above, the Project Reserve List corresponds to the identification phase, and incorporates the candidate projects to which local government departments have the intention to apply the PPP model, but due to the fact that the value-for-money evaluation and the financial affordability assessment have not yet been completed, they cannot be called PPP projects in the strict sense; the Project Management Database covers the stages of preparation, procurement, implementation, and transfer, and incorporates the PPP projects subject to life cycle management in accordance with related management measures.

1.2 Concept of PPP Market Transparency

Information transparency refers to the degree of information disclosure of a market, company or project. For the purposes of this Report, transparency of PPP market refers to the degree of information disclosure of PPP projects by responsible parties (competent authorities, government-authorized partners, corporate partners, intermediaries, etc.). In theory, information disclosure across the PPP market also covers the disclosure of project management methods, policy documents, and the information of all project participants. For example, the existing PPP expert database, institution library, etc. also contains mass data, but due to data availability and other reasons, the PPP market information transparency in this Report refers only to the degree of information disclosure of PPP projects, and transparency indexes of all kinds are compiled on this basis. Horizontally, we constructed transparency indexes by province, city, and industry. Vertically, our indexes were divided into overall transparency index, immediate disclosure index, disclosure in due time index, and phased index. Besides PPP projects, this Report has also

incorporated the information transparency of PPP intermediaries, which is introduced in a separate chapter.

PPP is a market-oriented market-based public infrastructure and services mechanism which requires the management means and service capabilities that are compatible with marketization which requires transparency for the PPP market to deliver real value for money. PPP information disclosure in China has improved over the last three years following the systematic promotion of the PPP Integrated Information Platform. It has become an essential tool for local governments to strengthen project management, promote project connection, and facilitate project implementation. At present, China is accelerating the disclosure of PPP project information and government service information, with an aim to continuously improving PPP management transparency.

In particular, in January 2017, the Finance Department of the Ministry of Finance issued the No. 1 Document, i.e. the *Interim Measures for Administration of Information Disclosure for Public-Private Partnership Integrated Information Platform* (Cai Jin [2017] No. 1). This No.1 Document further clarifies the responsible parties of the PPP project information disclosure, details disclosure content, time limit and methods to ensure timely and full disclosure of key information such as the basic information, implementation program, evaluation and assessment report, procurement documents, project contracts and other information of the PPP projects to be included in the database. It also requires disclosure priority of demonstration projects to ensure that projects operate in a transparent manner, strengthen government supervision and social supervision, and promote project implementation. PPP projects that more completely meet the information disclosure requirements of the No. 1 Document are projects which will be assessed as projects with high information transparency, and where projects fail to disclose the information as required by the No. 1 Document, they will be assessed as projects with low information transparency. Moreover, in order to ensure the objectiveness and fairness of the assessment, all relevant information beyond the scope of the No. 1 Document is not included in the assessment scope in this Report. The reason is that data used by the Research Group comes from the Integrated Information Platform of the China Public Private Partnerships Center, which was designed mainly based on capturing the information disclosure requirements detailed in the No. 1 Document.

1.3 Necessity and Significance of PPP Information Disclosure

First, improve business environment and encourage private capital to participate in public services. PPPs by nature are generally long term with the social capital providers (including private capital providers) often investing large sums of money over extended time period before any returns can be realized. Successful PPPs rely in part on the integrity of Government and the equity of the partnership arrangements. Therefore, improving the market transparency of the PPP processes can support greater participation in PPP projects, encourage competition which drives value and has the potential to create a fairer and more equal market environment. At the same time, improved PPP market transparency will also help support the partnering spirit between the government and enterprises, assist to eradicate corruption, and maintain a clean and efficient government image.

Second, promote social harmony and enhance public awareness and confidence. The adoption of PPP for the provision of public infrastructure and services is closely aligned to the interests of the public. PPP projects are usually infrastructure, goods and services provided for the general public, and therefore, the construction, operation and quality of which directly affects them. Additionally, PPP projects are ultimately paid either by taxpayers through taxation or by taxpayers directly as the end users. Therefore, strengthening the disclosure of PPP information will help the public to understand and supervise the PPP market and PPP projects in a more convenient manner, facilitate the understanding and cooperation of the public, and create a harmonious atmosphere for the progress of related work.

Third, improve supply efficiency and enhance performance management over public goods. PPP projects are mostly applied to infrastructure and other public goods and services. They are generally characterized by detailed information, frequently technical in nature and with complex pricing structures. Strengthening information disclosure will help professionals in various fields make scientific and rigorous appraisal concerning issues such as pricing benchmarks, financial affordability, and charging standards in PPP projects, thus realizing the scientific pricing of public goods and services. At the same time, higher PPP market transparency alleviates information asymmetry during the construction and operation of public goods, removes insider trading, realizes the

maintenance and appreciation of state-owned assets, and safeguards the rights and interests of taxpayers and consumers. Finally, sound information disclosure will also help resolve local debt and financial risks.

Fourth, raise governance level and build a new public management model. PPP is a market-oriented and socialized management model for the provision of public goods and services. It aims to, via reforms and innovations, break monopolies, introduce competition mechanisms, utilize market's professional and innovation capabilities, enrich public goods and services and improve the provision quality of public goods and services, to satisfy the growing demands of people for diverse public goods and services. Therefore, it is of great practical significance to improving governance and building a new public management model. Early in the 1980s and 1990s, China began to experiment with public-private partnerships in the field of infrastructure construction. However, due to the absence of institutional construction, the projects faced "variation and distortion". To solve such problems, in this round of PPP promotion, the competent department of the industry started with institutional construction by formulating a system in line with the concept of "top-level design + supporting policies + operating guidelines", covering the life cycle of PPP. Adequate information disclosure is an integral part of the system, where competent authorities could take PPP information disclosure as a means to urging local governments and all relevant parties to participate in PPP projects in a more regulated manner, thereby jointly promoting the continuous improvement of the new management model.

Fifth, promote PPP development and propel the comprehensive deepening of reform process. Promoting PPPs in the provision of public infrastructure and services is an important factor in the delivery of reform. It is also an important measure for advancing structural reform at the supply side, and an important means for implementing innovation-driven development and developing the new economy. Driving the development of PPP market fully reflects the core spirit of law-based governance, giving play to the decisive role of market in the allocation of resources, and better exerting the function of the government. The development of PPP market has promoted reform of the administrative system, the financial system, and the investment & financing systems. Therefore, the standardized development of PPP market brought about by improving its transparency is also of great value to other reforms. At present, China's PPP market is in a leading position in terms of disclosure work among similar government affairs, and even in the

whole world. In-depth assessment, analysis and summary of achievements and experience in PPP market's information disclosure work can provide reference value for other reforms.

Sixth, build up national image and demonstrate national confidence in political system. Many countries use PPPs for the delivery of infrastructure and services, as attracted the participation of multiple international organizations. After years of exploration and consideration of options, China has formed its own model and style of PPP projects, and has made innovations in many aspects of PPP models. Accordingly, the summary and analysis on the information transparency of PPP market is important in the shaping of an open and efficient image of the Chinese government as well as increasing its influence and participation in the international PPP market. Moreover, as infrastructure is also an important component of the Belt and Road Initiative, promoting PPP standardization through information disclosure helps China's PPP model to spread in the countries and regions along the Belt and Road, demonstrating China's soft power while exporting products and technologies.

1.4 Development of PPP Information Disclosure in China

Since the initiation of PPP projects in 2013, as deployed by the CPC Central Committee and the State Council, the Ministry of Finance has successively issued the *Interim Measures for Administration of Information Disclosure for Public-Private Partnership Integrated Information Platform* (Cai Jin [2017] No. 1), the *Circular on Regulating Project Database of the National PPP Integrated Information Platform* (Cai Ban Jin [2017] No. 92) and the *Circular on Further Regulating the Project Information Management of the National PPP Integrated Information Platform* (Cai Zheng Qi Han [2018] No. 2), among other documents. And the Ministry of Finance is responsible for planning and implementing the PPP reform and promoting the information disclosure of PPP projects.

I. The National PPP Integrated Information Platform has been established. In 2015, under the guidance of the national "Internet+" action plan, the Ministry of Finance established the PPP Integrated Information Platform — a PPP information network covering all regions of the country and 19 sectors, penetrating all aspects of project

implementation, and serving all market players. First, a channel for the collection and management of PPP project information that runs through the finance departments of "state-province-city-county" at all levels has been built up. Second, two platforms — information disclosure and online management, have been set up to publish PPP policies and regulations, news, share knowledge, and enable information tracking & management; and three functions: project management, transaction matchmaking, and information service are offered. Finally, four core application databases, i.e. Project Database, Expert Library, Institution Library and Data Bank are built: Project Database is used to collect and manage key information of PPP projects across the country; Expert Library and Institution Library are designed for the collection and management of the information on experts, consulting agencies, private capital, financial institutions and other parties involved; Data Bank collects and manages PPP related policies and regulations, work updates, guidebooks, training materials and best practices.

II. An information disclosure mechanism has been set up. It clarifies the accountability for information disclosure of PPP projects, the information to be disclosed and specific requirements at each stage, makes regulations for the management of Expert Library and Institution Library, and publishes requirements for information disclosure by PPP experts and consulting organizations.

III. The PPP information disclosure system has been innovated. The information on the addition and removal of PPP projects is disclosed on a monthly basis, and overall PPP project information statistics and release are carried out on a quarterly basis. PPP policies and work updates are published through multiple channels, including the "PPP column" on the official website of the Ministry of Finance, the Chinese and English websites of the China Public Private Partnerships Center (CPPPC), the WeChat public account "China PPP Center", the mobile application "China PPP Map" and other online media. So far, a PPP project information disclosure model featuring regularity, comprehensiveness and multiple approaches has been established in China.

Thanks to the care, support and joint efforts of all stakeholders, PPP information disclosure has achieved positive results. Project Database, Institution Library and Expert Library are gaining greater social influence and recognition, and have become useful tools for strengthening project management, advancing project connection, and promoting project implementation. The Project Database Quarterly Report is regarded as the "CSI 300 Index" in the PPP market. Financial institutions have even opened up a "green channel" for the credit

support granted to demonstration projects that have done a better job in information disclosure. According to statistics, as of the end of December 2020, the PPP Integrated Information Platform included 10 010 projects and 360 PPP intermediaries. Websites, WeChat accounts, etc. have become the authoritative publishing platforms for PPP news. On March 31, 2020, the Ministry of Finance released the *Guideline for PPP Project Performance Management*, proposing a complete appraisal system for PPP performance. While clarifying who to take accountability, the document has also incorporated truthfulness, openness, transparency and quality into specific assessment rules. The Guideline is expected to more accurately and effectively improve the quality of information disclosure.

PPP information disclosure has played a positive role in the China's PPP development. The Benchmarking Infrastructure Development 2020 released by the World Bank has evaluated the PPP policies and regulations in 140 economies from four dimensions: preparation of PPPs, procurement of PPPs, PPP contract management and unsolicited proposals (USPs) for PPPs. The report noted that China has established a basic PPP institutional framework, standardized the operation methods on key stages such as the value-for-money evaluation report and the financial affordability assessment report, and formulated a system for publicizing important information such as procurement documents and project progress, thus having created a favorable policy environment. In specific, China scored 80 points in Procurement of PPPs (average score of high-income economies, 73; average score of upper-middle-income economies, 62), ranking among the top in the world; 81 points in Contract Management (average score of high-income economies, 64; average score of upper-middle-income economies, 64); 54 points in Preparation (average score of high-income economies, 50; average score of upper-middle-income economies, 44); 50 points in USP (average score of high-income economies, 63; average score of upper-middle-income economies, 60).

The achievements and experience gained in disclosing PPP market information needs summary. At the same time, it is also necessary to analyze the content waiting for further improvement. The purpose of this Report is to summarize the disclosure work of the PPP market and analyze its strengths and deficiencies through index preparation. The rigorous and fair assessment on market transparency depends on scientific assessment methods. As for this Report, such a principle is articulated by the design of the PPP market transparency index system and index preparation methods, which is the topic of the next chapter.

1.5 Overview of PPP Information Disclosure in China①

Pursuant to the *Circular on Regulating the Operation of the Public-Private Partnership (PPP) Integrated Information Platform* (Cai Jin [2015] No.166), the Ministry of Finance has developed the Public-Private Partnership (PPP) Integrated Information Platform and Project Library. The assessment of PPP project information disclosure in this Report is based on the data available on the Information Platform. In this section, with reference to such data, an overview of the PPP market in China is provided below.

1.5.1 Overview and Stages Distribution in National Project Management Database

As of the end of 2020, the Project Management Database included a total of 9 924 projects, an increase of 484, or 5.1% over the same period last year; the investment value totaled RMB 15.2 trillion, growing by RMB 0.8 trillion, or 5.6% year-on-year; these projects covered 31 provinces and Xinjiang Production and Construction Corps, and 19 industries. A total of 7 091 projects were implemented, with an investment value of RMB 11.4 trillion, and an implementation rate of 71.5%, rising by 4.4 percentage points from the end of 2019. A total of 4 270 projects with an investment value of RMB 6.6 trillion were started, representing an operating rate of 60.2%, 1.6 percentage points higher than that at the end of 2019. 860, 1 973, and 7 091 projects in the Project Management Database were at preparation, procurement, and implementation phases respectively, with investment values of RMB 1.1 trillion, RMB 2.7 trillion, and RMB 11.4 trillion, respectively, as shown in Figure 1–2. There are no projects in the transfer stage.

In 2020, the PPP market's focus shifted from quantity and speed to quality. Throughout the year, 998 new projects were included in the Project Management Database, a year-on-year decrease of 436 or 30.4%. They contributed to an investment value of RMB 1.6 trillion, dropping by RMB 0.6 trillion or 27.3% year-on-year. Due to

① The data in this section mainly come from the Abstract of the Annual Report of National PPP Integrated Information Platform — Project Management Database 2020 released by the China Public Private Partnerships Center. Due to missing data, sampling deadline and other reasons, the samples included in index compilation in the following paragraphs do not completely correspond to the samples in this section.

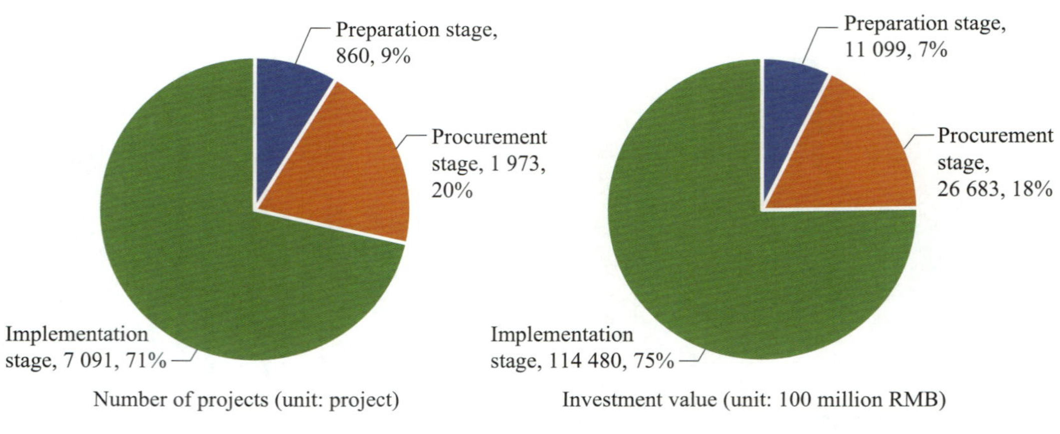

Figure 1–2 Management Database Projects in Each Stage in 2020

the change in investment value caused by the structural adjustment to inventory projects in the Management Database, the difference obtained from the investment value of newly-increased projects minus that of the removed projects was not the same as the net investment value increased.

The net increase of projects for the year recorded 484 (that is, the number of new projects in the Database at the end of 2020 minus that at the end of 2019), a year-on-year drop of 302 or 61.6%.

1.5.2 Distribution of Projects in Management Database by Region

In 2020, the top five provinces with most projects included into the Database were Guangxi (106 projects), Guizhou (102 projects), Yunnan (85 projects), Henan (82 projects), and Jiangxi (78 projects); the top five provinces in terms of investment value of newly-increased projects were Yunnan (RMB 280.9 billion), Guizhou (RMB 1 027 billion), Shanxi (RMB 98.5 billion), Sichuan (RMB 93.1 billion), and Henan (RMB 92.5 billion). See Figure 1–3 for the number and investment value of new projects in the Database by region in 2020.

In terms of the total number of projects in the Database, the top five provinces were Henan with 805 projects, Shandong (including Qingdao) 755, Sichuan 569, Guangdong 566, and Guizhou 549, together accounting for 32.7% of the total. Sorted by the total investment value, the top five were Yunnan with RMB 1.3 trillion, Guizhou RMB 1.2 trillion, Sichuan RMB 1.1 trillion, Henan RMB 1.0 trillion, and Zhejiang RMB 983.9 billion, accounting for 37.0% of the total. By region, the number and investment value of

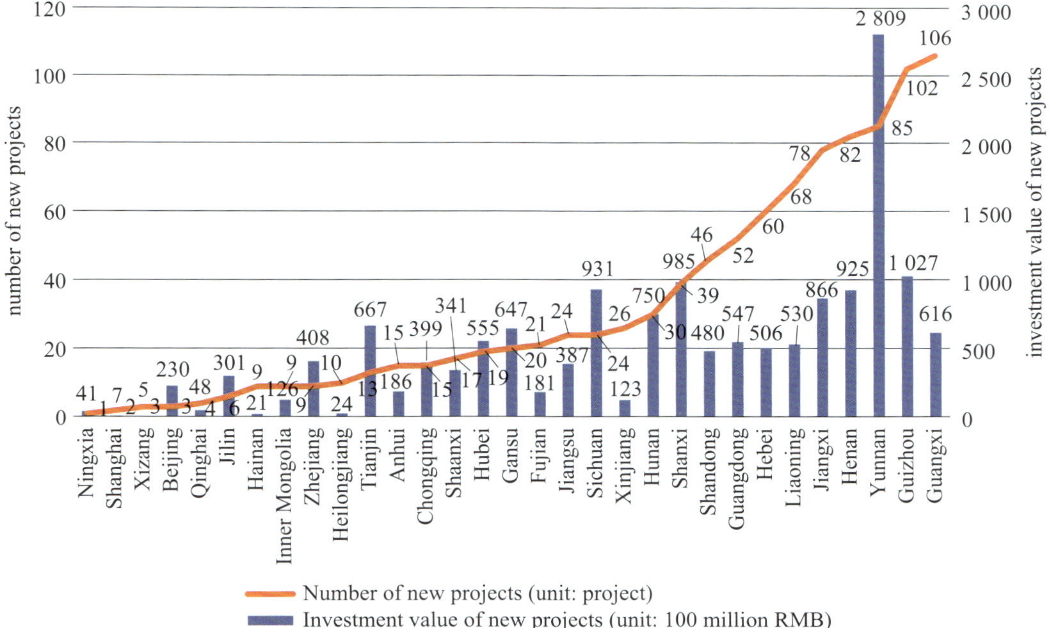

Figure 1–3 Number and Investment Value of New Projects in Management Database by Region in 2020

total projects in the Management Database at the end of 2020 are shown in Figure 1–4 and Figure 1–5.

1.5.3 Distribution of Projects in Management Database by Industry

In 2020, the top five industries with most new projects included to the Management Database were Municipal Engineering (393 projects), Transportation (107 projects), Ecological Construction and Environmental Protection (66 projects), Forestry (66 projects) and Education (66 projects); and the top five industries in terms of the investment value of newly-increased projects were Transportation (RMB 622.9 billion), Municipal Engineering (RMB 363.6 billion), Comprehensive Urban Development (RMB 114.3 billion), Ecological Construction and Environmental Protection (RMB 107.3 billion) and Forestry (RMB 78 billion). See Figure 1–6 for the number and investment value of new projects in the database by region in 2020.

By the end of 2020, the cumulative number and investment value of PPP projects in the Management Database by industry are shown in Figure 1–7 and Figure 1–8. In

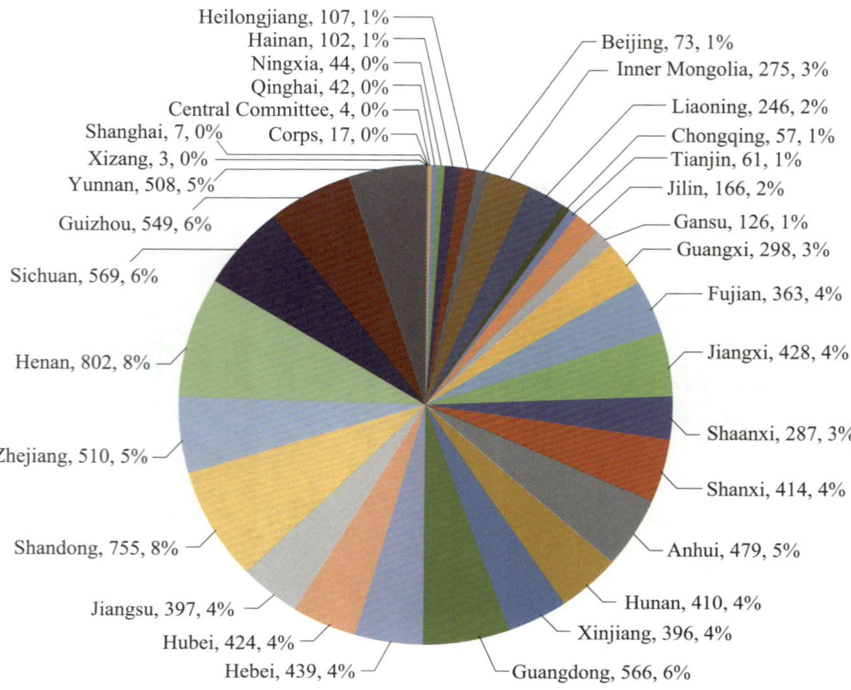

(unit: project)

Note: "Central Committee" refers to projects directly under the central Chinese government, the same below. "Corps" refers to the Xinjiang Production and Construction Corps, the same below.

Figure 1–4 Number of Projects in Management Database at the End of 2020 by Region

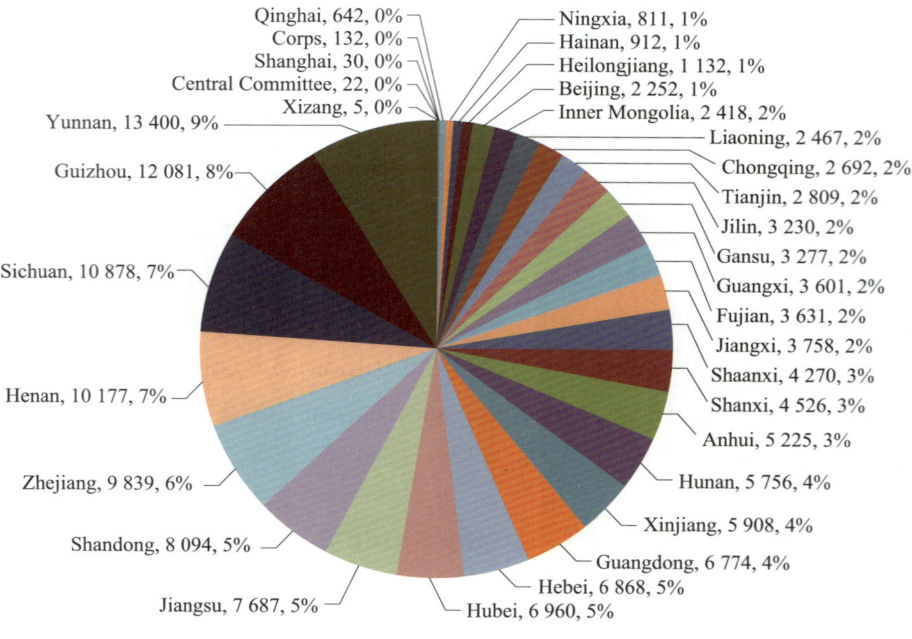

(unit: 100 million RMB)

Figure 1–5 Investment Value of Projects in Management Database at the End of 2020 by Region

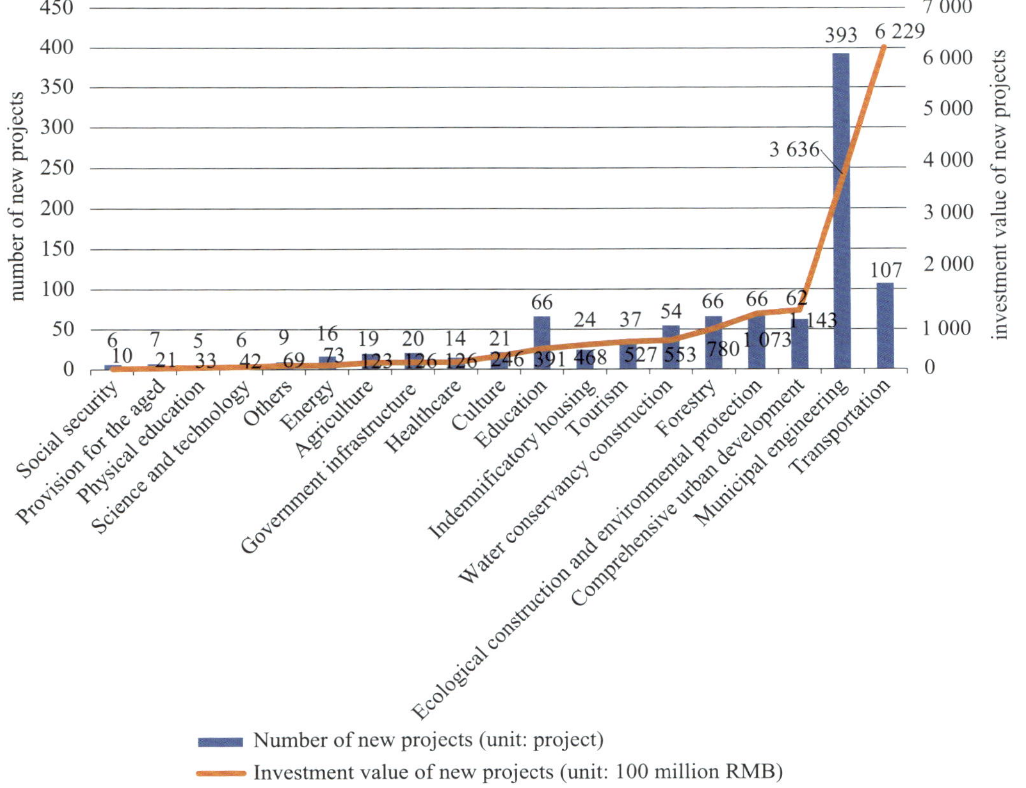

Figure 1–6 Number and Investment Value of New Projects in Management Database by Industry in 2020

specific, the top five industries with most projects in the Management Database were Municipal Engineering (4 051 projects), Transportation (1 361 projects), Ecological Construction and Environmental Protection (943 projects), Comprehensive Urban Development (621 projects) and Education (478 projects), together accounting for 75.1% of the total; and the top five industries in terms of the investment value of projects were Transportation (RMB 5.0 trillion), Municipal Engineering (RMB 4.4 trillion), Comprehensive Urban Development (RMB 2.0 trillion), Ecological Construction and Environmental Protection (RMB 1.0 trillion) and Tourism (RMB 417 billion), accounting for 84.4% of the total.

1.5.4 Proportion of viability gap funding projects increased steadily

Divided by the three return mechanisms, in 2020 alone there were 40 user-pays projects with an investment value of RMB 171.6 billion, accounting for 11.0% of the total

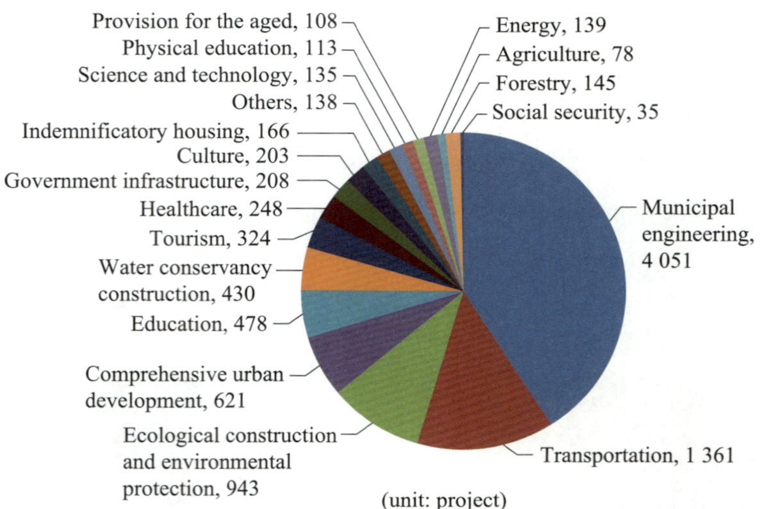

Figure 1–7 Number of Projects in Management Database at the End of 2020 by Industry

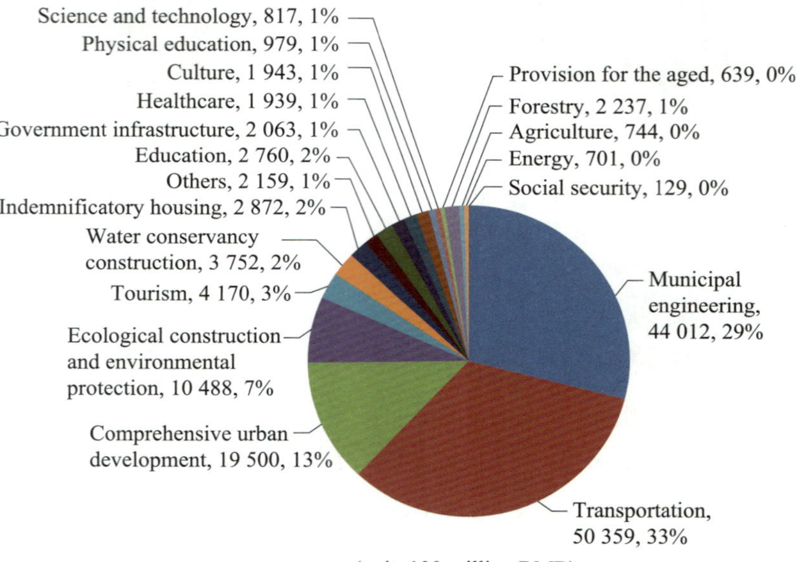

Figure 1–8 Investment Value of Projects in Management Database at the End of 2020 by Industry

investment value delivered by new projects in the database; 739 viability gap funding (that is, payment by both government and market) projects with an investment value of RMB 1.2622 trillion, accounting for 80.5% of the total; and 219 government-pays projects, with a net decrease of RMB 133.3 billion in investment value, accounting for 8.5% of the total.

As of the end of 2020, there were a total of 607 user-pays projects with an investment value of RMB 1.4 trillion, accounting for 6.1% and 9.3% of the total in the Management Database respectively; 5 806 viability gap funding projects with an investment value of RMB 10.4 trillion, accounting for 58.5% and 68.5% of the total; and 3 511 government-pays projects with an investment value of RMB 3.4 trillion, accounting for 35.4% and 22.2% of the total, as shown in Figure 1–9.

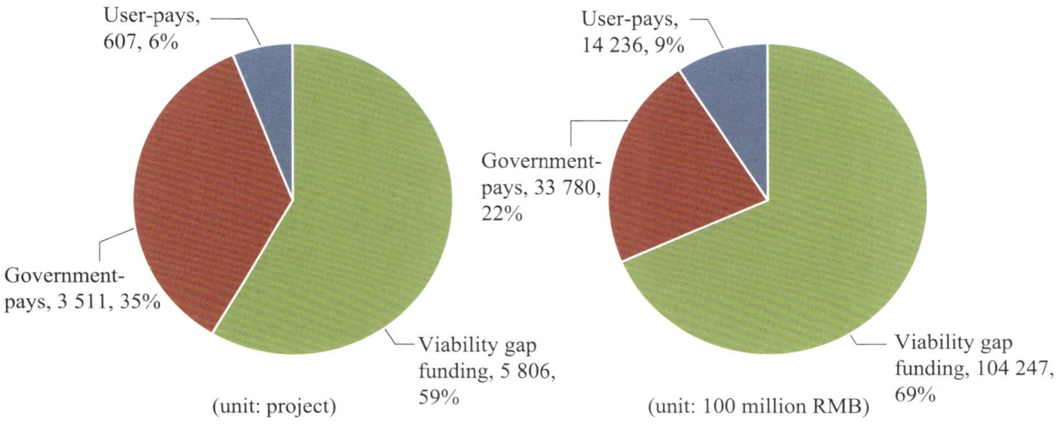

Figure 1–9 Number and Investment Value of Projects in Management Database by Payment Mechanism at the End of 2020

1.5.5 Proportion of BOT projects increased steadily

In 2020, the top three operation modes with most newly-added projects in the Management Database were BOT (743), TOT (110), and others (72); while the top three in terms of the investment value were BOT (RMB 1.2607 trillion), others (RMB 113 billion), and TOT (RMB 92.4 billion). See Figure 1–10 for the number and investment value of new projects in the Database by operation mode in 2020.

Ranking by the cumulative number of projects, the top three in the Management Database were BOT (7 789), others (971) and TOT+BOT (391), together accounting for 92.2% of the total number in the Project Database. By the cumulative investment value, the top three in the Management Database were BOT (RMB 1.2 trillion), others (RMB 2.0 trillion), and TOT+BOT (RMB 3 891 billion. The number and investment value of projects in the Management Database by operation mode by the end of 2020 are shown in Figure 1–11.

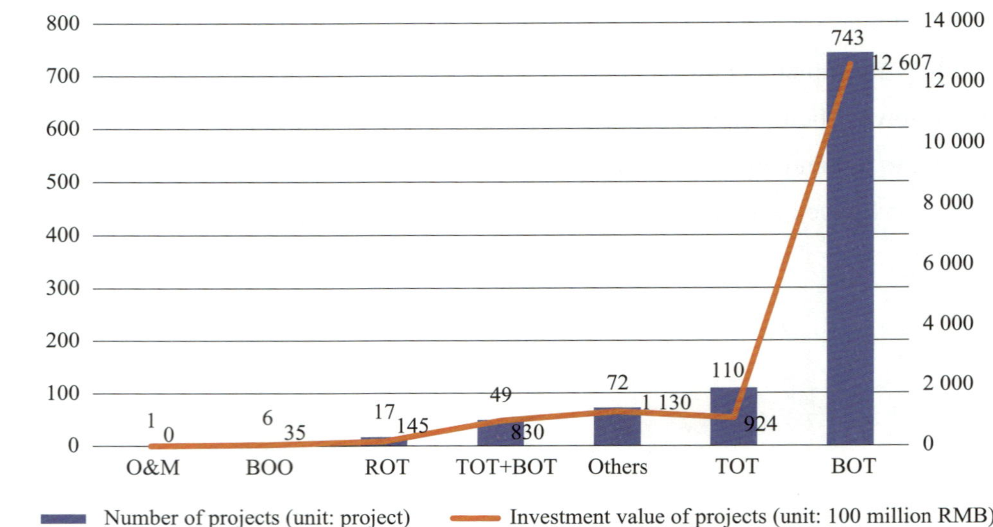

Figure 1–10 Number and Investment Value of Projects in Management Database by Operation Mode in 2020

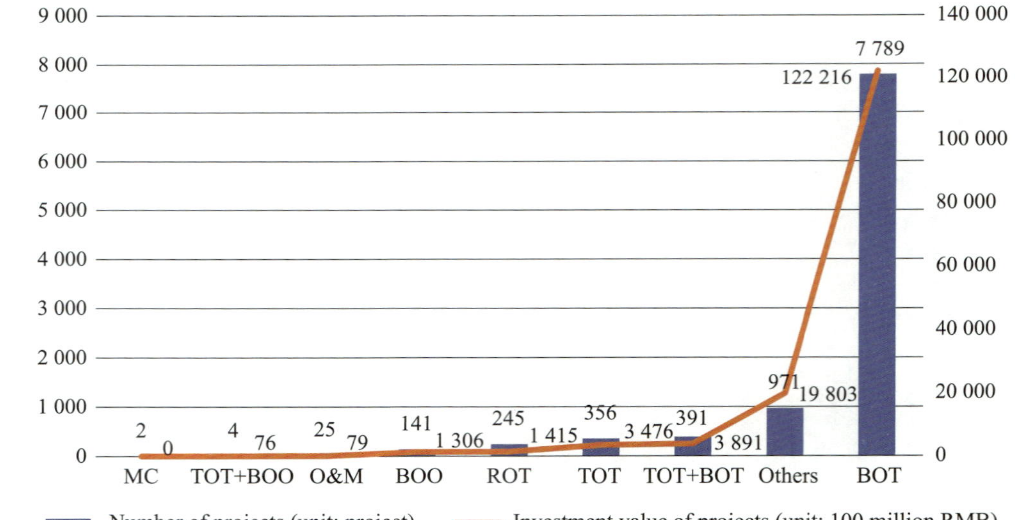

Figure 1–11 Number and Investment Value of Projects by Operation Mode by the End of 2020

1.5.6 Proportion of green and low-carbon projects increased steadily

Among the newly-increased projects in the Project Database in 2020, there were 646 green and low-carbon projects, with a total investment value of RMB 677.7 billion,

accounting for 64.7% and 43.2%, respectively. 118 of them have been implemented, representing an implementation rate of 18.3%. As of the end of 2020, there were 5 762 green and low-carbon projects in the Project Database, accounting for 58.1%; and they contributed to a cumulative investment value of RMB 5.5 trillion, accounting for 36.3%, of which 3 954 have been implemented, with an implementation rate of 68.6%.

2

Index System and Calculating Methodology

2.1 Construction of Index System

2.1.1 Basic Principles of Index System

The legitimacy of the Index System is directly related to the quality of the steps taken in index preparation and the validity of the interpretation of assessment results. To this end, the Index System that the Research Group established reflects all factors that affect the transparency of PPP information in an objective, reasonable and comprehensive manner, and also takes into account the availability and reliability of data. To establish a reliable PPP Market Transparency Assessment Index System, the Research Group defined key principles that should underpin the construction of an Index System. These key principles are hierarchy, commonality, continuity, as well as significance, impartiality and time-point.

(1) Principle of hierarchy within the Index System. Hierarchy refers to the multiplicity of levels within the Index System itself. Due to the multiple levels that PPP information covers based on PPP project life-cycles, the Index System must also be composed of a multi-level structure to reflect the features of each level in the PPP project life-cycle. At the same time, all the elements are linked to each other to form an organic whole, which is to reflect the full picture of PPP market transparency from the projects at different stages and levels. Specifically, with reference to the spirit of related administration measures, the index system for PPP market transparency can be divided into three levels, namely, the overall index, a secondary index based on the five phases of PPP projects, and underlying specific index for tasks within each phase of a PPP project. Therefore, the transparency index can be classified into a general index and then sub-indexes at identification, preparation, procurement, implementation, and transfer stages. Of course, given that different projects may be at different stages (i.e. phases in the project cycle), not every individual project's transparency index covers all the five stages.

(2) Principle of commonality and comparability of available information. The Research Group assessed the transparency of each PPP project, for which there is information unique to specific PPP project. Therefore, the Research Group selected the indicators that can be applied across all the project samples for the sake of comparability. Those inapplicable to all projects, such as "design documents and approval documents", "government's authorization documents (if any) for the adjustment and updates at the project procurement stage", "increase or decrease of the capital", etc., were not included in the Index System. However, the Research Group has provided some policy suggestions at the end of the Report on the administration measures for improving the disclosure of such information.

(3) Principle of continuity for on-going measurement of transparency. Since this is the third time we assess the transparency of PPP market, the Index System is required to not only reflect the progress made by China in PPP project information disclosure in 2020, but also seamlessly link with the systems in the previous three years, so that the index continuity will be maintained with consideration of potential future changes. In other words, the Index System shall have strong dynamic adaptability. The Research Group hopes that the information disclosure status of China's PPP market can be continuously assessed longitudinally through long-term tracking.

(4) Principle of significance in weighting scores. While the selection of indicators should be as comprehensive as possible, the selection should also be able to distinguish relative importance for transparency. For some particularly important indexes, as many fields as possible shall be selected. At the same time, the Research Group has set high scores for more important information and low scores for less important information through an expert survey. For example, the scores assigned to value-for-money assessment and financial affordability assessment might be higher than those to basic project information.

(5) Principle of impartiality. As an assessment report on policy effectiveness, this China PPP Market Transparency Report is expected to have certain impacts on regions and projects upon release. Therefore, the Research Group considers that this Report must adhere to the principle of fairness and impartiality, treat all projects equally and elaborate on each and every achievement and problem. It is necessary to truthfully present the objective conditions of information disclosure in different regions and different types of PPP projects, and at the same time, make as clear as possible

the objective and exogenous reasons that lead to discrepancies in the results in various regions and industries.

(6) Principle of common time-point. This Research Group assessed the disclosure of all project information in the Management Database on the PPP Integrated Information Platform of the Ministry of Finance as of Thursday, December 31, 2020, which falls into the concept of inventory, that is, the object of assessment is the accumulated information disclosure status of all PPP projects existing before this time-point. Restricted by the availability of data, the assessment did not address the dynamic characteristics such as the specific time of disclosure. For example, some indicators involved disclosure in due time, so theoretically, in addition to whether or not information was disclosed, the Research Group also assessed the timeliness of such disclosure, which is an important assessment basis as well. However, as the Research Group could not obtain detailed information such as the specific time point of disclosure, such information has not been included in the Index System this time.

2.1.2 Design Basis for Index System

(1) Design basis. To assess information disclosure in PPP market, the primary basis is the relevant policies as promulgated by the Ministry for Finance and/or the China Public Private Partnerships Center (CPPPC). On January 23, 2017, the Ministry of Finance promulgated the *Interim Measures for Administration of Information Disclosure for Public-Private Partnership Integrated Information Platform* (namely, the No. 1 Document). This is the main operating guide for local competent authorities to disclose information on PPP projects. Therefore, the rules in the No. 1 Document are the essential basis for the design of PPP market transparency index system. The Index System that the Research Group designed aligns with the requirements of the No. 1 Document. In principle, the information not required by the No. 1 Document was not included into the index system, for the sake of fairness to all regions.

(2) Data sources. According to the requirements of the China Public Private Partnerships Center, all local PPP projects must be included and published on the PPP Integrated Information Platform set up on the homepage of the CPPPC website. Considering the need for consistency of data sources, the Research Group has chosen the PPP Integrated Information Platform as the main source. Therefore, in this Report, the main basis for index design is the No. 1 Document, and the data mainly comes from the

PPP Integrated Information Platform. Because the No. 1 Document has come into force only recently, there are still some areas that need to be improved. For example, many fields are required to be disclosed by the No. 1 Document, but they are not displayed in the project data base component of the official CPPPC website. As a result, such fields were not included in the index system. After more information is disclosed on the website in the future, the Research Group will seek further improvements. Finally, due to the slight adjustment to several fields disclosed by the PPP Integrated Information Platform of the Ministry of Finance, the relevant indicators have also been updated in the evaluation this time.

(3) Assessment object. On November 10, 2017, the General Office of the Ministry of Finance issued the *Circular on Regulating Project Database of the National PPP Integrated Information Platform*, which requires the establishment of Project Reserve List and Project Management Database on the basis of the Project Database. The document defines that "the Project Reserve List corresponds to the identification stage, which incorporates the candidate projects that local government departments have the intention to adopt the PPP model, but have not completed the value-for-money assessment and the financial affordability assessment; and the Project Management Database covers the stages of preparation, procurement, implementation, and transfer". In conjunction with the policy advices of competent departments, the Research Group has limited the assessment object to projects that have at least commenced the preparation stage, that is, projects that have been entered into the Project Management Database. In addition, the Research Group also excluded several projects that could not be found on the PPP Information Integration Platform and eventually 9 662 samples were accepted for the analysis, an increase compared with 2019.

(4) Method of acquisition. The Research Group mainly relied on the data available on the website of CPPPC①, and referred to the requirements in the No. 1 Document to select and acquire the source data and then make categorization. Upon the analysis by the Research Group, the index system incorporated a total of 68 index fields. The Research Group has extracted them one by one, by direct reading and PDF files downloading from the CPPPC website.

---

① CPPPC has also provided some data directly to the Research Group, for which the Research Group would like to show gratitude.

Among the 68 fields, some fields needed to be acquired from PDF files. However, after reading them through, the Research Group found that there were a number of “forged” samples: for some projects, some PDF attachments were uploaded corresponding to certain fields, but they turned out to be blank or false files. This is because according to the system requirements, some items are mandatory. If the PDF files are not uploaded, the entire project cannot enter the database or perform the next steps for the project. As a result, some projects chose to upload false or blank PDF files. In order to identify and reduce such acts in the future and ensure robust accuracy and fairness, the Research Group conducted meticulous manual verification of all the PDF files of all projects and “punished” the “false uploads”. Specifically, for the fields related to PDF files, the scoring rules are as follows: if a true file is uploaded, it scores 1; if there is no upload, scores 0; if a fake file is uploaded, scores −1. In case of inadequate fields in an uploaded file, the Research Group marked it with 0.5.

2.1.3 Construction of Index System

The requirements of the No. 1 Document require that certain specified information in PPP projects should be immediately disclosed, and the remainder disclosed in “due time”. Among the requirements, the requirements on immediate disclosure were easy to identify and process, but those on disclosure in “due time” were quite difficult, because the Research Group had to define “due time”. However, as per the No.1 Document, “disclosure in due time” mostly refers to “disclosure within six months after entering into the implementation stage”. Therefore, the Research Group decided to follow the approach applied in the previous three years, that is, to select the projects that had entered the implementation stage by the end of June 2020 for assessment. For those projects, if they had not disclosed corresponding information as of December 31, 2020, the Research Group would conclude that they failed to disclose relevant information “in due time”, and as a result, performed poorly in terms of “disclosure in due time”.

Adopting such an approach led to a gap between the research samples for immediate disclosure and those for disclosure in due time. Specifically, as of the end of December 2020, the total number of samples entering the Management Database was 9 662, all of which could be used as assessment samples for immediate disclosure; however, there were only 5 801 projects having entered the implementation stage by the end of June

2020 and could be used for the assessment on disclosure in due time. For individual projects, some projects contain information for both immediate disclosure and disclosure in due time, and some contain information for immediate disclosure only, so they cannot be assessed under the same framework. Therefore, for the transparency of individual projects, the PPP information transparency index produced by the Research Group includes two independent fields — one on immediate disclosure, the other on disclosure in due time. Considering that the Research Group had to assess the transparency of the PPP market at regional and industry levels eventually, the Research Group used the analytic hierarchy process to weigh the index on immediate disclosure and the index on disclosure in due time, thus calculating the general index.

Both the index on immediate disclosure and the index on disclosure in due time include two levels — staged index and specific index. PPP projects are generally divided into five stages: identification stage, preparation stage, procurement stage, implementation stage, and transfer stage. However, there are no PPP projects having entered transfer stage in China, so it was not covered by both indexes. In addition, due to the lack of appropriate index fields on disclosure in due time, the corresponding index didn't contain the information at implementation stage either. Therefore, in the end the index on immediate disclosure included four stages: identification, preparation, procurement, and implementation; the index on disclosure in due time included three stages: identification, preparation, and procurement.

The hierarchy diagram of our final index system is shown in Figure 2–1. The specific index systems for immediate disclosure and disclosure in due time are shown in Table 2–1 and Table 2–2 respectively.

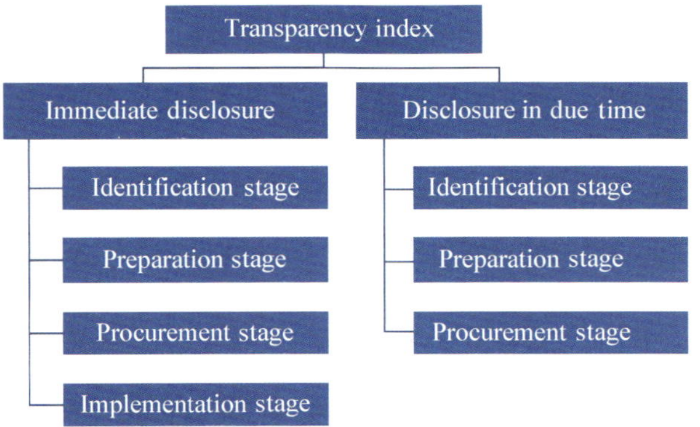

Figure 2–1 Hierarchy Diagram of PPP Transparency Index

Table 2–1 Index System for Immediate Disclosure

Primary index	Specific field	Remarks
Identification stage	Total investment	
	Partnership duration	
	Secondary industries	
	Operation mode	
	Return mechanism	
	Time of project initiation	
	Type of initiation	
	Name of initiator	
	Project profile	
	Contact person of project	
	Contact number of project	
	Contact person of financial affairs	
	Contact number of financial affairs	
	Land use area of project	
	Proposed development year	
	Selection of the mode of purchasing social capital	
	Description of implementation program	
	Cooperation scope (identification)	
	Value-for-money qualitative assessment indicators and weights, scoring standards, scoring results	
	Conclusions on whether value-for-money assessment passes or not (including opinions of the finance departments)	
	Financial expenditure liabilities of the project and those of the PPP projects implemented and to be implemented in the year and annual budget arrangements, and the ratio of expenditure for all the PPP projects out of the budget in each year in the expenditure of the general public budget	
	Conclusions on whether the financial affordability assessment passes or not	
Preparation stage	Proposed investment value of social capital	
	Proposed government investment value	
	Name of government approving implementation program	
	Approval time of implementation program by the government at the same level	
	Authorization documents of the people's government at the same level to implementing agencies, that is, the contracting parties of PPP project contracts	
	Government's approval documents with respect to implementation program	

(continued)

Primary index	Specific field	Remarks
Procurement stage	Prequalification announcements (including prequalification application documents)	
	Announcement of pre-bid winners and transaction results, the announcement of the bid-winning and transaction results and the letter of acceptance	
	Review opinions on proposed PPP contract by the competent industry authority at the same level	
	Review opinions on proposed PPP contract by the finance department at the same level	
	Review opinions on proposed PPP contract by the legal department at the same level	
	Whether people's government at the same level has approved the proposed PPP contract	
	Date of approval	
	Review opinions by the people's government at the same level on incorporating the government's financial expenditure liability which span two years into the mid-term financial plan	
	Date of review	
Implementation stage	Name of project company	
	Establishment time of project company	
	Registered capital of project company	
	Economic nature of project company	
	Subscription by shareholders	
	Authorization by the people's government at the same level to government's investment representatives	

Table 2–2 Index System for Disclosure in Due Time

Primary index	Specific field	Remarks
Identification stage	Value-for-money assessment report and approval documents	
	Financial affordability assessment report and approval documents	
	Proposals for new or renovated or expanded projects and approval documents	
	Feasibility study report	
	Design documents and approval documents	
	Assets appraisal report with respect to the stocked public assets or equities	

(continued)

Primary index	Specific field	Remarks
Preparation stage	Completion time of value-for-money assessment	
	Completion time of financial affordability assessment	
	Project implementation program as examined and approved and amendments thereto	
Procurement stage	Prequalification: announcement time	
	Prequalification: prequalification time	
	Procurement: announcement time	
	Procurement results: time of review on response documents	
	Procurement results: time of negotiation about confirmation	
	Procurement results: time of government review	
	Procurement results: time of contract signing	
	Procurement results: time of contract announcement	
	Procurement results: media for contract announcement	
	Project investment amount specified in contract	
	Procurement documents	
	Concluding observations with respect to prequalification, and the list of prequalification experts	
	Concluding observations with respect to response documents, and the list of review experts	
	List of the working group of negotiation about confirmation	
	Signed PPP project contracts	
	Government's responsibility confirmation documents for the expenditure of the project or the update or adjustment documents of the people's congress at the same level (or the NPC Standing Committee) including the financial expenditure liability of the project into budgets which span two years	

2.1.4 Explanatory Notes to Other Core Issues

This Report assesses whether information disclosure is in place, rather than the "quality" of the information disclosure. This Report has assessed the information disclosure of PPP projects, including completeness and importance, etc., but apart from obvious forging, the assessment does not touch upon the "quality" of specific content. Specifically, for a field (i.e. a defined information disclosure obligation contained in

the No. 1 Document), if a project has disclosed corresponding information, it wins scores in the assessment, no matter the work is done well or poorly. For example, the PDF files of financial affordability report, as important information, were verified by the Research Group manually one by one, and at the same time, experts may assign a higher score to them. These are the factors considered in the assessment. As to whether a financial affordability report is normative, scientific, has sufficient argument and reliable conclusion, etc., is not the research subject of this Report. Because logically speaking, even if the financial sustainability report may not be standardized or poor in quality, as long as the responsible party chooses to disclose the report in a real and public manner, it wins scores under the assessment process used. Of course, the Research Group may go beyond "information transparency assessment" in the future and conduct special assessments on the standardization of PPP work in a certain region or field reflected by these important reports.

2.2 Calculating Methodology

2.2.1 Introduction to Calculating Methodology

For multi-index assessment, weights directly affect the results. There are many ways to determine weights. According to different sources of raw data, they can be roughly divided into two categories: subjective weighting and objective weighting. Subjective weighting is to obtain results by experts based on subjective judgments, such as Delphi method, AHP (Analytic Hierarchy Process), expert scoring method, etc., which invites authoritative experts to compare the importance among different fields, but the approach compromises objectivity. Objective weighting is to obtain results based on the numerical calculations of fields. It does not rely on subjective judgments, so it has strong objectivity, but cannot necessarily reflect the importance relations among different fields, nor can it necessarily satisfy the requirements of decision makers. Representatives of objective weighting are principal components analysis and coefficient of variation. Both subjective and objective weightings have their advantages and disadvantages. In calculating the weights of the fields of each rule hierarchy on the upper-hierarchy targets, the Research Group used subjective weighting — AHP; when calculating the weights of specific fields on the upper-rule

hierarchy, the Research Group utilized expert scoring method.①

2.2.2 Analytic Hierarchy Process

Analytic Hierarchy Process (AHP) is a comprehensive assessment method for system analysis and decision making, which can quantify qualitative problems in a relatively rational manner. The main feature of AHP is that by building a hierarchical structure, it converts judgments into the importance comparison between two factors, thereby transforming qualitative decision into quantitative decision, which is easier to justify.

In an AHP model construct, a decision matrix is formed through investigation and judgment. When the decision matrix passes consistency check, it is accepted to calculate the weight of each index; if the consistency check fails, the element values of the decision matrix need adjustment until it passes the consistency check. Specifically, the steps of AHP are as follows:

Step 1: Establish hierarchical model. Upon the in-depth analysis on the factors that affect PPP information transparency, subdivide the factors into several hierarchies according to their subordination relationship. The top is target hierarchy, the middle is rule hierarchy, and the specific fields are at the lowest. The hierarchical model for this Report is shown in Figure 2–1.

Step 2: Build decision matrix. Construct decision matrix to compare the relative importance of two specific fields. As the schematic diagram of the PPP project transparency hierarchy in this Report shows, two classified indexes are involved. Therefore, three decision matrixes were built, namely the general index decision matrix (to judge the relative importance of immediate disclosure index and disclosure in due time index when compiling the general index of PPP market transparency), the immediate disclosure index decision matrix (to judge the relative importance of sub-indexes at identification, preparation, procurement, and implementation stages when compiling the

---

① The Research Group used the coefficient of variation method when calculating the weight of each specific indicator on the upper-rule hierarchy. It turned out that the results obtained by the coefficient of variation were in high consistency with those obtained by expert scoring. The decision to choose expert scoring method was made given that the method could better reflect the views on indicator importance of different sectors of the society, including industry authorities, university scholars, and social capital owners, rather than relying solely on the statistical characteristics of indicators. This makes it easier for each locality to locate problems in PPP information disclosure and make improvements in a targeted manner.

immediate disclosure index), and the disclosure in due time decision matrix (to judge the relative importance of sub-indexes at identification, preparation, and procurement stages when compiling the disclosure in due time index).

In general, to compare the influence of n factors $c_1, c_2, \cdots, c_n$ on the factors on upper hierarchy, the decision matrix requires that the relative importance of two factors on the factors on upper hierarchy be compared each time, and the relative importance is usually expressed in values of 1-9. Value is assigned to each factor that constitutes the decision matrix c_{ij} (the meaning of the values is shown in Table 2–3, which is usually assigned by experienced experts). All comparison results constitute "paired comparison matrix", also called "positive reciprocal matrix".

Table 2–3 Meaning of Decision Matrix Scale

Scale c_{ij}	Definition	Meaning
1	Equally important	The impact of c_i is the same as that of c_j
3	Slightly more important	The impact of c_i is slightly stronger than that of c_j
5	Relatively more important	The impact of c_i is stronger than that of c_j
7	More important	The impact of c_i is obviously stronger than that of c_j
9	Extremely more important	The impact of c_i is absolutely stronger than that of c_j
2, 4, 6, 8	Middle value of two adjacent scales	The impact ratio of c_i to c_j is between two adjacent scales
1/2, $\cdots$, 1/9	Reciprocal	The impact ratio of c_i to c_j is the reciprocal of the α_{ij} above

$$C = \begin{pmatrix} c_{11} & c_{12} & \cdots & c_{1n} \\ c_{21} & c_{22} & \cdots & c_{2n} \\ \vdots & \vdots & \vdots & \vdots \\ c_{n1} & c_{n2} & \cdots & c_{nn} \end{pmatrix}$$

$$C = (c_{ij})_{n\times n},\ c_{ij}>0,\ c_{ji}=\frac{1}{c_{ij}},\ c_{ii} = 1.$$

If the positive reciprocal matrix C meets $c_{ij}\times c_{jk}=c_{ik}$, then C is called complete consistency matrix.

Step 3: Calculate the maximum eigenvalue of decision matrix and its eigenvector. The process of determining the weight of each index with decision matrix is actually to

obtain the eigenvector of the decision matrix. By solving the maximum eigenvalue of the reciprocal matrix, the corresponding eigenvector can be obtained and then normalized to be the weight vector.

$$CW = \lambda_{max} W$$

Step 4: Consistency check. First, calculate the consistency index *CI* of the *n* decision matrix:

$$CI = \frac{\lambda_{max} - n}{n-1}$$

Secondly, calculate the average random consistency index *RI*. 1) Randomly select numbers from 1-9 and their reciprocals to form a *n* positive reciprocal matrix and calculate its maximum eigenvalue. 2) Repeat 1 000 times to obtain the maximum eigenvalues of 1 000 random positive reciprocal matrices, and calculate the mean value of the 1 000 max. eigenvalues *k*. 3) Obtain the average random consistency index *RI*.

$$RI = \frac{k - n}{n-1}$$

Finally, calculate the consistency ratio *CR* and check consistency.

$$CR = \frac{CI}{RI}$$

When $CR<0.1$, it is generally considered that the inconsistency degree of matrix *A* is within tolerance range, and its eigenvector can be used as a weight vector. Otherwise, the decision matrix needs to be modified (repeat Steps 2 and 3) until *CR* is less than 0.1.

Step 5: Calculate weight vector. By normalizing the eigenvector corresponding to the maximum eigenvalue of the decision matrix that has passed consistency check, the weight of the factor on the factors of upper hierarchy can be obtained.

Accordingly, the Research Group invited 11 representatives from universities and colleges (3), government (3), corporate partners (3) and intermediary consulting (2) to fill in the three decision matrices, then calculated the weights of each stage through the AHP described above, and finally obtained the mean values of the weights assigned by these experts. Appendix I shows the decision matrix survey forms for experts. Table 2–4

shows the table of weights calculated based on the decision matrixes provided by experts. For immediate disclosure, the weights of the sub-indexes at identification, preparation, procurement, and implementation stages were 0.19, 0.19, 0.4, and 0.22; regarding disclosure in due time, the weights of the sub-indexes at identification, preparation, procurement stages were 0.25, 0.30 and 0.45; and when being consolidated into the general index of PPP market transparency, the weights of the two disclosure modes were 0.61 and 0.39 respectively.

Table 2–4　Table of Weights Based on Decision Matrixes by Experts

Transparency index of immediate disclosure		Transparency index of disclosure in due time		General index	
Stage	Weight	Stage	Weight	Sub-index	Weight
Identification stage	0.19	Identification stage	0.25	Disclosure in due time	0.39
Preparation stage	0.19	Preparation stage	0.30	Immediate disclosure	0.61
Procurement stage	0.40	Procurement stage	0.45	—	—
Implementation stage	0.22	—	—	—	—

2.2.3　Weight Calculation Method

After the weighting of each middle hierarchy on upper hierarchy was finalized through AHP, it was also required to determine the weighting of the bottom hierarchy (that is, each specific field) on upper hierarchy. In this regard, the Research Group applied the experts scoring method.

Based on the information earlier in this Report, especially the "principle of significance", the Research Group scored the specific fields by means of expert scoring, giving them certain weights. The fields were divided into "common", "important" and "especially important", corresponding to 1 point, 2 points, and 3 points respectively. The higher the point is, the field is more significant. 11 experts from college, government, business, and consulting were invited for scoring. Table 2–5 and Table 2–6 show the results of expert scoring. It needs to be further noted that the scores of the above indicators were compared with each other within a certain stage, rather than directly compared among all. To clarify this, the Research Group also listed the specific weights corresponding to the scores in each stage in Table 2–5 and Table 2–6.

Table 2–5 Expert Scoring Results on Specific Fields of Immediate Disclosure

Stage	Specific field	Score	Weight
Identification stage	Total investment	2.455	5.52
	Partnership duration	2.273	5.11
	Secondary industries	1.091	2.45
	Operation mode	2.182	4.91
	Return mechanism	2.909	6.54
	Time of project initiation	1.636	3.68
	Type of initiation	1.455	3.27
	Name of initiator	1.182	2.66
	Project profile	2.000	4.50
	Contact person of project	1.455	3.27
	Contact number of project	1.455	3.27
	Contact person of financial affairs	1.455	3.27
	Contact number of financial affairs	1.455	3.27
	Land use area of project	2.000	4.50
	Proposed development year	2.000	4.50
	Selection of the mode of purchasing social capital	2.455	5.52
	Description of implementation program	2.364	5.32
	Cooperation scope (identification)	2.182	4.91
	Value-for-money qualitative assessment indicators and weights, scoring standards, scoring results	2.545	5.72
	Conclusions on whether value-for-money assessment passes or not (including opinions of the finance departments)	2.636	5.93
	Financial expenditure liabilities of the project and those of the PPP projects implemented and to be implemented in the year and annual budget arrangements, and the ratio of expenditure for all the PPP projects out of the budget in each year in the expenditure of the general public budget	2.818	6.34
	Conclusions on whether the financial affordability assessment passes or not	2.455	5.52
Preparation stage	Proposed investment value of social capital	2.182	18.20
	Proposed government investment value	2.273	18.90
	Name of government approving implementation program	1.727	14.40

(continued)

Stage	Specific field	Score	Weight
Preparation stage	Approval time of implementation program by the government at the same level	1.727	14.40
	Authorization documents of the people's government at the same level to implementing agencies, that is, the contracting parties of PPP project contracts	2.000	16.70
	Government's approval documents with respect to implementation program	2.091	17.40
Procurement stage	Prequalification announcements (including prequalification application documents)	2.364	11.20
	Announcement of pre-bid winners and transaction results, the announcement of the bid-winning and transaction results and the letter of acceptance	2.545	12.10
	Review opinions on proposed PPP contract by the competent industry authority at the same level	1.909	9.10
	Review opinions on proposed PPP contract by the finance department at the same level	2.000	9.50
	Review opinions on proposed PPP contract by the legal department at the same level	1.909	9.10
	Whether people's government at the same level has approved the proposed PPP contract	2.455	11.60
	Date of approval	2.455	11.60
	Review opinions by the people's government at the same level on incorporating the government's financial expenditure liability which span two years into the mid-term financial plan	2.727	12.90
	Date of review	2.727	12.90
Implementation stage	Name of project company	1.636	15.60
	Establishment time of project company	1.545	14.80
	Registered capital of project company	1.818	17.40
	Economic nature of project company	1.455	13.90
	Subscription by shareholders	2.000	19.10
	Authorization by the people's government at the same level to government's investment representatives	2.000	19.10

Table 2–6 Expert Scoring Results on Specific Fields of Disclosure in Due Time

Stage	Specific field	Score	Weight
Identification stage	Value-for-money assessment report and approval documents	3.000	18.0
	Financial affordability assessment report and approval documents	3.000	18.0
	Proposals for new or renovated or expanded projects and approval documents	2.333	14.0
	Feasibility study report	2.667	16.0
	Design documents and approval documents	2.677	16.1
	Assets appraisal report with respect to the stocked public assets or equities	3.000	18.0
Preparation stage	Completion time of value-for-money assessment	1.556	33.3
	Completion time of financial affordability assessment	1.556	33.3
	Project implementation program as examined and approved and amendments thereto	1.556	33.3
Procurement stage	Prequalification: announcement time	1.778	5.5
	Prequalification: prequalification time	1.667	5.2
	Procurement: announcement time	1.889	5.9
	Procurement results: time of review on response documents	1.556	4.8
	Procurement results: time of negotiation about confirmation	1.889	5.9
	Procurement results: time of government review	1.778	5.5
	Procurement results: time of contract signing	1.778	5.5
	Procurement results: time of contract announcement	1.889	5.9
	Procurement results: media for contract announcement	1.444	4.5
	Project investment amount specified in contract	2.556	8.0
	Procurement documents	2.889	9.0
	Concluding observations with respect to prequalification, and the list of prequalification experts	2.111	6.6
	Concluding observations with respect to response documents, and the list of review experts	2.111	6.6
	List of the working group of negotiation about confirmation	1.222	3.8
	Appendixes to PPP project contracts	2.556	8.0
	Responsibility confirmation documents for expenditure by the government at the same level	3.000	9.3

2.2.4 Indicator Synthesis

In multi-index assessment, synthesis refers to the integration of assessment values of different fields on different aspects of a subject through a certain formula to produce a holistic assessment. There are many mathematical methods that can be used for synthesis. Common synthesis models are weighted arithmetic mean, weighted geometric mean, or their combination. All three have their features and applicable occasions, without absolute difference in advantages or disadvantages. After comprehensively comparing the three methods, the Research Group chose weighted arithmetic mean, the formula of which is as follows:

$$d = \sum_{i=1}^{n} w_i d_i$$

Wherein, d is the general index, w_i is the normalized weight of each assessment index, d_i is the assessment score of single index, and n is the number of assessment indexes. Synthesis is based on a bottom-to-top layer-by-layer sequence. First, calculate the indexes on each hierarchy, and then weigh and consolidate the indexes to obtain the general index (see Chapter 4 for detailed calculation process).

Specifically, the disclosure status of each field from the website was firstly acquired and then given a score (a total of four scores, namely, 1 represents disclosure and no obvious forging; 0 represents no disclosure; 0.5 represents partial disclosure; -1 stands for "forged" disclosure). Subsequently, the scores of these fields were consolidated by the expert scoring method or coefficient of variation to calculate the scoring average (percentage system) at a certain stage (for example, disclosure in due time at identification stage). Subsequently, weights were generated by Analytic Hierarchy Process, sub-indexes at different stages were synthesized into immediate disclosure index or disclosure in due time index. Finally, the immediate disclosure index or disclosure in due time index was weighted to obtain the PPP market transparency index.

It should be noted that based on the Index System and calculation methods, theoretically, a project's general transparency index (or staged index) may reach 100 points, indicating that the project has correctly and completely disclosed the information required by the Research Group; the lowest score can be negative, indicating that the project has disclosed much false information. 0 indicates that the project has not disclosed

any information required by the Research Group, or it has disclosed some information, which was yet offset by certain forged disclosure. Of course, such circumstances were rare, especially upon the synthesis of a number of fields.

It needs to be emphasized that when calculating the general index, some projects did not cover all five stages, in order to ensure index stability, weighting normalization was used to ensure the consistency of relative weights. For example, for immediate disclosure index, the weights of identification, preparation, procurement, and implementation stages were 0.19, 0.19, 0.4, and 0.22, respectively. But for a project with only the first three stages, the weights would be:

Recognition stage=0.19/(0.19+0.19+0.4)=0.244

Preparation stage=0.19/(0.19+0.19+0.4)=0.244

Procurement stage=0.4/(0.19+0.19+0.4)=0.512

3

Primary Results and Overall Analysis

3.1 Introduction to Sample Data

3.1.1 Sample Overview

As previously outlined, the Index System was classified into two groupings: the immediate disclosure index and the disclosure in due time index. Among them, the immediate disclosure index covered 9 962 projects, an increase of 564 compared with the 9 398 projects in 2019; the disclosure in due time index involved 5 801 projects, representing an increase of 639 compared with the previous year. Furthermore, among the 9 962 total samples in 2020, 795, 1 889 and 6 978 projects were at the stages of preparation, procurement, and implementation, respectively. As can be seen from Figure 3–1, compared with 2019, the proportion of samples entering the implementation and procurement stages to the overall sample size in 2020 has increased slightly, while the proportion of samples still in preparation stage has declined.

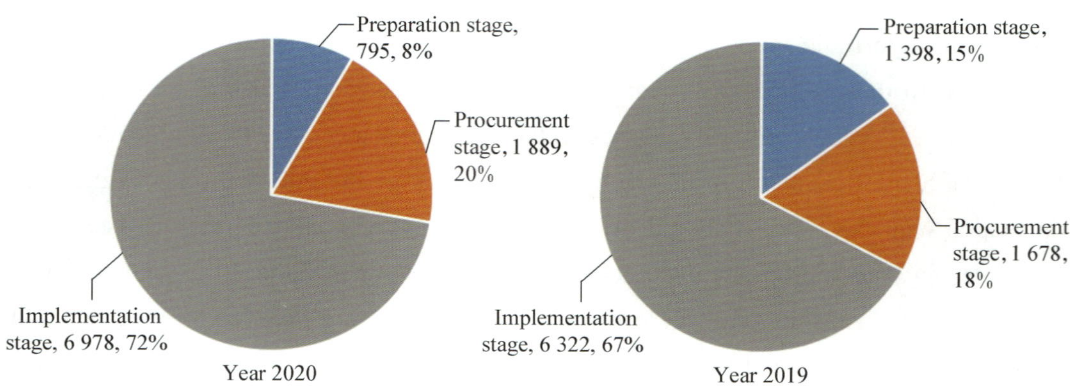

Figure 3–1 Distribution of Sample Projects by Stage in 2019 and 2020

In the following paragraphs we will find the total transparency index in 2020 changed little from 2019.

3.1.2 Index Methodology

Chapter 2 highlights the index system which consists of a total of 68 index fields, based on the CPPPC website, of which 31 index fields were manually read from the website to verify authenticity. Among the remaining 37 fields obtained directly from the website or CPPPC, they were assigned "1" if the field recorded disclosed information or "0" if there was no information disclosed in the field. While as for the manually read fields, a more detailed scoring system was applied: "1" point was allocated for complete disclosure, "0.5" points for partial disclosure, "0" points for no disclosure, and "–1" points for false or erroneous disclosure (e.g. if there is a blank PDF file).

Standard definitions were developed to define Partial and False Disclosure, to support consistency in the points allocation. Partial disclosure was defined as a field which contained multiple items of information, but only part of which had been disclosed. For example, if the field "value-for-money qualitative assessment indicators and weights, scoring standards, scoring results" included only the scoring standards or results, then 0.5 point would be assigned. Similarly, the value-for-money assessment report and financial affordability report requires the disclosure of the "value-for-money assessment report and approval documents by the competent industry authority and the finance industry at the same level" as well as the "financial affordability report and approval documents by the finance department at the same level". Some projects only disclosed the value-for-money assessment report and the financial affordability report, but no approval documents, or vice versa. In these instances, a score of 0.5 was also assigned. False disclosure with a penalty of "–1" which primarily applies to those circumstances where an uploaded PDF file was a blank document, or an erroneous document, or the information contained did not match with the field. It should be noted that in a very small number of cases some PDF files without appropriate documents lodged were not penalized. In these cases there were justifiable reasons (e.g. the project commenced before policies took effect) and under such circumstance, it was not assessed as false disclosure, and there no penalty was awarded, to avoid any unfair assessment.

Here we take the "value-for-money assessment report and approval documents by the competent industry authority and the finance industry at the same level" in disclosure in due time as an example to introduce our manual data collection. As shown in Figure

3–2, among the 5 801 samples subject to disclosure in due time, 4 829 have completely disclosed the "value-for-money assessment report and approval documents by the competent industry authority and the finance industry at the same level", 941 made partial disclosure, 15 no disclosure, and 16 had disclosed false or wrong documents. From 2019 to 2020, the complete disclosure rate under this index dropped from 81% to 83%, the false disclosure rate from 0.54% to 1%, and the non-disclosure rate decline sharply from 11% to 0%.

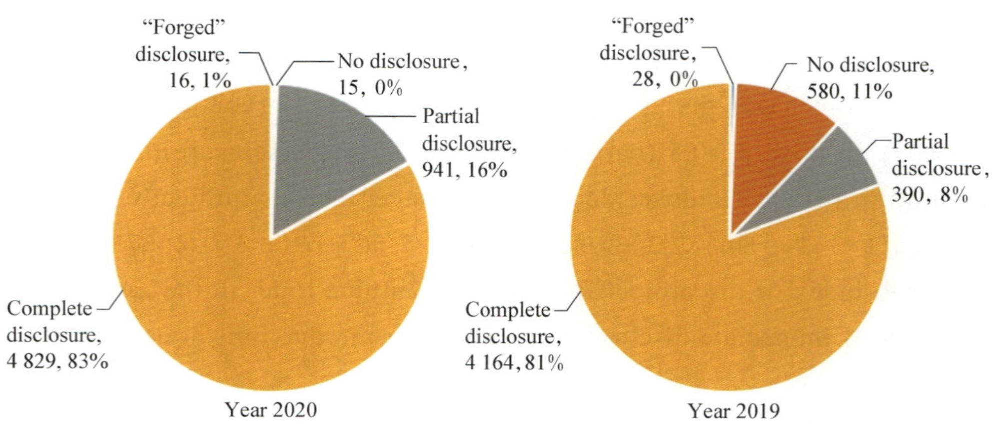

Figure 3–2 Disclosure of Value-for-money Assessment Report and Attachment

Once the scores were assigned, the final score of each field was determined by multiplying the score by the weighting (relative importance) determined through expert scoring (as outlined in Chapter 2).

3.2 Calculation of National General Index

3.2.1 Index Synthesis

With the score of each index, the Research Group would calculate the score of a PPP project at a certain stage (standardized to be a percentage out of 100), which is the sub-index at the stage. Take the disclosure in due time index at identification stage as an example: the stage contains six information items: "value-for-money assessment report and approval documents by the competent industry authority and the finance industry at the same level", "financial affordability report and approval documents by the finance department at the same level", "proposals for

new or renovated or expanded projects and approval documents" and "feasibility study report or fund application report or report for project approval, and approval documents by competent authority; assets appraisal report with respect to the stocked public assets", "design documents and approval documents", and "asset evaluation report with respect to the stocked public assets or equity, and various programs and others (if applicable) that may be involved in the transfer of stocked assets or equity". The six fields scored 3 points, 3 points, 2.333 points, 2.667 points, 2.667 points and 3 points respectively in expert scoring. Then, the total score of disclosure in due time at the identification stage was 16.667 points. Suppose a project was given 1 (complete disclosure), 1 (complete disclosure), 0.5 (partial disclosure), 0.5 (partial disclosure), 0 (no disclosure), and −1 (false disclosure) in the six fields at identification stage, then the project's score at the stage was $[1\times3+1\times3+0.5\times2.333+0.5\times2.667+0\times2.667+(-1)\times3]/16.667\times100=33.33$ was the sub-index of the project for disclosure in due time. In the same way, the sub-indexes of immediate disclosure and disclosure in due time at each stage were produced.

Table 3–1 summarizes the sub-indexes of immediate disclosure at different stages. Of the 9 962 immediate disclosure samples, the average scores were 95.58 at the identification stage, 90.41 at the preparation stage, 78.85 at the procurement stage, and 764.85 at the implementation stage. The results demonstrate that immediate information disclosure at the identification and preparation stages was generally satisfactory, however poorer at the procurement and implementation stages. From the perspective of management mechanism, most of the information required to be disclosed at the identification and preparation stages must be submitted before PPP projects are included into the database. Due to the rigorous review by competent authorities for database entry, the scores were generally higher. While after coming to the procurement and implementation stages, project progress wouldn't be hindered by the failure to upload information to the PPP Integrated Platform in time as required. As the information disclosure at these stages was not under proper regulation, lower scores were seen. Compared with 2019, the scores at the identification, preparation and procurement stages all showed increase, while a score drop was seen at the implementation stage.

Table 3–1 Immediate Disclosure Indexes at Different Stages

Stage	Year 2020			Year 2019		
	Sample size	Mean value	Standard deviation	Sample size	Mean value	Standard deviation
Identification stage	9 662	95.58	3.30	9 398	89.71	4.38
Preparation stage	9 662	90.41	16.61	9 398	84.48	25.39
Procurement stage	8 866	78.85	23.24	8 000	73.61	21.19
Implementation stage	6 978	64.85	32.15	6 322	71.17	28.86

Table 3–2 shows the distribution of immediate disclosure indexes at different stages, implying that negative scores are possible where false or erroneous documents were published; and conversely projects with strong information disclosure have the potential to score 100 points. Conversely projects with strong information disclosure has the potential to score 100 points. The Research Group paid attention to these "abnormal" projects and dealt with them specifically, in a bid to urge responsible departments to make up for shortcomings as soon as possible, and promote standardized management of PPP projects. However, we are more concerned with the information disclosure performance of most projects, since it represents the information transparency across the entire PPP market. Therefore, Table 3–2 also highlights scores at the 75 and 25 percentiles. By comparing the distribution of the transparency indexes at all stages of immediate disclosure in 2020 and 2019, we can see that the immediate disclosure at the identification stage in 2020 was better than that in 2019, as proven by the fact that both the upper quartile and the lower quartile in 2020 were higher than those in 2019; and the 25 percentile and the 75 percentile at the identification stage of immediate disclosure in 2020 were 94.27 and 100 points, respectively, both higher than the 88.64 and 92.21 points in 2019. Regarding those with higher scores, few differences were seen in the preparation stage of immediate disclosure between 2019 and 2020, as the 75 percentiles and maximum values in the two years were exactly the same. But as for the procurement stage, lower-scored projects did slightly better in immediate disclosure in 2020 than in 2019, since the 25 quantile in 2020 was 76.71 points, contrasted by 74.14 points in 2019. Finally, at the implementation stage, both the upper quartile and the lower quartile in 2020 were lower than those in 2019; the 25 and 75 quantiles in the implementation stage of immediate disclosure in 2020 were 53.91 and 90.43 points, respectively — lower than

the corresponding 61.74 and 100 points in 2019. This indicates that for those projects with low scores, their information disclosure at the implementation phase of immediate disclosure in 2020 was poorer than that in 2019. In general, the conclusions made based on careful examination of the index distribution are consistent with the information provided by Table 3–1. In terms of immediate disclosure, the projects performed better in the identification and preparation phases in 2020 than in 2019, coupled with a slightly poorer performance at the procurement and implementation stages than in 2019.

Table 3–2 Immediate Disclosure Indexes at Different Stages

Stage	Year 2020			
	Minimum value	25 percentile	75 percentile	Maximum value
Identification stage	66.26	94.27	100	100
Preparation stage	–17.425	83.33	100	100
Procurement stage	0	76.71	88.36	100
Implementation stage	0	53.91	90.43	100
Stage	**Year 2019**			
	Minimum value	**25 percentile**	**75 percentile**	**Maximum value**
Identification stage	58.44	88.64	92.21	97.56
Preparation stage	–34.09	66.67	100	100
Procurement stage	0	74.14	87.07	100
Implementation stage	0	61.74	100	100

Table 3–3 shows the disclosure in due time sub-indexes at different stages. Out of the 5 801 assessment objects, the average score at the identification stage was 50.50, 97.83 at the preparation stage, and 74.80 at the procurement stage. Disclosure was poorer at the identification stage relative to the preparation stage. One explanation for this could be that the information required at the identification stage includes value-for-money assessment report, financial affordability assessment report and some other core documents, and a number of projects failed to properly disclose these documents. Comparison of performance in disclosure in due time between 2019 and 2020 shows that the average scores at the preparation stage in the two years didn't vary much, the average score of the procurement stage in 2020 was slightly higher than that in 2019, and that of

the identification stage in 2019 was 5.87 points higher than that in 2019.

Table 3–3 Disclosure in Due Time Indexes at Different Stages

Stage	Year 2020			Year 2019		
	Sample size	Mean value	Standard deviation	Sample size	Mean value	Standard deviation
Identification stage	5 801	50.50	13.71	5 162	44.63	20.03
Preparation stage	5 801	97.83	6.86	5 162	95.81	11.66
Procurement stage	5 801	74.80	11.01	5 162	70.37	16.18

Table 3–4 reports the distribution of the transparency indexes at each stage of disclosure in due time, including minimum and maximum values, upper quartile and lower quartile. From the table, we can conclude that in terms of disclosure in due time, most projects disclosed the required information in the preparation and procurement stages, with 100% disclosure at the 75 percentile for the preparation stage; while 25% of the projects received a score that was less than 43.97 at the identification stage. Therefore, if action is to taken to improve the overall transparency of PPP projects concerning disclosure in due time, the focus should be on the complete disclosure of several core reports such as value-for-money assessment report and financial affordability reports. Only after these shortcomings are addressed will the transparency of disclosure in due time increase greatly. Comparing with the same in 2019, in 2020 the scores of the identification, preparation and procurement stages were all slightly higher.

Table 3–4 Disclosure In Due Time Indexes at Different Stages

Stage	Year 2020			
	Minimum value	25 percentile	75 percentile	Maximum value
Identification stage	–51.97	43.97	54.97	100.00
Preparation stage	0.00	100	100	100.00
Procurement stage	0.00	70.42	84.78	94.12
Stage	Year 2019			
	Minimum value	25 percentile	75 percentile	Maximum value
Identification stage	–63.96	43.97	52.97	100
Preparation stage	0	100	100	100
Procurement stage	–9.68	62.29	85.12	90.66

3.2.2 General Index

With transparency index at each stage, the Research Group synthesized the immediate disclosure index and disclosure in due time index based on the weights of the sub-index at each stage obtained by AHP as explained in the Chapter 2. Table 3–5 shows the general indexes of immediate disclosure and disclosure in due time, as well as their mean values, which were 80.37 and 74.67, respectively. Compared with 2019, the two indicators in 2020 basically remained stable, with slight increase.

Table 3–5 Immediate Disclosure and Disclosure in Due Time Indexes

Index	Year 2020			Year 2019		
	Sample size	Mean value	Standard deviation	Sample size	Mean value	Standard deviation
Immediate disclosure	9 962	80.37	8.57	9 398	79.14	13.95
Disclosure in due time	5 801	74.67	3.02	5 162	71.57	13.90

Also the immediate disclosure index and the disclosure in due time index, were synthesized for the national PPP market transparency index based on the weights of immediate disclosure index and disclosure in due time index calculated by AHP. The conclusion is, by the end of December 2019, the national PPP market transparency index was 78.15 (80.37×0.61+74.67×0.39), slightly higher than 2019 at 76.19. Figure 3–3 shows

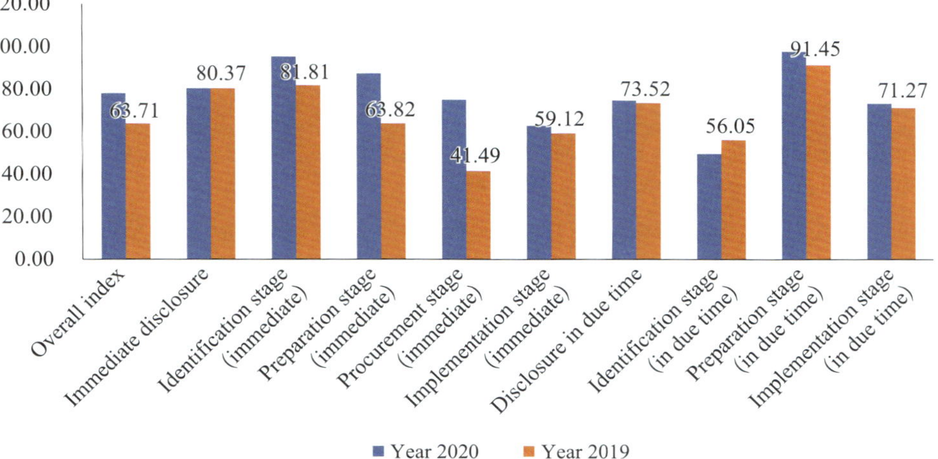

Figure 3–3 National PPP Market Transparency Index and Sub-index by Stage

the national PPP market transparency index, immediate disclosure index, disclosure in due time index, and the average transparency sub-index by stage. Consistent with the results shown from Table 3–1 to Table 3–4 above, Figure 3–3 indicates that the major changes from 2019 to 2020 include higher scores in the identification, preparation and procurement phases, and lower scores in the execution phase.

3.3 Heterogeneity Analysis of National General Index

Based on the analysis above, the national PPP market transparency index was calculated based on the average transparency index of around 9 600 PPP projects across China. As discussed previously, the average transparency may have masked the heterogeneity between individual projects. Therefore, in order to offer a more in-depth and intuitive display of the transparency of the national PPP market, in this section, the analysis needs to focus on different perspectives, such as industry sector, type, etc., A more detailed discussion at the provincial and municipal levels will also be provided in the following two chapters.

3.3.1 PPP Transparency Index by Sector

Figure 3–5 examines the PPP market transparency by sector. Figure 3–4 examines the PPP market transparency by sector. Although some differences were noted, they were not substantial. For example, the highest transparency index was 79.8 for the science and technology sector, and the lowest was 76.5 for the indemnificatory housing sector, showing a gap of merely 3.3 points. Upon analysis on the immediate disclosure index and the disclosure in due time index by industry, as well as the sub-indexes at different stages, findings are similar. Therefore, generally PPP projects in different sectors showed no significant heterogeneity in information disclosure requirements and practices. It also means the existing rules and regulations for the disclosure of PPP project information are generally applicable to all sectors. Since PPP projects in different sectors are often managed and supervised by authorities with expertise in the respective industry sector, the above results also indicated that these authorities have managed PPP project information disclosure in a similar manner. Furthermore, Figure 3–4 shows that all the industries other than social security made improvement in the transparency index in 2020 compared with 2019.

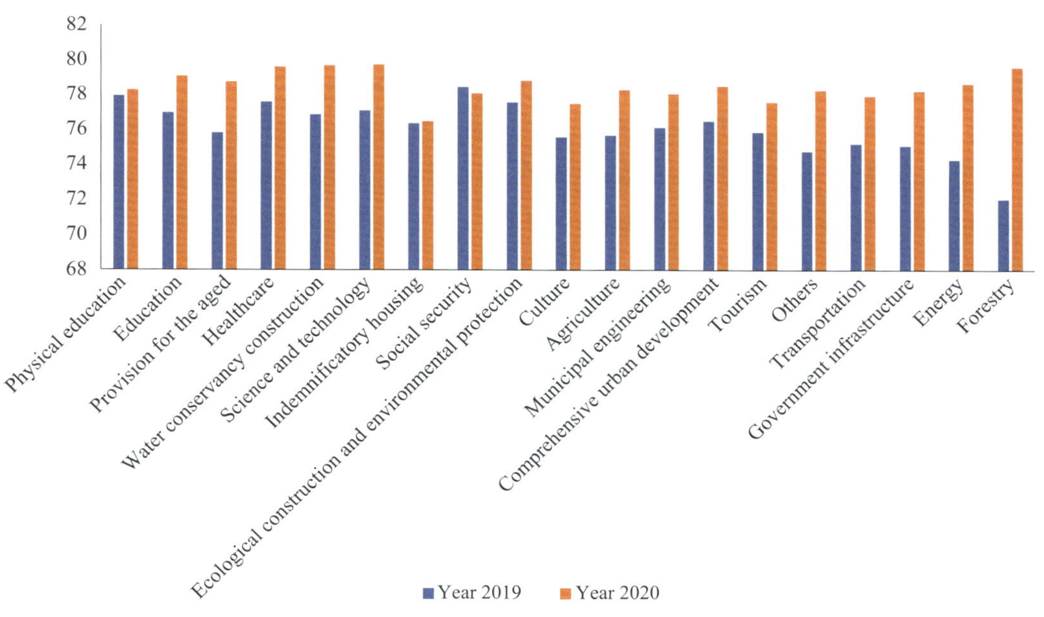

Figure 3–4 PPP Market Transparency Index by Sector

3.3.2 Transparency Indexes of Demonstration Projects and Non-demonstration Projects

As for demonstration and non-demonstration projects, as shown by Figure 3–5, the score gap between demonstration projects and non-demonstration ones in 2020

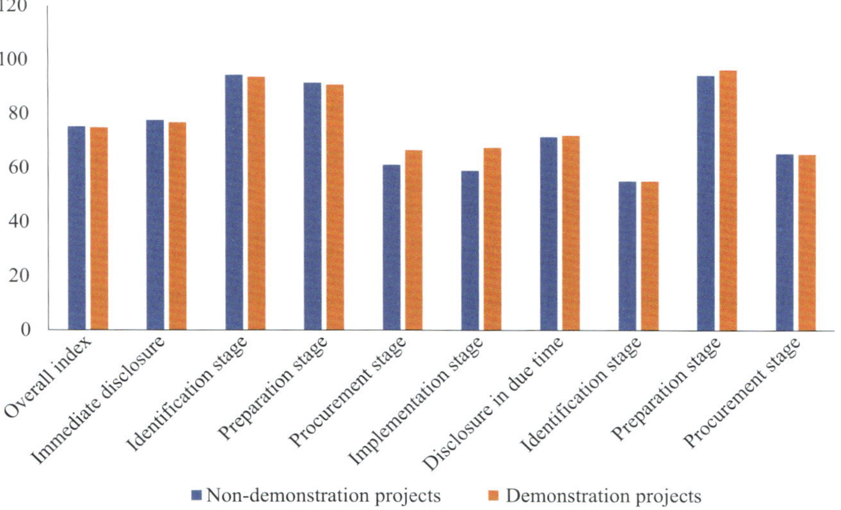

Figure 3–5 Transparency Indexes of Demonstration Projects and Non-demonstration Projects in 2020

was not significant[①], with the general index of the former slightly higher than that of the latter. According to the evaluation results in the past three years, the overall index of demonstration projects increased from 74.9 in 2018 to 77.19 in 2019, and then to 78.90 in 2020 — indicating a moderate growth rate; similarly, the overall index of non-demonstration projects grew from 75.3 in 2018 to 76.01 in 2019, and then 78.23 in 2020 — a minor increase as well. This indicates that the variable "whether it is a demonstration project", as time goes by, is increasingly ungrounded to justify the difference in transparency scores between projects.

① Our 2018 report showed a similar result, that is, a small gap was seen between the general transparency index of demonstration projects and that of non-demonstration projects.

4

Provincial Rankings and Analysis

4.1 Analysis on General Provincial Index

4.1.1 Provincial Ranking

The previous Chapter provides the 2020 national PPP market transparency index, while this Chapter will focus on provincial results. The calculation of the transparency index for each province was based on arithmetic average of the immediate disclosure index and the disclosure in time index for each province and multiplied by the weightings outlined in Chapter 2. (Based on the findings outlined in Chapter 2, the weight of immediate disclosure was 0.61, and the weight of disclosure in due time was 0.39). Table 4–1 shows the number of PPP projects and the transparency indexes of the 32 provincial-level units (provinces, municipalities, autonomous regions, and Xinjiang Production and Construction Corps, the same below) in 2019. From it the Research Group have come up with the following conclusions:

First, overall, the provincial average PPP market transparency index in 2020 was 78.02[①], a slight rise from last year (73.68). A possible reason is the addition of new projects. Moreover, 78.02 is higher than the mean value of all scores provided in the fiscal transparency reports by the Shanghai University of Finance and Economics research groups in the past 10 years (the provincial average fiscal transparency score in 2017 was only 48.3 points). It implies that as regulated by relevant departments, the PPP market is making faster progress in information disclosure than other financial segments.

Second, the PPP market information transparency index at the provincial level maintained at a satisfactory level, as the transparency scores of most provinces were concentrated between 70 and 85. However, compared with 2019, the provincial scores were more scattered. Specifically, in 2019 all of them were within the scope of 70–80,

---

① It is the simple arithmetic average of the general transparency indexes of all provinces, so it is slightly different from the previous national general index.

while in 2020, several provinces delivered a PPP transparency index above 82 or below 70. It indicates as the PPP projects continue to advance, the transparency scores of the provinces began to gradually differentiate. In specific, the top five in transparency ranking were Yunnan (84.98), Shandong (83.72), Hebei (82.99), Hunan (82.69) and Jiangsu (82.63). Beijing, Ningxia, Shanghai, Hainan, and Xizang performed relatively poorly, occupying the last five places in the ranking. Comparing with last year's ranking, we found that the province that made the greatest progress in PPP project information disclosure was Qinghai (79.22), rising by 12 places from the previous year to No.14. Among all provinces, Guangxi recorded the largest decline in the list, as its information transparency index dropped from 77.03 in 2019 to 76.40 in 2020. Despite a decline of less than 1 points, since the score gap between provinces was small, Qinghai ranked No.27 in 2020, plummeting by 14 places from the previous year. Provinces such as Tianjin, Hunan, Sichuan, Yunnan, and Jiangsu rose significantly in the list compared with 2019, while the ranks of Guangxi, Gansu, and Ningxia saw great decline.

Table 4–1 Provincial PPP Market Transparency Index and Ranking in 2020

Province	Project quantity in 2020	Transparency index in 2020	Ranking in 2020	Variance from last year	Project quantity in 2019	Transparency index in 2019
Yunnan	495	84.98	1	+4	481	80.17
Shandong	434	83.72	2	+2	765	80.20
Hebei	734	82.99	3	−1	390	81.29
Hunan	160	82.69	4	+6	418	77.64
Jiangsu	386	82.63	5	+4	398	77.69
Jilin	376	81.82	6	−3	170	80.52
Xinjiang	389	81.71	7	+4	381	77.48
Shaanxi	278	81.25	8	−1	280	77.94
Inner Mongolia	123	80.61	9	−3	283	78.07
Gansu	786	80.52	10	−9	124	81.97
Henan	42	79.91	11	+3	752	76.17
Anhui	474	79.65	12	−4	474	77.84
Guangdong	551	79.30	13	−1	519	77.20

(continued)

Province	Project quantity in 2020	Transparency index in 2020	Ranking in 2020	Variance from last year	Project quantity in 2019	Transparency index in 2019
Qinghai	262	79.22	14	+12	38	70.81
Sichuan	552	78.99	15	+5	557	73.05
Shanxi	103	78.47	16	0	396	74.15
Liaoning	406	78.22	17	–2	184	75.80
Hubei	419	78.22	18	+3	417	72.96
Heilongjiang	293	78.17	19	+4	107	72.09
Zhejiang	359	77.60	20	–3	513	73.86
Tianjin	55	77.45	21	+7	49	68.28
Fujian	241	77.35	22	–4	351	73.80
Guizhou	507	77.17	23	–4	512	73.76
Corps	418	77.05	24	+3	18	69.28
Jiangxi	529	76.91	25	0	355	71.52
Chongqing	16	76.56	26	–4	43	72.23
Guangxi	57	76.40	27	–14	204	77.03
Beijing	69	74.73	28	+1	70	67.49
Ningxia	43	73.83	29	–5	47	71.57
Shanghai	7	72.40	30	+1	5	60.77
Hainan	95	69.76	31	–1	96	62.89
Xizang	3	56.45	32	0	1	52.22

Notes: ① The projects contained in this table refer to the 9 962 PPP projects subject to immediate disclosure. The 5 801 PPP projects subject to disclosure in due time are a subset of it. ② "+"indicates an increase in the ranking, "–"indicates a fall in the ranking, the same below.

4.1.2 Provincial Rankings of Immediate Disclosure and Disclosure in Due Time

Figure 4–1 and Figure 4–2 show the provincial distribution of immediate disclosure indexes and disclosure in due time indexes of all provinces in 2019 and 2020. The results show that disclosure in due time index of each province was generally higher than the immediate disclosure index. This finding is consistent with that in Chapter 3, which implies again that all provinces have done a poorer job in immediate disclosure than in disclosure in due time on PPP projects.

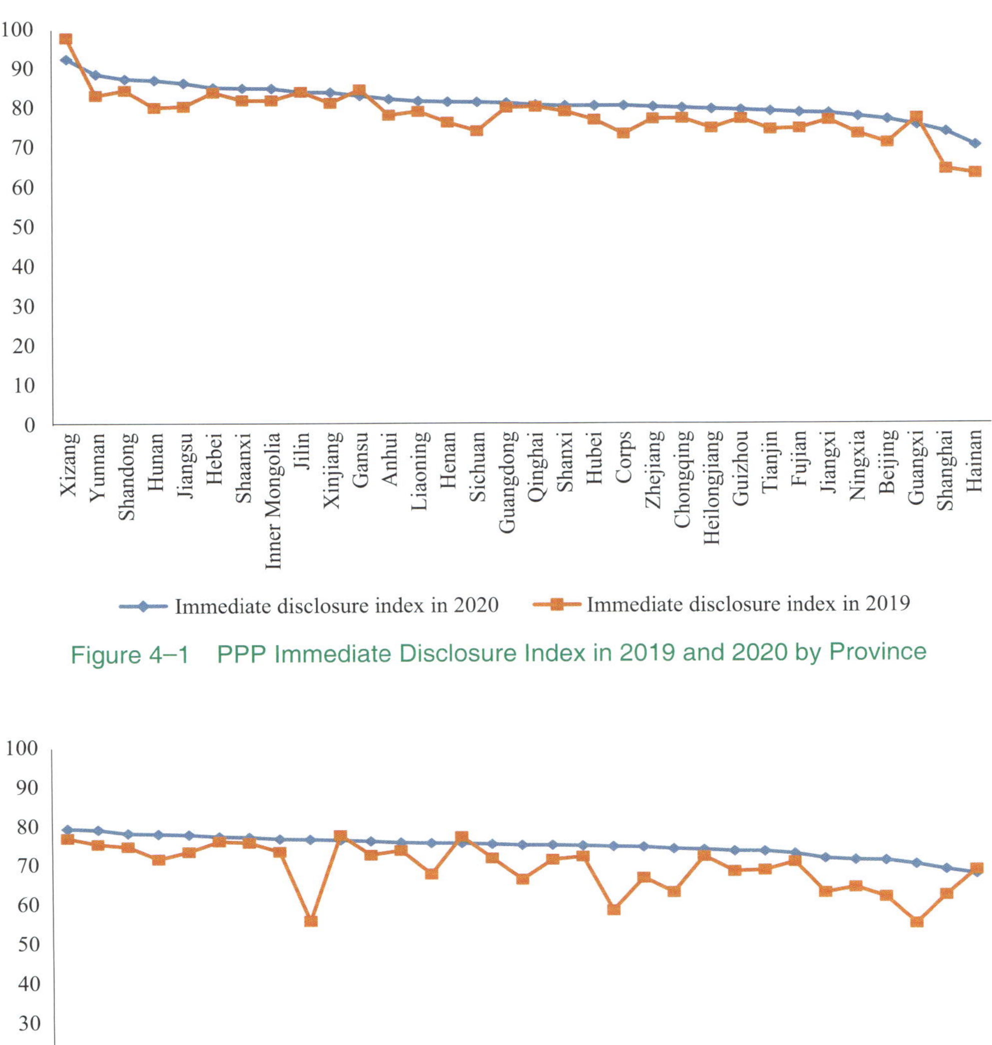

Figure 4–1 PPP Immediate Disclosure Index in 2019 and 2020 by Province

Note: Among them, as there were no projects subject to disclosure in due time in Xizang, Xizang did not participate in the corresponding ranking.

Figure 4–2 PPP Disclosure in Due Time Index in 2019 and 2020 by Province

While the provincial rankings of general transparency index, disclosure in due time index, and immediate disclosure index were generally consistent, it is important to qualify the impact of weightings on the results. As the weight allocated for immediate disclosure is higher than that for disclosure in due time (0.61 versus 0.39), it is more likely for the provinces that perform better in immediate disclosure to rank higher in the list of general index. For example, excluding Xizang, the top five provinces with the highest immediate disclosure index were also the top five in the ranking of general index. However, there still existed some differences in the provincial rankings of disclosure in due time index and immediate disclosure index. The No.4 in the ranking of immediate disclosure index Hunan ranked twelfth in terms of disclosure in due time, indicating that the province did do well in immediate disclosure, but less desirable in disclosure in due time. Another example is Shanghai, which ranked last in terms of immediate disclosure, and the second from bottom in disclosure in due time, indicating that the city needs to put more efforts on both categories of disclosure. The gap between the two lists further indicates that each region has its own advantages and disadvantages in disclosing the information of PPP projects, and it is necessary for them to learn from each other, so that the overall transparency of PPP projects will come to a higher stage.

Comparison between the data in 2020 and 2019 shows no obvious trends in the cross-phase changes of both immediate disclosure and disclosure in due time indexes. That is, all provinces delivered a mixed performance in terms of PPP project information disclosure. As for immediate disclosure, there are 28 provinces and cities showing increase in index and 4 decline. Concerning the immediate disclosure index, the largest improvement came from Shanghai, the score of which climbed from 64.60 in 2019 to 74.05 in 2020, followed by Sichuan, Hainan, and Xinjiang Production and Construction Corps; while the largest drop was obtained by Xizang, from 97.89 in 2019 to 92.53 in 2020. As for disclosure in due time, there are 28 provinces and cities showed increase and another 3 decline. The largest increase in the disclosure in due time index was in Qinghai, rising from 55.71 in 2019 to 76.60 in 2020. Guangxi recorded the smallest increase in the same category, from 76.12 in 2019 to 77.38 in 2020, representing a growth of 1.26 points only. Anhui Province dropped the most significantly in the disclosure in due time index, from 77.22 in 2019 to 75.49 in 2020. On the whole, most provinces delivered a higher disclosure in due time index, implying the growing efforts spared by them to the management of the disclosure in due time of PPP projects.

4.1.3 Relationship between Transparency Index and Project Quantity

During index compilation, some experts and representatives from local finance departments suggested quantitative factors should also be taken into consideration. The rationale is that some provinces manage larger numbers of PPP projects, which may increase the difficulty in supervision and information disclosure, which in turn may result in a lower PPP transparency index. Therefore, in order to examine the relationship between the quantity of PPP projects managed in each region and its PPP market transparency, Figure 4–3 maps provincial PPP transparency indexes and project quantities. It indicates that the quantity of PPP projects does not have a significant negative relationship with the provincial PPP market transparency index, but instead shows certain positive correlation In the statistical sense, the speculation that "a region is managing too many PPP projects, so it scores low in the information transparency" does not seem to hold true.

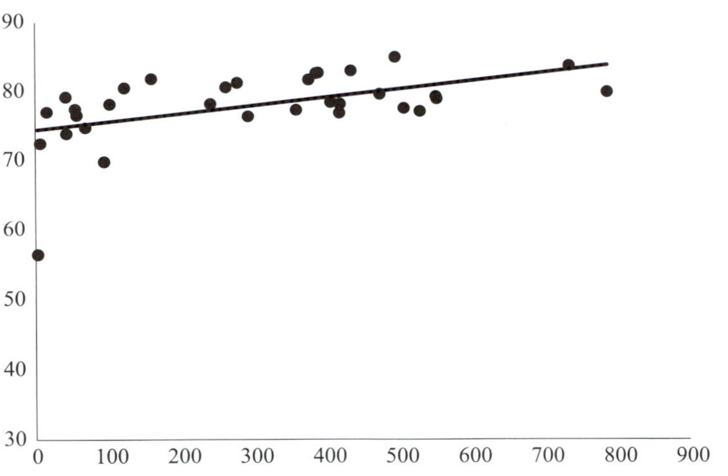

Figure 4–3 Scatter Diagram of Provincial Project Quantity and Transparency Index

Another doubt is that for the provinces with few PPP projects, which is deemed statistically insignificant, whether it is necessary to include them in the national ranking. In our report, no provincial-level units with too few projects were deleted. Instead, all were included in the rankings in order to thoroughly and objectively reflect the PPP information disclosure work done by each province. This is because it is hard to define a

scope for sample size, for which different readers might have different standards. Instead, they're free to intentionally omit the provinces they believe are operating few projects, and such omission doesn't affect the relative rankings of other provinces. Apart from that, it is also worthy of probing why the number of projects in a region is positively correlated with the region's PPP transparency index. One possible reason is that in regions with a large number of PPP projects, their competent authorities tend to arrange more management personnel or dedicated persons in charge.

4.2 Analysis on Provincial Index by Stage

4.2.1 Immediate Disclosure

The following is the analysis over the results of information disclosure by provinces in each stage of immediate disclosure and disclosure in due time. Table 4–2 shows the provincial rankings of 2020 PPP project immediate disclosure index and disclosure in due time index, as well as the variance from the previous year. As for immediate disclosure, Xizang, Yunnan, Shandong, Hunan and Jiangsu ranked as top five, while Ningxia, Beijing, Guangxi, Shanghai and Hainan were in the last five places. Xizang showed the largest rise in rank, from No.32 in 2019 to No.1 in 2020. The province with the most decline was Guangxi, which fell by 14 places from No.16 in 2019 to No.30 in 2020. In terms of disclosure in due time, Hebei, Hunan, Xinjiang, Guizhou, and Xinjiang Production and Construction Corps ranked among the top five, with Hubei, Zhejiang, Sichuan, Gansu, and Inner Mongolia coming in last. Qinghai presented the largest surge in the ranking of disclosure in due time index, leaping from No.30 in 2019 to No.8 in 2019. The province recording the most significant decline were Qinghai, dropping by 29 places from the previous year to No.30.

Table 4–2 Provincial Rankings of Immediate Disclosure Index and Disclosure in Due Time Index

Ranking	Immediate disclosure index in 2020	Variance from 2019	Disclosure in due time index in 2020	Variance from 2019
1	Xizang	+31	Hebei	2
2	Yunnan	+3	Hunan	6

(continued)

Ranking	Immediate disclosure index in 2020	Variance from 2019	Disclosure in due time index in 2020	Variance from 2019
3	Shandong	−1	Xinjiang	12
4	Hunan	+8	Guizhou	16
5	Jiangsu	+5	Corps	21
6	Hebei	−2	Heilongjiang	15
7	Shaanxi	−1	Shanxi	16
8	Inner Mongolia	−1	Qinghai	22
9	Jilin	−6	Yunnan	−3
10	Xinjiang	−2	Shandong	−1
11	Gansu	−10	Shaanxi	3
12	Anhui	+3	Anhui	−10
13	Liaoning	+1	Hainan	14
14	Henan	+8	Henan	−9
15	Sichuan	+11	Guangxi	−11
16	Guangdong	−5	Jilin	−9
17	Qinghai	−8	Jiangxi	8
18	Shanxi	−5	Shanghai	13
19	Hubei	+1	Fujian	−7
20	Corps	+8	Jiangsu	−10
21	Zhejiang	−2	Ningxia	−2
22	Chongqing	−5	Chongqing	2
23	Heilongjiang	0	Liaoning	−6
24	Guizhou	−6	Guangdong	−13
25	Tianjin	0	Beijing	3
26	Fujian	−2	Tianjin	3
27	Jiangxi	−6	Hubei	−5
28	Ningxia	−1	Zhejiang	−10
29	Beijing	0	Sichuan	−13
30	Guangxi	−14	Gansu	−29
31	Shanghai	−1	Inner Mongolia	−18
32	Hainan	−1		

Table 4–3 shows the provincial rankings of 2020 PPP project immediate disclosure index, and the sub-indexes of all stages in immediate disclosure.

Table 4–3 Provincial Rankings of Immediate Disclosure Index and Sub-index at Each Stage in 2020

Ranking	Immediate disclosure index	Identification stage	Preparation stage	Procurement stage	Implementation stage
1	Xizang	Xizang	Xizang	Jiangsu	Yunnan
2	Yunnan	Yunnan	Corps	Hunan	Inner Mongolia
3	Shandong	Hunan	Xinjiang	Gansu	Shandong
4	Hunan	Shanghai	Yunnan	Shandong	Hunan
5	Jiangsu	Gansu	Hebei	Xinjiang	Jiangsu
6	Hebei	Shandong	Gansu	Yunnan	Hebei
7	Shaanxi	Xinjiang	Shandong	Shaanxi	Jilin
8	Inner Mongolia	Qinghai	Shanxi	Guangdong	Corps
9	Jilin	Beijing	Guangxi	Inner Mongolia	Sichuan
10	Xinjiang	Shaanxi	Jilin	Beijing	Ningxia
11	Gansu	Jiangsu	Hubei	Fujian	Shaanxi
12	Anhui	Hebei	Henan	Anhui	Anhui
13	Liaoning	Guangxi	Inner Mongolia	Qinghai	Zhejiang
14	Henan	Tianjin	Chongqing	Jiangxi	Henan
15	Sichuan	Jilin	Jiangxi	Hebei	Chongqing
16	Guangdong	Liaoning	Jiangsu	Sichuan	Guizhou
17	Qinghai	Heilongjiang	Liaoning	Zhejiang	Hubei
18	Shanxi	Chongqing	Hunan	Jilin	Guangdong
19	Hubei	Guangdong	Shaanxi	Ningxia	Heilongjiang
20	Corps	Sichuan	Qinghai	Heilongjiang	Shanghai
21	Zhejiang	Shanxi	Guizhou	Tianjin	Fujian
22	Chongqing	Jiangxi	Heilongjiang	Henan	Hainan
23	Heilongjiang	Henan	Tianjin	Hubei	Xinjiang
24	Guizhou	Anhui	Anhui	Guizhou	Shanxi
25	Tianjin	Zhejiang	Guangdong	Chongqing	Liaoning
26	Fujian	Corps	Zhejiang	Shanxi	Beijing

(continued)

Ranking	Immediate disclosure index	Identification stage	Preparation stage	Procurement stage	Implementation stage
27	Jiangxi	Hubei	Sichuan	Liaoning	Gansu
28	Ningxia	Inner Mongolia	Fujian	Hainan	Guangxi
29	Beijing	Ningxia	Beijing	Corps	Qinghai
30	Guangxi	Fujian	Ningxia	Shanghai	Tianjin
31	Shanghai	Guizhou	Shanghai	Guangxi	Jiangxi
32	Hainan	Hainan	Hainan	Xizang	Xizang

Yunnan, Shandong, Jilin and Hebei performed well and consistently across all stages. Yunnan Province ranked high in all the stages of identification, preparation, procurement and implementation, which earned it No.2 in the general ranking of immediate disclosure index. Hebei delivered desirable results in the identification, preparation and implementation stages, but ranked No.15 in the procurement stage, resulting in its sixth place in the overall ranking. Better disclosure at the procurement stage is expected to improve the province's overall ranking. Xinjiang ranked high in the identification, preparation and procurement phases, but its poorer performance in the execution stage lowered its place in the general immediate disclosure index ranking.

Ningxia, Beijing, Guangxi, Shanghai and Hainan occupied the last five places in the ranking of immediate disclosure index. In particular, Shanghai ranked No.4 in the identification stage, but its poor performance during other stages lowered its overall ranking. The Xizang Autonomous Region came in first in the identification and preparation stages, which led to its ranking at the top of the list. Xinjiang Production and Construction Corps, Shanghai and Hainan performed poorly at all stages of information disclosure.

Shandong did not rank high in all stages, but it eventually occupied the third place in the overall ranking of immediate disclosure index. In contrast, Hunan ranked third, second, and fourth in the identification, procurement, and execution stages, respectively — which were higher than those of Shandong, but it was behind Shandong in the general ranking. This implies the impact of the distribution of PPP projects in different stages on the final results. Where a province has a higher percentage of PPP projects in preparation stage and the disclosure work done at this stage is excellent, then the province can easily achieve a high score. This is partly due to the calculation methods in Chapter 3,

whereby the procurement and implementation stage weighting were "consolidated" into the preparation and identification stages. If a province does not have many PPP projects at preparation stage, its slight inadequacies at procurement and implementation stages may adversely affect the final general transparency index. For better clarification, Table 4–4 shows the distribution of PPP projects by stage in each province. It is easy to find out that Hunan had a significantly higher proportion of projects at the preparation stage than Shandong. It should also be noted that the purpose of highlighting the distribution difference in stages is to explain the results and possible reasons. It does not imply project companies should deliberately slow down the progress of PPP projects to raise the index.

Table 4–4 Quantity of PPP Projects by Stage in Each Province in 2020

Province	Total quantity	Preparation stage	Procurement stage	Implementation stage
Anhui	474	22	26	426
Beijing	69	1	5	63
Fujian	359	19	30	310
Gansu	123	1	20	102
Guangdong	551	29	80	442
Guangxi	293	22	107	164
Guizhou	529	87	124	318
Hainan	95	6	13	76
Hebei	434	25	88	321
Henan	786	97	215	474
Heilongjiang	103	6	22	75
Hubei	419	38	100	281
Hunan	389	47	68	274
Jilin	160	15	27	118
Jiangsu	386	20	66	300
Jiangxi	418	28	48	342
Liaoning	241	53	85	103
Inner Mongolia	262	16	47	199
Ningxia	43	1	6	36
Qinghai	42	2	13	27

(continued)

Province	Total quantity	Preparation stage	Procurement stage	Implementation stage
Shandong	734	50	122	562
Shanxi	406	64	147	195
Shaanxi	278	30	57	191
Shanghai	7	2	2	3
Sichuan	552	19	130	403
Tianjin	55	9	14	32
Xizang	3	2	1	
Xinjiang	376	13	43	320
Corps	16	2	4	10
Yunnan	495	42	110	343
Zhejiang	507	22	50	435
Chongqing	57	5	19	33

4.2.2 Disclosure in Due Time

Table 4–5 shows the list of the top 10 provinces for the 2020 PPP project disclosure in due time index and sub-indexes at each stage. Hebei Province and Yunnan Province performed well at various stages. In particular, Hebei Province ranked second at both identification and procurement stages. Thanks to its outstanding performance in the identification stage, Guangxi Autonomous Region ranked No.3 in the disclosure in due time index ranking. Since the information disclosure in procurement stage was of the highest importance (according to the calculation results of the expert decision matrix, the weight of procurement stage was 0.45), Hebei and Yunnan occupied the first and second places in terms of disclosure in due time with a high score in procurement stage.

Table 4–5 Provincial Rankings of Disclosure in Due Time Index and Sub-index at Each Stage in 2020

Ranking	Disclosure in due time index	Identification stage	Preparation stage	Procurement stage
1	Hebei	Qinghai	Shanghai	Yunnan
2	Yunnan	Hebei	Jilin	Hebei
3	Jilin	Guangxi	Chongqing	Jilin

(continued)

Ranking	Disclosure in due time index	Identification stage	Preparation stage	Procurement stage
4	Xinjiang	Yunnan	Qinghai	Xinjiang
5	Shandong	Gansu	Hebei	Henan
6	Guangxi	Xinjiang	Shandong	Shandong
7	Henan	Shandong	Tianjin	Jiangsu
8	Jiangsu	Jiangxi	Liaoning	Gansu
9	Qinghai	Anhui	Yunnan	Hunan
10	Gansu	Jilin	Guangdong	Guangxi
11	Guangdong	Guangdong	Heilongjiang	Heilongjiang
12	Hunan	Tianjin	Guangxi	Guangdong
13	Heilongjiang	Shaanxi	Fujian	Sichuan
14	Anhui	Jiangsu	Anhui	Inner Mongolia
15	Shaanxi	Henan	Hubei	Shanxi
16	Shanxi	Fujian	Shanxi	Shaanxi
17	Sichuan	Hunan	Henan	Anhui
18	Fujian	Zhejiang	Jiangsu	Fujian
19	Tianjin	Guizhou	Zhejiang	Hubei
20	Hubei	Hubei	Xinjiang	Qinghai
21	Jiangxi	Shanxi	Jiangxi	Tianjin
22	Inner Mongolia	Heilongjiang	Sichuan	Guizhou
23	Guizhou	Sichuan	Hunan	Jiangxi
24	Zhejiang	Inner Mongolia	Shaanxi	Zhejiang
25	Liaoning	Corps	Beijing	Liaoning
26	Corps	Liaoning	Guizhou	Beijing
27	Chongqing	Chongqing	Gansu	Corps
28	Beijing	Shanghai	Hainan	Hainan
29	Shanghai	Ningxia	Inner Mongolia	Chongqing
30	Hainan	Beijing	Corps	Shanghai
31	Ningxia	Hainan	Ningxia	Ningxia

The last five on the list were occupied by Chongqing, Beijing, Shanghai, Hainan and Ningxia. According to Table 4–3, Beijing, Shanghai, Ningxia and Hainan also performed poorly in immediate disclosure (see the previous analysis), ranking among the last on the list. It indicates that their PPP information disclosure approaches are in need of improvement.

Figure 4–4 consolidates the indexes of provincial units at each stage of immediate disclosure and disclosure in real time. The comparison highlights that the disclosure of information at identification and preparation stages was more complete, while the indexes at procurement and implementation stages were generally lower. Such results are basically in line with expectations as the more detailed information at the identification and preparation stages is likely to determine if a PPP project progresses, and is often more valued by the regulatory authorities and social participants, hence resulting in the higher corresponding indexes.

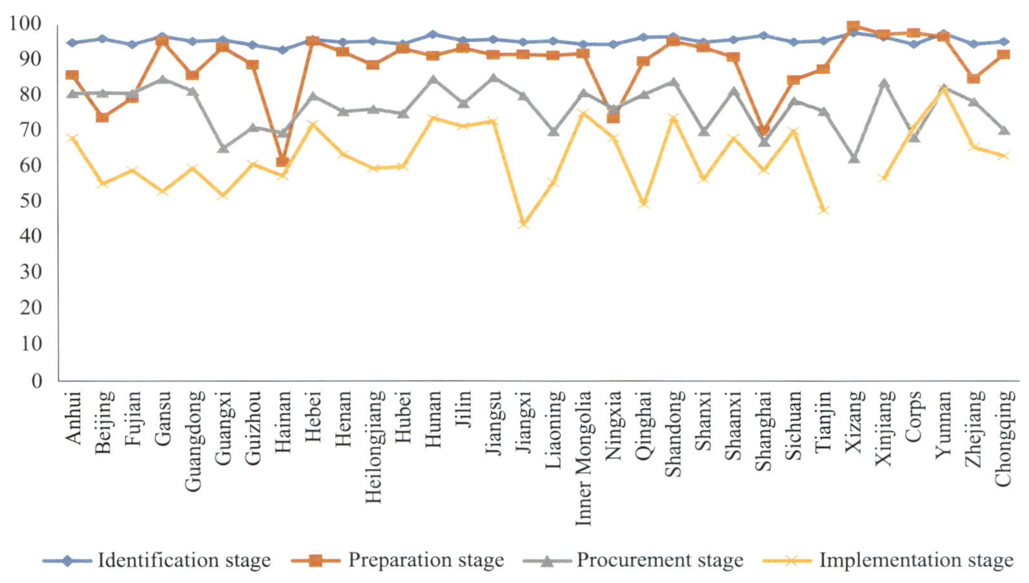

Figure 4–4 Provincial Distribution of Immediate Disclosure Transparency Indexes by Stage in 2020

Figure 4–5 shows the indexes of provincial units at various stages of disclosure in due time. Unlike the case in immediate disclosure, the information disclosure performance at identification stage does not appear to be as comprehensive as in the preparation and procurement stages. This may be attributed to the identification stage

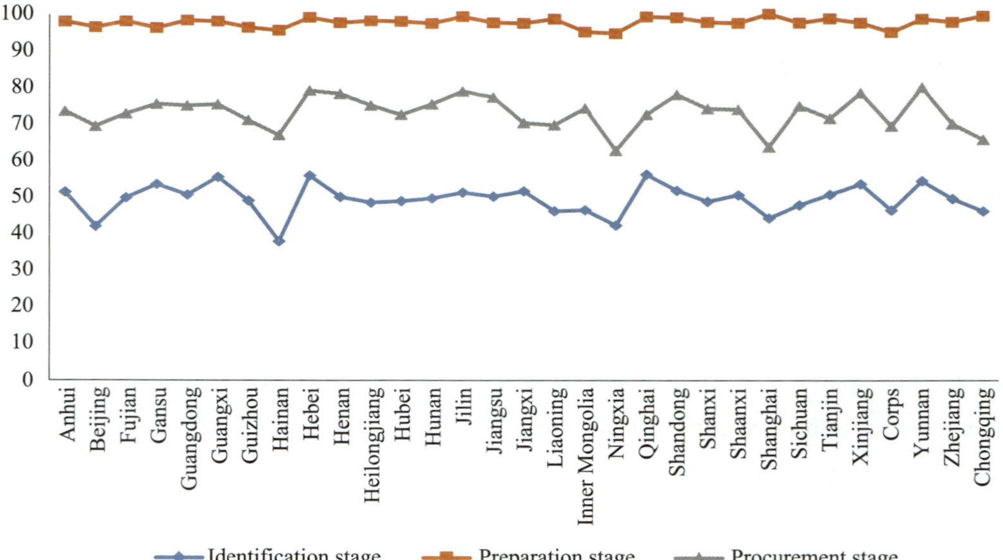

Figure 4–5 Provincial Distribution of Disclosure in Due Time Indexes by Stage in 2020

requiring two important PDF files, namely the "Two Assessments" (value-for-money assessment and financial affordability assessment). The Research Group conducted a very strict review of the two files, and there were many projects with no disclosure or false disclosure, consequently contributing to a generally low index of each province at this stage.

4.3 Analysis on Provincial Transparency Indexes of "Two Assessments and One Program"

The "Two Assessments and One Program" refer to the "value-for-money assessment report and approval documents by the competent industry authority and the finance industry at the same level", the "financial affordability report and approval documents by the finance department at the same level" and "attachments to implementation program". The "Two Assessments and One Program" takes a very important position at the identification stage and preparation stage of a PPP project, and is also an indispensable step in the normal operation of PPP projects in China, enough to determine whether a PPP project can be implemented smoothly or not. Accordingly, this section briefly summarizes

the disclosure of these key reports in all provinces.

The "Two Assessments and One Program" documents contain extensive amounts of complex information, prepared in PDF files and published on the website. It is not unusual for the PDF files to extend to tens or even hundreds of pages for the public to review. Three PDF files were the focus of the Research Group for manual reading and checking — "value for money", "financial affordability", "implementation program". Table 4–6 shows the provincial rankings of the scores of the three PDF files. It can be seen that the rankings are highly consistent with that of disclosure in due time index. For example, Hebei Province took the first place in "value-for-money assessment report and approval documents by the competent industry authority and the finance industry at the same level" and the second place in the "financial affordability report and approval documents by the finance department at the same level". The province's excellent performance in the two indicators earned it the first place in the disclosure in due time index. Shanghai ranked the last in the same ranking, mainly attributable to its low score in the disclosure of the three documents, which showed that the city needs to dedicate more efforts to this aspect. Chongqing took the second place in the ranking of "attachments to implementation program", but due to its low scores in "value-for-money assessment report and approval documents by the competent industry authority and the finance industry at the same level" and "financial affordability report and approval documents by the finance department at the same level", its general index of disclosure in due time ranked No.27. Jilin performed well in "Two Assessments and One Program", ranking among top four in all three documents, which resulted in the third place in the overall ranking of disclosure in due time index. Shandong, Guangxi and Henan delivered a mixed performance in "Two Assessments and One Program", making them rank from No.5 to No.7 in the general list.

Table 4–6 Provincial Transparency Rankings of "Two Assessments and One Program"

Ranking	Disclosure in due time index	Value-for-money	Financial affordability	Implementation program
1	Hebei	Hebei	Qinghai	Shanghai
2	Yunnan	Qinghai	Hebei	Jilin
3	Jilin	Yunnan	Tianjin	Chongqing
4	Xinjiang	Jilin	Jilin	Qinghai

(continued)

Ranking	Disclosure in due time index	Value-for-money	Financial affordability	Implementation program
5	Shandong	Tianjin	Yunnan	Hebei
6	Guangxi	Guangxi	Fujian	Shandong
7	Henan	Jiangxi	Guangdong	Tianjin
8	Jiangsu	Guangdong	Guangxi	Liaoning
9	Qinghai	Fujian	Jiangxi	Yunnan
10	Gansu	Shandong	Henan	Guangdong
11	Guangdong	Henan	Sichuan	Fujian
12	Hunan	Shaanxi	Shandong	Heilongjiang
13	Heilongjiang	Xinjiang	Shanxi	Guangxi
14	Anhui	Shanxi	Gansu	Anhui
15	Shaanxi	Gansu	Xinjiang	Hubei
16	Shanxi	Guizhou	Chongqing	Zhejiang
17	Sichuan	Jiangsu	Shaanxi	Shanxi
18	Fujian	Hubei	Hubei	Henan
19	Tianjin	Zhejiang	Jiangsu	Sichuan
20	Hubei	Heilongjiang	Zhejiang	Jiangsu
21	Jiangxi	Anhui	Anhui	Xinjiang
22	Inner Mongolia	Hunan	Guizhou	Jiangxi
23	Guizhou	Chongqing	Heilongjiang	Hunan
24	Zhejiang	Sichuan	Hunan	Shaanxi
25	Liaoning	Liaoning	Inner Mongolia	Beijing
26	Corps	Inner Mongolia	Corps	Hainan
27	Chongqing	Corps	Beijing	Guizhou
28	Beijing	Shanghai	Shanghai	Gansu
29	Shanghai	Ningxia	Liaoning	Inner Mongolia
30	Hainan	Beijing	Ningxia	Corps
31	Ningxia	Hainan	Hainan	Ningxia

In the future, the Research Group will consider carrying out a number of special assessments to check not only whether these key fields or core PDF files are disclosed, but also the content quality of these reports, with an aim to further promote the standardization and transparency of PPP projects.

5

Municipal Rankings and Analysis

5.1 Municipal Distribution of PPP Projects

Drawing on the same methodology for comparative analysis of the PPP market transparency indexes at national level and at provincial level in Chapter 3 and Chapter 4, this Chapter presents some analysis on the transparency of the PPP market in some cities with a large number of PPP projects. In the 338 prefecture-level cities (autonomous prefecture, prefecture, league, etc., are all defined as "city" hereinafter), 328 cities have introduced the PPP model, as shown by Table 5–1. The PPP model is far-reaching, especially in 22 provinces and autonomous regions, that is, Guangdong, Shandong, Henan, Xinjiang, Anhui, Yunnan, Liaoning, Hunan, Guangxi, Jiangsu, Hubei, Inner Mongolia, Hebei, Shanxi, Zhejiang, Jiangxi, Shaanxi, Jilin, Sichuan, Fujian, Guizhou and Ningxia, where PPP projects have covered all prefecture-level cities.

Table 5–1 Number of Cities in Each Province Having Introduced PPP Model

Province	Number of cities with PPP	Total number of cities	Province	Number of cities with PPP	Total number of cities
Yunnan	16	16	Jiangxi	11	11
Inner Mongolia	12	12	Hebei	11	11
Jilin	9	9	Henan	17	17
Sichuan	21	21	Zhejiang	11	11
Ningxia	5	5	Hainan	3	3
Anhui	16	16	Hubei	13	13
Shandong	17	17	Hunan	14	14
Shanxi	11	11	Gansu	13	14
Guangdong	21	21	Fujian	9	9
Guangxi	14	14	Guizhou	9	9

(continued)

Province	Number of cities with PPP	Total number of cities	Province	Number of cities with PPP	Total number of cities
Xinjiang	14	14	Liaoning	14	14
Shaanxi	10	10	Qinghai	6	8
Jiangsu	13	13	Heilongjiang	12	13
Xizang	2	7			

Some cities have mature PPP markets, while others are relatively new to PPP projects. For the purposes of this Report, the Research Group selected the cities that have introduced a large number of PPP projects for analysis. Specifically, 46 cities were selected as samples for analysis of municipal PPP market transparency. They were cities above the prefecture level with more than 50 projects registered in the PPP Integrated Information Platform as of Thursday, December 31, 2020. For the results of the PPP Market Transparency Index in cities above the prefecture level with more than 30 projects, please see Annex Ⅳ. The 46 cities are: Jining of Shandong, Aksu of Xinjiang, Rizhao of Shandong, Yuxi of Yunnan, Honghe of Yunnan, Chengde of Hebei, Kunming of Yunnan, Weifang of Shandong, Nanyang of Henan, Xinxiang of Henan, Heze of Shandong, Tangshan of Hebei, Dongguan of Guangdong, Xuzhou of Jiangsu, Urumqi of Xinjiang, Bijie of Guizhou, Nanjing of Jiangsu, Xi'an of Shaanxi, Pingdingshan of Henan, Jinan of Shandong, Luoyang of Henan, Linyi of Shandong, Chifeng of Inner Mongolia, Chengdu of Sichuan, Fuyang of Anhui, Hangzhou of Zhejiang, Quanzhou of Fujian, Zhengzhou of Henan, Wuhan of Hubei, Lishui of Zhejiang, Bayingolin of Xinjiang, Wenzhou of Zhejiang, Ningde of Fujian, Zunyi of Guizhou, Linfen of Shanxi, Xinyang of Henan, Yibin of Sichuan, Zhumadian of Henan, Zhangzhou of Fujian, Qingdao of Shandong, Yichun of Jiangxi, Ganzhou of Jiangxi, Taizhou of Zhejiang, Fuzhou of Fujian, Qiannan of Guizhou, and Qiandongnan of Guizhou.

5.2 Municipal PPP Market Transparency Index

5.2.1 Municipal Ranking

Of the 47 cities selected, all of which could be described as relatively mature PPP markets, the overall ranking of PPP market transparency index in 2020 is shown in Table

5–2. Jining of Shandong, ranked first, with an index of 82.81 points, 6.86 points higher than the national average; followed by Aksu of Xinjiang and Rizhao of Shandong, scoring 84.59 and 83.94 points, respectively. Besides them, cities with a total score greater than 80 include Yuxi of Yunnan, Honghe of Yunnan, Chengde of Hebei, Kunming of Yunnan, Weifang of Shandong, Nanyang of Henan, Xinxiang of Henan, Heze of Shandong, Tangshan of Hebei, Dongguan of Guangdong, Xuzhou of Jiangsu, Urumqi of Xinjiang, and Bijie of Guizhou. These are cities where PPP information was well disclosed.

Table 5–2 Overall Transparency Indexes of Selected Cities in 2020

Ranking	City	Project quantity in 2020	Overall index in 2020	Variance from general index in 2019	Overall index in 2019
1	Jining, Shandong	177	87.22	+5.60	81.62
2	Aksu, Xinjiang	54	85.96	+4.55	81.41
3	Rizhao, Shandong	56	85.78	−0.35	86.13
4	Yuxi, Yunnan	53	85.72	−0.74	86.46
5	Honghe, Yunnan	60	85.19	+3.13	82.06
6	Chengde, Hebei	62	85.09	+7.03	78.06
7	Kunming, Yunnan	97	84.98	+3.57	81.41
8	Weifang, Shandong	58	84.96	+3.17	81.79
9	Nanyang, Henan	112	83.41	+9.83	73.58
10	Xinxiang, Henan	74	83.16	+2.31	80.85
11	Heze, Shandong	62	82.91	+1.33	81.58
12	Tangshan, Hebei	55	82.48	+1.16	81.32
13	Dongguan, Guangdong	51	82.41	+7.23	75.18
14	Xuzhou, Jiangsu	69	82.35	+2.92	79.43
15	Urumqi, Xinjiang	57	82.26	−3.98	86.24
16	Bijie, Guizhou	82	81.94	+4.58	77.36
17	Nanjing, Jiangsu	66	81.62	+1.53	80.09
18	Xi'an, Shaanxi	68	81.61	+3.55	78.06
19	Pingdingshan, Henan	70	81.50	−0.98	82.48
20	Jinan, Shandong	66	81.33	+1.46	79.87

(continued)

Ranking	City	Project quantity in 2020	Overall index in 2020	Variance from general index in 2019	Overall index in 2019
21	Luoyang, Henan	108	81.00	+6.01	74.99
22	Linyi, Shandong	61	80.56	+4.70	75.86
23	Chifeng, Inner Mongolia	68	80.54	+3.45	77.09
24	Chengdu, Sichuan	68	80.47	+2.08	78.39
25	Fuyang, Anhui	59	80.24	+3.63	76.61
26	Hangzhou, Zhejiang	61	80.06	+0.18	79.88
27	Quanzhou, Fujian	62	79.56	+3.71	75.85
28	Zhengzhou, Henan	58	79.25	+2.82	76.43
29	Wuhan, Hubei	52	79.21	+5.67	73.54
30	Lishui, Zhejiang	135	78.65	+8.24	70.41
31	Bayingolin, Xinjiang	81	78.56	+2.59	75.97
32	Wenzhou, Zhejiang	70	78.29	+1.20	77.09
33	Ningde, Fujian	55	78.06	+3.16	74.9
34	Zunyi, Guizhou	56	78.06	+4.39	73.67
35	Linfen, Shanxi	86	78.00	+0.50	77.5
36	Xinyang, Henan	59	77.90	+0.65	77.25
37	Yibin, Sichuan	51	77.78	+5.35	72.43
38	Zhumadian, Henan	55	77.50	+4.60	72.9
39	Zhangzhou, Fujian	63	77.45	+3.18	74.27
40	Qingdao, Shandong	81	76.94	−3.34	80.28
41	Tianjin	93	76.53	+6.19	70.34
42	Yichun, Jiangxi	59	76.47	+5.54	70.93
43	Ganzhou, Jiangxi	62	76.35	+4.27	72.08
44	Taizhou, Zhejiang	54	75.88	+2.59	73.29
45	Fuzhou, Fujian	53	74.30	+3.02	71.28
46	Qiannan, Guizhou	56	73.47	−3.44	76.91

By comparison with the indexes in 2019, it can be found that some prefecture-level cities scored significantly higher in 2020 than in 2019. Among them, the largest increase was delivered by Aksu of Xinjiang, the 2020 overall score of which increased by 15.39 points compared to 2019, and followed by Dongguan of Shandong, with an increase of 13.62 points from 2019. However, it can also be found that the indexes of many cities above the prefecture

level decreased in 2020 from 2019, especially Qiannan Prefecture of Guizhou and Haikou of Hainan. They recorded the largest decline from 2019 by 13.10 and 12 points, respectively.

5.2.2 Comparison with National Average

The distribution diagram of the general transparency indexes of 46 cities shows a minor gap between most cities as the PPP model is in full swing in all these locations. However, it should also be noted that the PPP market information transparency indexes of some cities were much lower than those of the rest. By variation in the market transparency index, the 46 cities can be roughly classified into two groups, as shown in Figure 5–1. The first group includes 25 cities with leading PPP market transparency performance across the nation, i.e. those ranking between Jining of Shandong and Fuyang of Anhui; the second group includes 21 cities that lagged behind the national average, i.e. those ranking between Hangzhou of Zhejiang and Qiandongnan of Guizhou. As most of the cities analyzed manage large numbers of PPP projects, business unfamiliarity should not be a factor for poor PPP market transparency indexes delivered by the cities in the second group. Instead, it means that some cities do need to strengthen their efforts related to PPP information disclosure to avoid the negligence in standardized management.

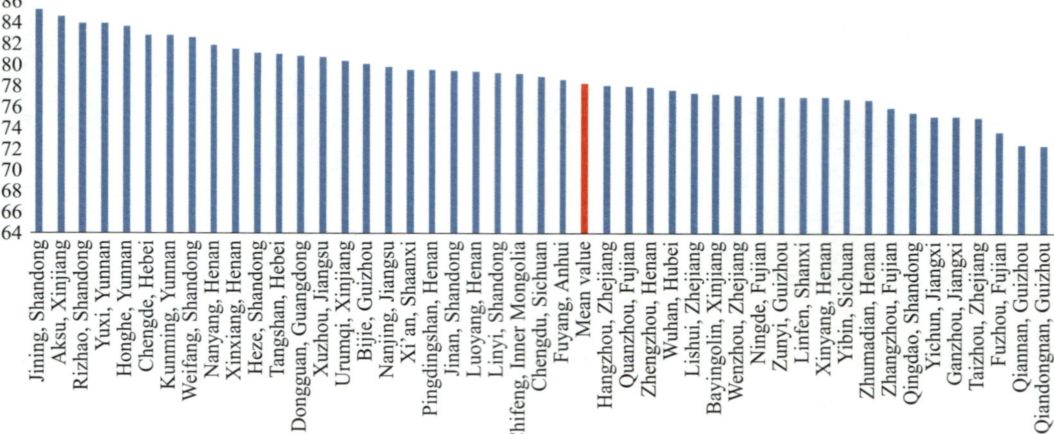

Figure 5–1 Distribution of Transparency Indexes of Selected Cities in 2020

5.2.3 Analysis on Municipal Index by Immediate Disclosure/ Disclosure in Due Time

Figure 5–2 and Figure 5–3 show the distribution of the immediate disclosure indexes

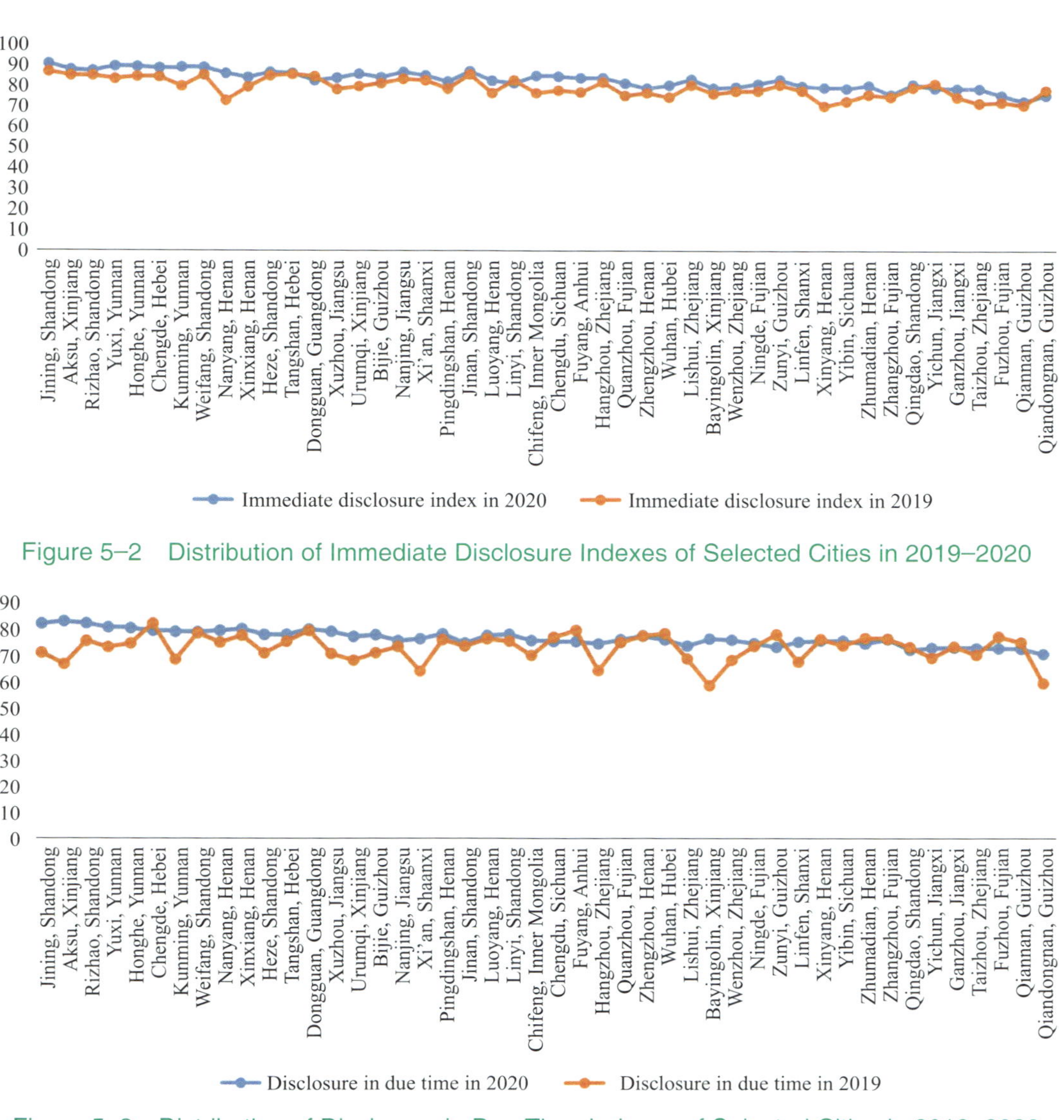

Figure 5–2 Distribution of Immediate Disclosure Indexes of Selected Cities in 2019–2020

Figure 5–3 Distribution of Disclosure in Due Time Indexes of Selected Cities in 2019–2020

and the disclosure in due time indexes of 46 cities. As shown in Figure 5–2, the average immediate disclosure index 82.89 in 2020 was higher than the 79.02 in 2019, representing a minor variance. At the same time, it can be observed from Figure 5–3 that all the cities other than Bayingolin of Xinjiang, Qiannan of Guizhou, and Wuhan of Hubei scored similarly in terms of disclosure in due time in 2020 and 2019. Also, the majority of cities from Urumqi of Xinjiang to Ganzhou of Jiangxi scored higher in both immediate disclosure and disclosure in due time indexes in 2020 than 2019; while Qiannan of Guizhou did the opposite. It indicates that the good performance of cities in PPP

project information transparency was attributable to their high scores in both immediate disclosure and disclosure in due time. On the other hand, there were cites delivering worse performance in both dimensions.

As far as immediate disclosure is concerned, the top three cities that made the largest improvement in 2020 compared with 2019 are: Nanyang of Henan (from 86.14 to 72.83 points), Kunming of Yunnan (from 79.86 to 89.18 points), and Xinyang of Henan (from 70.07 to 79.20 points). The cities recorded with the largest drop are: Qiandongnan of Guizhou, Yichun of Jiangxi, and Dongguan of Guangdong. In terms of disclosure in due time, the top three cities that delivered the largest increase in score in 2020 are: Bayingolin of Xinjiang, Qiannan of Guizhou, and Wuhan of Hubei; on the contrary, the largest decrease was seen in Zunyi of Guizhou, Fuzhou of Fujian, and Fuyang of Anhui. Figure 5–4 indicates that the overall immediate disclosure index is higher than the index of disclosure in due time in 2020, calling for more efforts in the information disclosure in due time by cities.

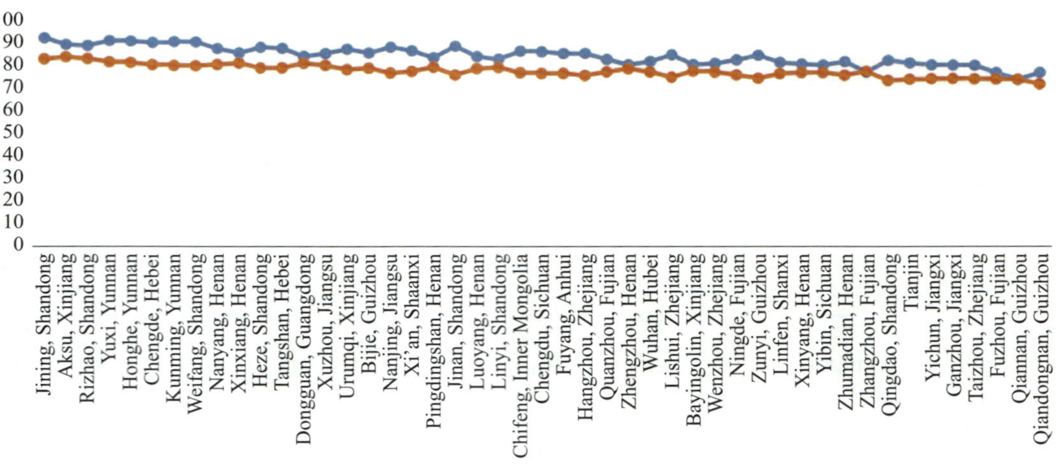

Figure 5–4 Distribution of Immediate Disclosure Indexes and Disclosure in Due Time Indexes of Selected Cities in 2020

5.2.4 Analysis on Municipal Index by Stage

The municipal sub-indexes at different stages are shown in Figure 5–5 and Figure 5–6. Figure 5–5 shows the immediate disclosure index of each city at the stages of identification, preparation, procurement and implementation. The results indicate that in

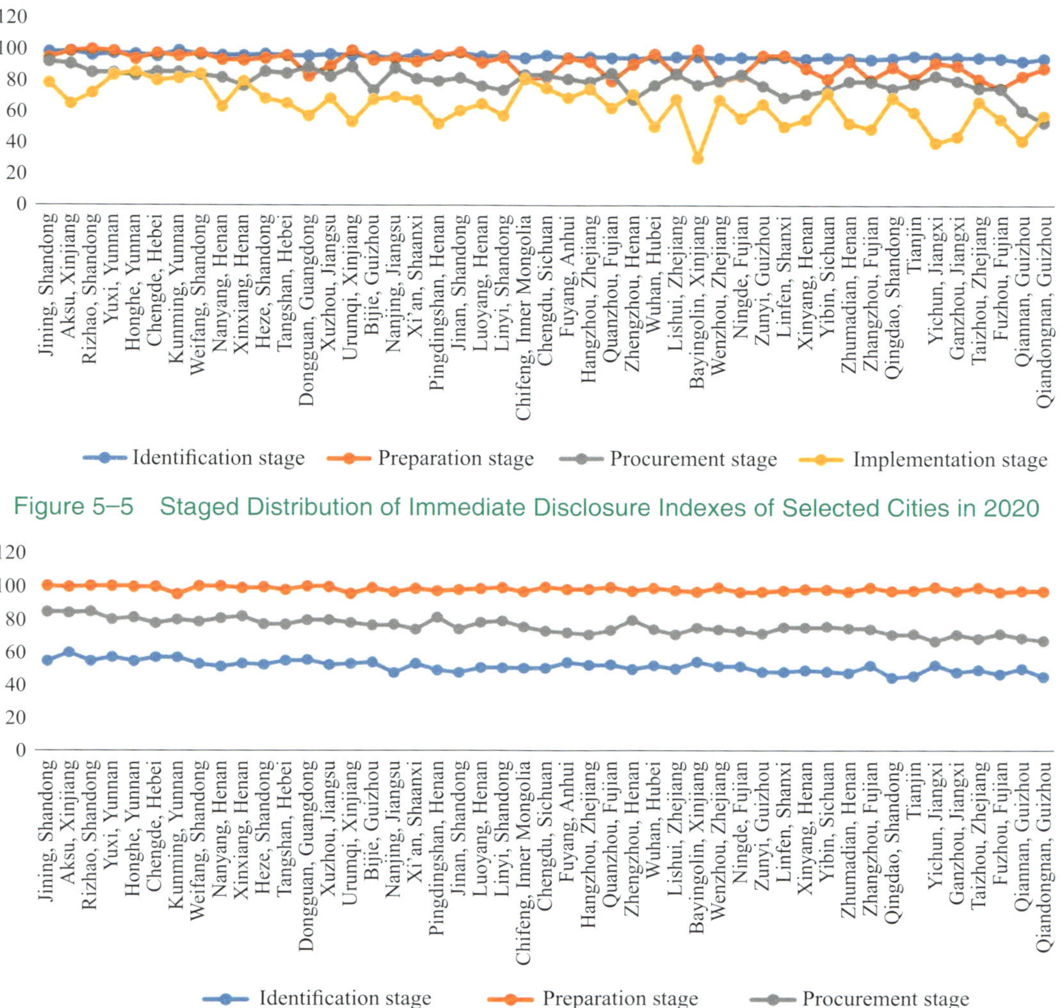

Figure 5–5 Staged Distribution of Immediate Disclosure Indexes of Selected Cities in 2020

Figure 5–6 Distribution of Disclosure in Due Time Indexes of Selected Cities in 2020 by Stage

relation to immediate information disclosure requirements, cities have performed better during the identification and preparation phases, with scores generally higher than those at other stages. The reason may be that the high completeness of basic information in identification and preparation stages helps attract social capital and directly improves the tendering results of PPP projects. As a result, it is likely most project management departments will pay more attention to immediately disclosing information required at the two stages, resulting in average indexes of 95.50 and 90.71 respectively. The average information transparency indexes at procurement and implementation stages were 79.59 and 64.21 respectively, lower than the other two, along with high fluctuation. Meanwhile,

it should also be noted that the immediate disclosure indexes of some cities in the preparation stage were lower than those in procurement and implementation stages.

Conversely, for disclosure in due time, the index at identification stage was significantly lower than preparation and procurement phases. The identification stage average index was 51.31, while the index at the preparation stage averaged up to 98.29. The likely reason for such difference relates to the requirement raised by disclosure in due time at the identification stage as to disclose value-for-money assessment report, financial affordability assessment report and other essential attachments. All of these were rigorously reviewed by the Research Group. Many reports were found problematic and/or "forged". Therefore, the non-standard reporting of value-for-money and financial affordability led to the poorest performance of disclosure in due time at identification stage among all stages. No outstanding fluctuation is found in the disclosure in due time index of the three stages among 47 cities.

The results are a signal to local authorities that due attention should be made to the information disclosure effort for the "Two Assessments", and the quality level, as well as a reminder to the national competent authorities to keep tightening the regulatory requirements for "Two Assessments". Due to the pervasiveness of the problem, it is necessary to propose a more detailed and operable policy guide for these key tasks.

5.3 Analysis on Municipal Transparency Indexes of "Two Assessments and One Program"

This section is a continuation of the provincial analysis, examining the transparency of the "Two Assessments and One Program" in key cities. Table 5–3 shows the performance of Rizhao of Shandong, Jining of Shandong, Yuxi of Yunnan and Dongguan of Guangdong in disclosing the "Two Assessments and One Program" is worthy of recognition. Rizhao and Jining ranked first in the disclosure of information relating to value-for-money and financial affordability, with a perfect score. According to the definition above, it means there was neither incomplete disclosure nor "false" disclosure of information found in the two cities. Although Aksu, Xinjiang did not rank among the top five in each of the three indicators, its relatively high ranking in all of them resulted in its first place in the disclosure in due time index as a whole.

Table 5–3 Municipal Transparency Rankings of "Two Assessments and One Program"

Ranking	Disclosure in due time index	Value-for-money	Financial affordability	Implementation program
1	Aksu, Xinjiang	Rizhao, Shandong	Rizhao, Shandong	Rizhao, Shandong
2	Rizhao, Shandong	Jining, Shandong	Jining, Shandong	Jining, Shandong
3	Jining, Shandong	Yuxi, Yunnan	Yuxi, Yunnan	Yuxi, Yunnan
4	Yuxi, Yunnan	Dongguan, Guangdong	Dongguan, Guangdong	Dongguan, Guangdong
5	Honghe, Yunnan	Xuzhou, Jiangsu	Nanyang, Henan	Nanyang, Henan
6	Xinxiang, Henan	Heze, Shandong	Weifang, Shandong	Weifang, Shandong
7	Dongguan, Guangdong	Nanyang, Henan	Xuzhou, Jiangsu	Chengde, Hebei
8	Nanyang, Henan	Quanzhou, Fujian	Bijie, Guizhou	Xuzhou, Jiangsu
9	Chengde, Hebei	Aksu, Xinjiang	Heze, Shandong	Yichun, Jiangxi
10	Xuzhou, Jiangsu	Zhangzhou, Fujian	Quanzhou, Fujian	Chengdu, Sichuan
11	Kunming, Yunnan	Qiannan, Guizhou	Aksu, Xinjiang	Honghe, Yunnan
12	Weifang, Shandong	Bijie, Guizhou	Zhangzhou, Fujian	Heze, Shandong
13	Pingdingshan, Henan	Chengdu, Sichuan	Chengde, Hebei	Quanzhou, Fujian
14	Linyi, Shandong	Honghe, Yunnan	Qiannan, Guizhou	Aksu, Xinjiang
15	Tangshan, Hebei	Xinxiang, Henan	Chengdu, Sichuan	Zhangzhou, Fujian
16	Heze, Shandong	Chengde, Hebei	Luoyang, Henan	Taizhou, Zhejiang
17	Bijie, Guizhou	Yichun, Jiangxi	Honghe, Yunnan	Wenzhou, Zhejiang
18	Luoyang, Henan	Tangshan, Hebei	Fuyang, Anhui	Qiannan, Guizhou
19	Zhengzhou, Henan	Xi'an, Shaanxi	Xinxiang, Henan	Linyi, Shandong
20	Urumqi, Xinjiang	Wuhan, Hubei	Linfen, Shanxi	Bijie, Guizhou
21	Bayingolin, Xinjiang	Luoyang, Henan	Yichun, Jiangxi	Xinxiang, Henan
22	Xi'an, Shaanxi	Wenzhou, Zhejiang	Tangshan, Hebei	Wuhan, Hubei
23	Zhangzhou, Fujian	Fuyang, Anhui	Bayingolin, Xinjiang	Xi'an, Shaanxi
24	Quanzhou, Fujian	Chifeng, Inner Mongolia	Xi'an, Shaanxi	Luoyang, Henan
25	Wuhan, Hubei	Kunming, Yunnan	Wuhan, Hubei	Xinyang, Henan
26	Wenzhou, Zhejiang	Weifang, Shandong	Xinyang, Henan	Hangzhou, Zhejiang

(continued)

Ranking	Disclosure in due time index	Value-for-money	Financial affordability	Implementation program
27	Xinyang, Henan	Jinan, Shandong	Chifeng, Inner Mongolia	Fuyang, Anhui
28	Chifeng, Inner Mongolia	Pingdingshan, Henan	Taizhou, Zhejiang	Yibin, Sichuan
29	Yibin, Sichuan	Xinyang, Henan	Kunming, Yunnan	Jinan, Shandong
30	Nanjing, Jiangsu	Linfen, Shanxi	Jinan, Shandong	Ningde, Fujian
31	Fuyang, Anhui	Linyi, Shandong	Ningde, Fujian	Tangshan, Hebei
32	Chengdu, Sichuan	Bayingolin, Xinjiang	Yibin, Sichuan	Lishui, Zhejiang
33	Linfen, Shanxi	Taizhou, Zhejiang	Wenzhou, Zhejiang	Linfen, Shanxi
34	Jinan, Shandong	Ningde, Fujian	Hangzhou, Zhejiang	Qingdao, Shandong
35	Ningde, Fujian	Zunyi, Guizhou	Pingdingshan, Henan	Ganzhou, Jiangxi
36	Zhumadian, Henan	Fuzhou, Fujian	Fuzhou, Fujian	Pingdingshan, Henan
37	Hangzhou, Zhejiang	Zhumadian, Henan	Ganzhou, Jiangxi	Qiandongnan, Guizhou
38	Lishui, Zhejiang	Zhengzhou, Henan	Zunyi, Guizhou	Zhengzhou, Henan
39	Zunyi, Guizhou	Nanjing, Jiangsu	Zhengzhou, Henan	Zhumadian, Henan
40	Ganzhou, Jiangxi	Ganzhou, Jiangxi	Linyi, Shandong	Zunyi, Guizhou
41	Yichun, Jiangxi	Hangzhou, Zhejiang	Zhumadian, Henan	Chifeng, Inner Mongolia
42	Taizhou, Zhejiang	Yibin, Sichuan	Lishui, Zhejiang	Bayingolin, Xinjiang
43	Fuzhou, Fujian	Lishui, Zhejiang	Nanjing, Jiangsu	Fuzhou, Fujian
44	Qiannan, Guizhou	Urumqi, Xinjiang	Urumqi, Xinjiang	Nanjing, Jiangsu
45	Qingdao, Shandong	Qingdao, Shandong	Qiandongnan, Guizhou	Urumqi, Xinjiang
46	Qiandongnan, Guizhou	Qiandongnan, Guizhou	Qingdao, Shandong	Kunming, Yunnan

Yichun of Jiangxi, despite its desirable performance in disclosing value-for-money and financial affordability reports, ranked among the last in the index of disclosure in due time, mainly attributable to its poor work regarding implementation program. Urumqi, Xinjiang and Kunming, Yunnan ranked among the last in disclosing information on value-for-money and financial affordability, with average performance in terms of implementation program.

5.4 Relevance of Economy & Finance to General Index

In this section, the cities listed in the *2017 China City Statistical Yearbook* are selected as an object of research. In specific, they are 289 cities at the prefecture level and above, including 4 municipalities directly under the Central Government, 15 deputy provincial capital cities, 17 provincial capital cities and 253 prefecture-level cities. Based on the data of these cities and the 2020 PPP Information Disclosure Index, in combination with the quantitative analysis method, a scatter diagram concerning the 2020 PPP Market Transparency Index (vertical axis) and the gap between fiscal revenue and expenditure in 2017 (horizontal axis) is obtained. The selection of data on these 289 cities in 2017 is out of the following considerations: First, the cities cover 90% of the Chinese population and can basically represent the situation nationwide. Second, the data on GDP per capita, fiscal revenue, and fiscal expenditure in 2017 is chosen to avoid endogenous problems; while the source — *2017 China City Statistical Yearbook* can also ensure the authority of the data.

Figure 5–7 shows a positive correlation between the 2020 PPP Market Transparency Index and the gap between fiscal revenue and expenditure in 2017. That is, the larger the gap, the higher the 2020 PPP Market Transparency Index is. This may be because a region

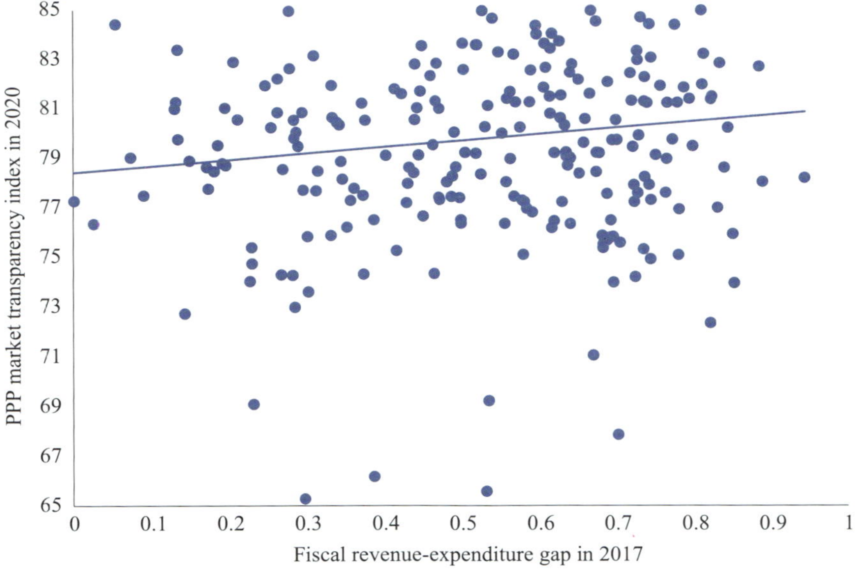

Figure 5–7 Relevance between Fiscal Revenue-Expenditure Gap in 2017 and PPP Market Transparency Index in 2020

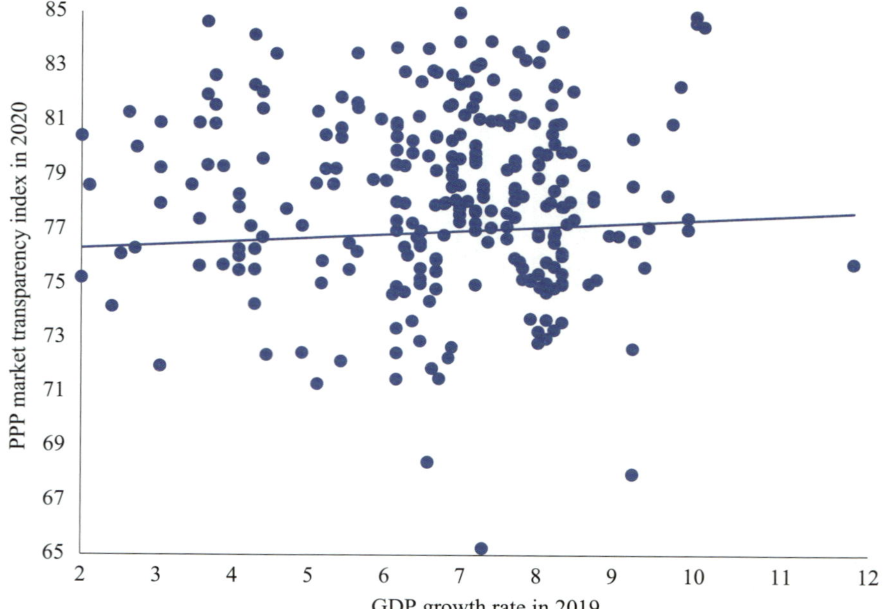

Figure 5–8 Relevance between GDP Growth Rate in 2019 and PPP Market Transparency Index in 2020

with larger fiscal gap is more motivated to seek financing through PPP. To attract social capital, it is more obligated to standardize its work on PPP projects, so the transparency index of the region will be higher. Figure 5–8 shows that GDP per capita is negatively correlated with the PPP transparency index in 2020, that is, the more slowly a region grows economically, the higher its PPP transparency index.

6

Evaluation of Information Disclosure by PPP Intermediaries

6.1 Significance of Evaluating Intermediaries' Transparency

PPP projects reflect the long-term partnerships between public and private capital, and are subject to long-term quality test. Therefore, interested parties have more and higher requirements for professional consulting services in PPP projects than in traditional projects, and it is a common practice by foreign countries to resort to professional consulting agencies in PPP projects. In order to improve the quality and efficiency of project development and implementation, the Ministry of Finance issued an array of files, indicating that for the purpose of optimizing project design and scheme, professional intermediary technologies and services shall be introduced into PPP projects. For instance, in 2014, the *Operational Guidelines for Public-Private Partnership Model (Trial)* (Cai Jin [2014] No.113) noted to actively employ professional third parties into prominent performance. In 2015, the Ministry of Finance issued the *Circular on Further Effectively Implementing the Demonstration of Public-Private Partnership Projects* (Cai Jin [2015] No.57), further putting forward that professional intermediaries of high competence shall be employed for providing technical support to demonstration projects.

In practical terms, PPP projects involve multi-parties and intricacies. During the process of identification, preparation, procurement, implementation, and transferring, PPP projects require various expertise in audit, law and finance. It is unlikely for government officers to equip with all required techniques and easily have the entire process under control. With core competitiveness and practical experiences in respective fields, intermediaries can help government to design value-for-money assessment reports and feasibility study reports, thus increasing the leverage held by government during its negotiation with social capital.

However, many companies transformed into PPP intermediaries as relevant consulting services demands upsurge along with PPP projects' boom in China. Consequently, there is an unevenness of capacity among Chinese PPP intermediaries.

Some might even not be qualified for providing necessary professional techniques. Therefore, relevant regulatory departments set a high priority on supervising PPP intermediaries, and hence formulated the *Interim Measures for the Administration of PPP Consulting Agency Database* (Cai Jin [2017] No.8) and the like. Those files stipulated that the information submitted by PPP intermediaries shall be subject to verification and disclosure, and the information inquiry function in the PPP Consulting Agency Database shall be made available to the whole society. By actively accepting the supervision by service receivers and all sectors of society, PPP intermediaries shall improve the quality of PPP consulting services, and build up a standardized and orderly PPP consulting services market.

To examine and promote the information transparency of PPP intermediaries in China and hence to well maintain a favorable market environment for the sustainable development of PPP market, referring to the aforesaid compilation of PPP project information transparency index, the Research Group has compiled transparency indexes for PPP intermediaries, thereby evaluating the information transparency of PPP intermediaries.[①] However, given the wide disparity between PPP intermediary information transparency and PPP project information transparency in terms of index system and assessment object, the Research Group provided separate index compilation and analysis rather than compiling these two into one single index system.

6.2 Construction of Index System and Calculating Methodology

Prior to the results of PPP intermediary information transparency index, a brief introduction of the index system and calculating methodology of PPP intermediary information transparency evaluation is provided in this section.

6.2.1 Design Principle and Basis for Index System

(1) Design principle for index system. Due to the multiple layers of meaning contained by intermediary information, index system should correspondingly be

① It needs to be stated again that this evaluation is restricted to the disclosure of information by PPP intermediaries, rather than the evaluation of information quality or PPP intermediaries' overall operation compliance, scale and market share.

composed with multiplicity to reflect the nature of each layer. Therefore, referring to the compilation of PPP project information transparency index, the Research Group also divided the compilation of PPP intermediary information transparency index and evaluation into several categories. Specifically, with reference to the spirit of related administration measures and the status of the PPP Consulting Agency Database in the PPP Integrated Information Platform, the index system for PPP intermediary information transparency was divided into three levels, namely, the overall index, a secondary index (including institutions' basic information, the information on the PPP projects undertaken by the institutions, as well as their website information), and underlying specific index.

(2) Data sources and design basis for index system. According to the requirements of the China Public Private Partnerships Center, all information concerning PPP intermediaries must be published on the PPP Consulting Agency Database Information Disclosure System of the PPP Integrated Information Platform set up on the homepage of the CPPPC website. Considering the need for consistency of data sources, the Research Group chose the specific index fields in the Database as the evaluation basis and main source. The fields are divided into two parts — institutions' basic information and the information on the PPP projects undertaken by the institutions. In addition, for further enrichment of the index system, the Research Group logged in to the official websites of the institutions one by one to check the disclosure of information related to PPP, thereby constituting the secondary index — website information.

(3) Assessment object. In conjunction with the policy advices of competent departments and in consideration of practical operability, the Research Group limited the assessment objects to intermediaries that had been included into the PPP Consulting Agency Database Information Disclosure System of the PPP Integrated Information Platform and meanwhile published on the Platform, amounting to 360 institutions.

(4) Data acquisition. The Research Group mainly relied on the data available on the website of CPPPC[①], and logged in to the official website of each intermediary to acquire the source data and then make categorization. Upon the analysis by the Research Group, the index system incorporated a total of 28[②] index fields. The Research Group has extracted them one by one, by direct reading, copying and pasting from the CPPPC website.

---

① The data in this Chapter were all manually collected by the Research Group.

② Compared with last year, our assessment this year deleted the indicator — the year of establishment.

6.2.2 Index System for Evaluation of PPP Intermediary Information Disclosure

Subject to the aforesaid principles and methods, the hierarchy diagram of PPP intermediary information transparency index system is shown in Figure 6–1. The index system for the evaluation of PPP intermediary information transparency consisted of the overall index, three secondary sub-indexes (basic information, project information, and website information of intermediaries), and the lowest hierarchy — specific indexes.

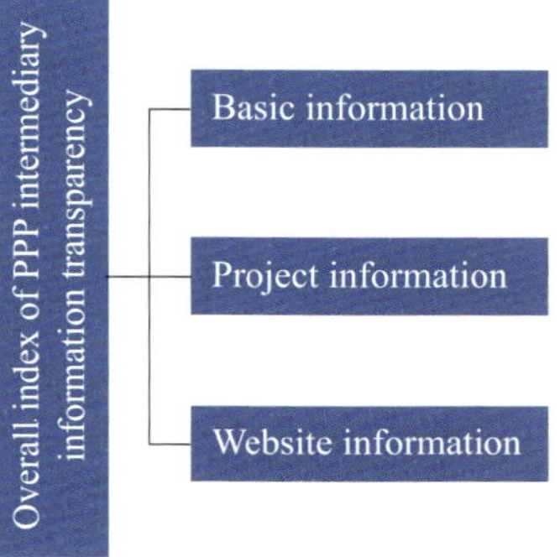

Figure 6–1 Hierarchy Diagram of PPP Intermediary Information Transparency Index

The specific index system for the evaluation of PPP intermediary information disclosure is shown in Table 6–1. The scoring system for these specific indexes was simplified. Most indexes were assigned "1" if the field recorded disclosed information or "0" if there was no information disclosed in the field. While for exceptional indexes containing multiple items of information, an intermediate score of "0.5"was specially designed. Take the index field of "website information" as an example, "1" was given to an institution with its website published on the official website of CPPPC; "0.5" for an institution with a website available for access through search engines like Baidu, but unpublished at CPPPC; otherwise, "0" points. Regarding the news published on the intermediary websites, the following scoring system was applied: "0" points for non-coverage, "0.5" points for coverage but the latest three pieces of news were released more than 30 days from the date of data acquisition, and "1" point for coverage and the latest three pieces of news were released no more than 30 days from the date of data acquisition. Clearer distinction could be achieved by such design.

Table 6–1 PPP Intermediary Information Transparency Assessment Index System

Secondary index	Specific field
Basic information	Name of company
	Organization introduction
	Business scope
	Date of incorporation
	Corresponding address
	Postal code
	Official website
	Performance statistics
	Evaluation by principal
	Key executives
	Honors
	Qualifications
	Record of withdrawals
Project information	Name of project
	Project phase
	Region
	Industry
	Investment volume
	Demonstration level
	Performance category of consulting service industry
	Project manager (PM)
	Business experience of PM in PPPs
	Name of principal
	Signature page of consulting service contract
Website information	Executive profiles on website
	Business qualifications
	Business projects
	Latest news

6.2.3 Calculating Methodology for Indicator Synthesis

For multi-index assessment, weights directly affect the results. Considering the comparability with last year's evaluation results, we applied the same index synthesis approach as last year. Specifically, in the process of synthesizing specific indicators into secondary indexes, the coefficient of variation was applied. The basic idea of the method is to weight each field based on its degree of variation in observed values. Specifically, if the coefficient of variation of a field is large, it means that the field has greater explanatory power in measuring the overall difference in assessment object, and such field should be given a bigger weight.

For the specific process of determining index weight by the coefficient of variation method: first, calculate the coefficient of variation of each field, which indicates the absolute degree of variation of each field:

$$CV_i = \frac{S_i}{\overline{x}_i}, i = 1, 2, 3, \cdots, n$$

Wherein, S_i is the standard deviation of each field, $\overline{x}_i$ is the mean value of each field. Then, normalize the coefficient of variation of each field to obtain the weight of each field:

$$q_i = \frac{CV_i}{\sum_{i=1}^{n} CV_i}, i = 1, 2, 3, \cdots, n$$

Finally, the secondary indexes were synthesized into the general index. At this point, the secondary indexes — intermediary information, project information and website information were given a weight of 1/3 each.

6.3 Analysis on Intermediary Transparency Index

6.3.1 Basic Features

Table 6–2 is the basic descriptive statistics of the PPP intermediary information transparency index, which shows that the average transparency index of 358 intermediaries

recorded 70.16. Specific to the three secondary sub-indexes, Table 6–2 also indicates that the intermediaries scored the highest in disclosing project information, which was 89.62 points, followed by the disclosure of their basic information on the PPP Integrated Information Platform, with an average of 67 points. Under the index system designed by the Research Group, the information collected from the official websites of the intermediaries scored the lowest in terms of transparency, which was 53.86 points only. Chronologically, intermediaries delivered slightly lower scores in 2020 than in 2019; the information disclosure in three sub-indexes all showed certain decline, which was primarily due to the less satisfactory results made in website announcement and website construction by intermediaries. From the perspective of policies, similar to the situation last year, we still call for more efforts to the information disclosure surrounding intermediary websites.

Table 6–2 Description Statistics of Index

Variable	Year 2019			Year 2020		
	Observed value	Mean value	Standard deviation	Observed value	Mean value	Standard deviation
Overall index	357	75.20	17.25	358	70.16	20.83
Basic information	357	76.09	22.41	358	67.00	29.67
Project information	357	90.89	20.06	358	89.62	12.46
Website information	357	58.63	39.00	358	53.86	39.11

Figure 6–2 shows the histograms of the overall transparency index of PPP intermediaries, as well as their scores in the three secondary indexes. Most PPP intermediaries delivered good performance in disclosing project information and their own basic information; while the disclosure of website information presented polarization, which means that some institutions did well, and some poorly. This result leads to the large standard deviation of website information disclosure as shown in Table 6–2.

Table 6–3 provides the list of intermediaries ranking among top 10 in terms of the PPP Intermediary Transparency Index. It shows that the top ten all did a good job in information disclosure, with nearly a full mark across the 28 intermediary information disclosure indicators we've designed. Specifically, Henan Yongzheng Project Management Co., Ltd., Huachun Construction Engineering Project Management Co., Ltd., and China CNTC International Tendering Corporation ranked the top three.

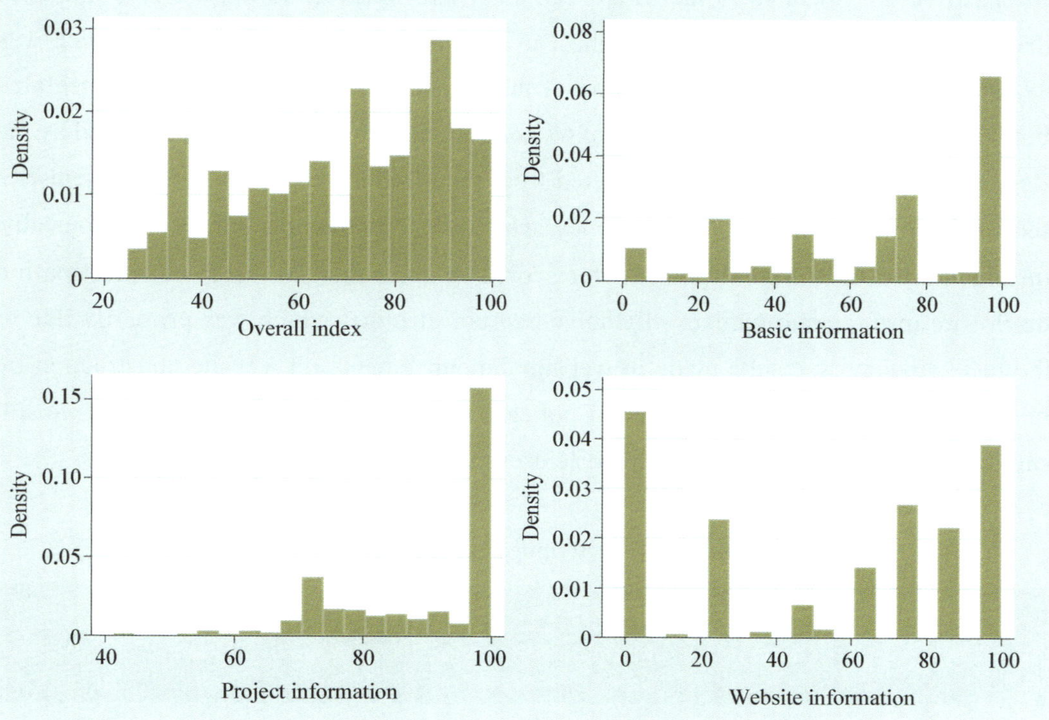

Figure 6–2 Histograms of Overall Index and Sub-Indexes of PPP Intermediary Information Transparency

Compared with the previous year, the top ten did not vary much. In other words, most of the top ten intermediaries in 2019 maintained their positions among the top ten in 2020. Henan Yongzheng Project Management Co., Ltd., Tianhe Guozi Holding Group Co., Ltd. and China Nuclear Industry HuaWei Engineering Design and Research Co., Ltd. made great progress and climbed towards the top ten.

Table 6–3 Top 10 PPP Intermediaries in the Ranking of Information Transparency Index

Ranking	Name of intermediary	Overall index	Variance from last year
1	Henan Yongzheng Project Management Co., Ltd.	99.756	+15
2	Huachun Construction Engineering Project Management Co., Ltd.	99.071	−1
3	China CNTC International Tendering Corporation	99.048	+3
4	Tianhe Guozi Holding Group Co., Ltd.	99.045	+16

(continued)

Ranking	Name of intermediary	Overall index	Variance from last year
5	CAMCE WHU Design & Research Co., Ltd.	99.041	+2
6	China Nuclear Industry HuaWei Engineering Design and Research Co., Ltd.	99.022	+15
7	Hanjing Project Management Ltd.	99.010	+9
8	Beijing Dayue Consulting Co., Ltd.	98.962	+11
9	Anhui Tendering Group Inc.	98.956	−7
10	Shanghai Jumbo Consulting Co., Ltd.	98.863	−1

6.3.2 Relevance between PPP Intermediary Information Disclosure and Project Volume

Figure 6–3 shows the relationship between the PPP intermediary information transparency index and the number of PPP projects engaged. The conclusion is highly aligned with that last year: the more PPP projects an intermediary is involved in, the higher its score is. In terms of both theory and practice, the number of PPP projects and the information disclosure by intermediaries are in a relationship of mutual promotion.

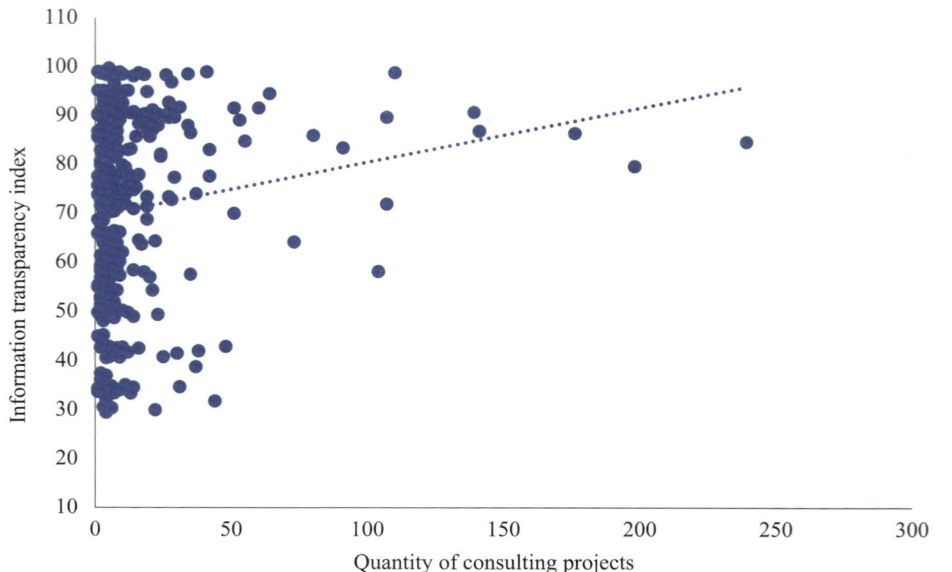

Figure 6–3 Relationship between PPP Intermediary Information Transparency Index and Quantity of Consulting Projects

The larger number of projects an institution is engaged in means the institution is larger in scale and more standardized in management, leading to higher attention to information disclosure, and then higher score in information transparency; in turn, the better an intermediary does in information disclosure, the more attractive it is to customers, so that it is able to participate in more PPP projects. As a result, a significant positive correlation is developed between the PPP intermediary information transparency index and the number of PPP projects participated by intermediaries.

6.3.3 Relevance between PPP Intermediary Information Disclosure and Company Qualifications

The relevance between the information transparency index and qualifications of intermediaries is studied in this section. According to Figure 6–4, the longer an intermediary operates, the better it does in information disclosure. That is, there is a prominent positive correlation between the "age" of intermediaries and the information transparency index. This is also quite similar to what was discovered in the previous year.

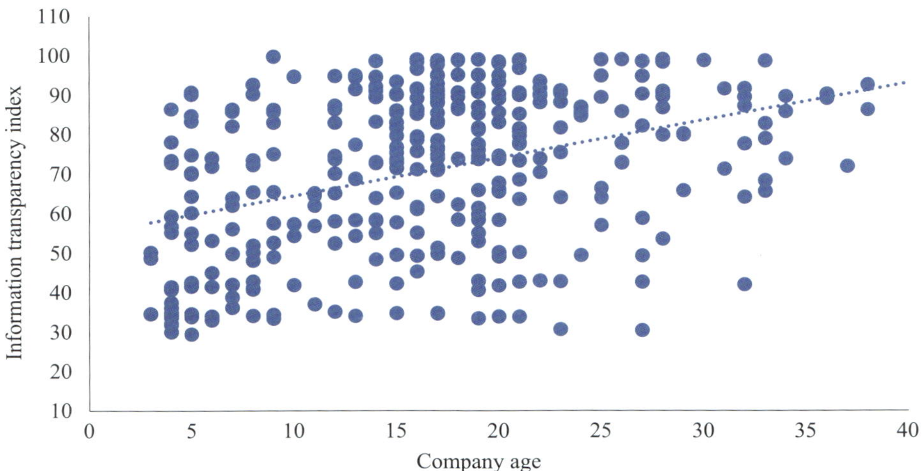

Figure 6–4 Relationship between PPP Intermediary Information Transparency Index and Company Age

7

Report Summary and Outlook

7.1 Report Summary

PPPs is the acronym for Public-Private Partnerships. At present, China's PPP model is not only a means of market-oriented investment and financing by government, but also has become a comprehensive and systematic market and social reform for the provision of public infrastructure and services. Therefore, all stakeholders (both internal and external) have high expectations for the further development and implementation of PPP, hoping it could play a key role in leading the reform of public finance system and assisting the public sector in deepening reform. In this context, standardized arrangements for the management of PPP projects are particularly important. In particular, the timely and complete information disclosure of PPP projects is the basis for standardized management of PPP projects. From 2017, a number of documents issued by the Ministry of Finance have made provisions concerning the information disclosure of PPP projects. In particular, the *Interim Measures for Administration of Information Disclosure for Public-Private Partnership Integrated Information Platform* (Cai Jin [2017] No. 1) released in early 2017 specified all the requirements for information disclosure of PPP projects. When it came to 2018, the removal of PPP projects from management database became a key mission in PPP management. In specific, more than 2 000 PPP projects that failed to meet the management specifications were cleaned and removed from management database, while many new projects were added to the database as well. From the beginning of 2019, as more PPP projects come to the implementation stage, how to effectively promote the disclosure in due time of PPP projects becomes increasingly important. Meanwhile, the public has higher and higher requirements for the quality of PPP project information disclosed. On March 31, 2020, the Ministry of Finance released the Guideline for PPP Project Performance Management, proposing a complete appraisal system for PPP performance. While clarifying who to take accountability, the document has also incorporated truthfulness, openness, transparency and quality into specific

assessment rules.

Against this backdrop, the Research Group of Shanghai University of Finance and Economics, following the evaluation of the information disclosure of PPP projects in the past three years, carried out a detailed assessment on the latest status as of December 31, 2020. The Research Group assessed in detail the information disclosure work of 9 662 projects included into the management database as of the end of 2020, and compiled a set of "2020 China PPP Market Transparency Index", which incorporates 68 index fields and is divided into transparency index of immediate disclosure, transparency index of disclosure in due time, and transparency sub-indexes at each stage, i.e. identification, preparation, procurement, and implementation. Regarding the synthesis of indexes, the Research Group adopted an approach combining analytic hierarchy process (AHP) and expert scoring: for specific indexes under sub-indexes, different scores were set according to the importance determined by selected experts; and for the synthesis of sub-indexes, the Research Group adopted AHP, a method commonly used in the compilation of similar indexes, thus guaranteeing the reliability of the index preparation method. In the end, through the statistical analysis of final results, the Research Group obtained the following findings:

First, the overall national PPP market transparency index 2020 was 78.15, a slight improvement from 2019. As of December 31, 2020, the overall national PPP market transparency index recorded 78.15 (out of 100, the same below), an increase of about 2 points from 76.19 in 2019. In specific, the transparency index of immediate disclosure was 80.37, an increase of 1.2 points from last year (79.14), while the transparency index of disclosure in due time was 74.67, three points higher from last year (71.57). Further analysis on heterogeneity shows no obvious difference in the transparency scores between industries or between demonstration and non-demonstration projects.

Second, the overall PPP market information transparency index at the provincial level rose steadily, yet with a larger gap between different provinces. The transparency indexes of most provinces ranged from 70 to 85, but there are also a few provinces that presented a PPP transparency index higher than 82 or lower than 70. The top five provinces are Yunnan (84.98), Shandong (83.72), Hebei (82.99), Hunan (82.69) and Jiangsu (82.63).

Third, most cities delivered PPP market transparency indexes higher than

those in 2019. The Research Group selected 46 cities that managed a relatively large large number of PPP projects (>50 projects in the management database) for more detailed analysis. Comparison with the indexes in 2019 shows that some cities above the prefecture level scored significantly higher in 2020 than in 2019. Among them, the largest increase was delivered by Aksu of Xinjiang, the 2020 overall score of which increased by 15.39 points compared to 2019; and followed by Dongguan of Guangdong, with increase of 13.62 points from 2019. However, it can also be found that the indexes of many cities above the prefecture level decreased in 2020 from 2019, especially Qiannan of Guizhou and Haikou of Hainan. They recorded the largest decline from 2019 by 13.10 and 12 points, respectively.

Fourth, PPP intermediaries showed minor cross-phase differences in information disclosure, with their transparency indexes positively related to qualifications and business volumes. Based on the assessment of information disclosure by PPP projects, we made a further analysis on the status quo of information disclosure by PPP intermediaries in this year's report. The main findings are as follows: the average transparency index of intermediaries was 70.16. In secondary indexes, projects engaged by intermediaries scored relatively high in terms of information disclosure, but some of them delivered less satisfactory performance in active information disclosure; further analysis also found that intermediaries' information transparency indexes showed a clear positive correlation with the number of PPP projects they were engaged in and how long they had been operating.

7.2 Policy Suggestions

To conclude the above analysis, in 2020 China has made steady progress regarding the information disclosure in PPP market compared with the previous year. The results observed in this Report suggest the progress in PPP information disclosure is leading reform in infrastructure and services. Notwithstanding these achievements, the Research Group also identified issues related to the disclosure of PPP market information. Therefore, the following are offered as policy improvement opportunities and enhancements, with a view to further improving the PPP information disclosure work, further raising the information disclosure transparency in the PPP market, and promoting the standardized management of PPP projects in China.

First, to improve the operational norms for the disclosure of "inapplicable" information and temporary major events. PPP projects cover a wide range of sectors and fields, which have varied cooperation methods, return mechanisms, etc. It is difficult to ascertain in analyzing results if information is required to be disclosed but not lodged, or if it is not applicable. Accordingly, this limits the extent of research scope when analyzing PPP information disclosure performance. A possible remedy may be to require the project to insert a notation to the effect of "the information item does not apply to this project". From this, it is possible to discern whether the information item is inapplicable, or if the project has failed to disclose the information. In addition, there should be similar requirements for the management of disclosure on major temporary events. For instance, for the disclosure of information on temporary major events such as "material breach and withdrawal of performance bond, handling of public complaints, etc.", projects should be requested to state that "as of now, the project has no material breach and withdrawal of performance bond, handling of public complaints and other issues to be disclosed" or similar expressions, if there are no corresponding events. This practice is common in the information disclosure management standards of listed companies, commercial banks and other institutions.

Second, to improve the classification of management of information subject to immediate disclosure and disclosure in due time. As mentioned above, classification is an important measure. However, through investigation by the Research Group and discussion with experts, it was determined the classification criteria require further improvement. For example, some information subject to disclosure in due time may be transferred to immediate disclosure; and some immediate disclosure work which is time-consuming, may be transferred to disclosure in due time category. Input through the professional opinions of the representatives from project companies, consulting agencies and the academic community will support improvement in the classification of management information.

Third, to strengthen the supervision and inspection of the disclosure of key information in PPP projects. Based on the above analysis, the Research Group identified there were substantial differences in the implementation of information disclosure at different stages. For example, for disclosure in due time, the assessment results of value-for-money report and financial affordability report at identification stage was less desirable compared with others. Accordingly, it is a recommendation of the

Research Group that the supervision and inspection over disclosure outcomes should be strengthened. Random inspection may be utilized to supervise the disclosure of these project reports. In addition, concerning the information to be disclosed at implementation stage, it may be necessary to improve the system and regulations, urging responsible parties to disclose relevant information in a proactive and timely manner. For example, it is feasible to link the information disclosure work of the project company at the implementation stage with government payment by means of contractual covenants, etc. Finally, automatically screening the documents by keyword identification may be helpful in the prevention of false uploads. The screening could require attachments without certain keywords were not approved for upload, thereby improving the quality of information disclosure.

Fourth, to further clarify the disclosure accountability and division of labor. Since the *Interim Measures for Administration of Information Disclosure* for Public-Private Partnership Integrated Information Platform took effect on March 1, 2017, there has been significant progress in PPP information disclosure, as also verified by the assessment results we obtained over the past three years. However, there are still some challenges to be resolved in the disclosure of PPP information. Any lack of accountability is likely to bring a series of systemic problems to PPP information disclosure. According to the Article 4 of Cai Jin [2017] No. 1, "Local finance departments at all levels will, in conjunction with the related departments of the government at the same level, promote, guide, coordinate and supervise the PPP project information disclosure work within their respective administrative region and carry out the following work in combination with local conditions". In the actual implementation, finance departments need to coordinate water conservancy bureaus, transportation bureaus, sports bureaus, social capital and third-party consulting agencies to collect and consolidate information. As the information disclosure work has limited binding power to the related departments of the government at the same level other than the finance department, it is difficult for local financial systems to update the data in a timely manner. Such circumstance may be mitigated in regions without abundant financial resources, for if the progress of information disclosure does not match with that of project construction, the government can choose to delay payment to punish relevant departments. However, the restraint can hardly be realized in regions with poor financial resources, which make the conditions worse in those places where it is already difficult to attract high-quality social capital based on their local

conditions. Therefore, it is necessary to further clarify the accountability and to build supporting incentive mechanisms.

Fifth, to promote the information disclosure by PPP intermediaries. PPP projects reflect long-term partnerships, and are subject to long-term quality test. There are higher requirements for solutions and agreements in PPP projects than in traditional projects, and it is a common practice by foreign countries to resort to professional consulting agencies in PPP projects. Therefore, PPP intermediaries play an important role in the compliant operation and management of PPP projects. The discussion in Chapter VI shows that there is still much room for the improvement of the information disclosure by PPP intermediaries. Roughly, there are two aspects. On the one hand, it is necessary for PPP intermediaries to disclose their own information. More fields may be added to the PPP Consulting Agency Database for them to fill in, such as the number of employees, personnel structure, leading teams, etc. On the other hand, during the operation of PPP projects, it is necessary to strengthen the disclosure of such information as intermediaries' participation, dedication, types of projects they were involved before, and the classification of intermediaries. The following information may be disclosed as well: the proportion of projects that have been engaged by an intermediary and removed from the Management Database; whether it is serving a local government and a social capital owner that has cooperation with the government at the same time (to avoid conflicts related to business ethics). Such requirements pose pressure on PPP intermediaries, so that they can be more cautious in their participation in PPP projects.

7.3 Outlook

That's all for the 2019 China PPP Market Transparency Report. Based on the index compilation and analysis in 2017–2019, and by means of index preparation, substantial data and analysis on the information disclosure of PPP projects in China as of the end of 2020 are provided. The Report has maintained the continuity of the index system and index compilation methods. While there have been several continuous refinements to assess the information transparency of the China PPP market, there are still many deficiencies in terms of index system setting, index preparation methods, and specific analysis. The Research Group recommends that future changes should consider:

First, the index system can be improved. As stated in the Report, due to the absence of information and many other reasons, the PPP market transparency index was intentionally divided into immediate disclosure index and disclosure in due time index. As the PPP integrated information platform grows mature, and especially when the time of disclosure can be accurately incorporated into the database, it is expected to combine the two in the future. Moreover, in addition to assessing whether related information is disclosed, it is also possible to further assess disclosure timeliness. With the advancing of the PPP, more and more projects will enter implementation and transfer stages, and the information disclosure work at these stages will be of higher significance, then the index system may also appropriately focus on those stages.

Second, information quality may be included in the assessment. As we have mentioned in the preceding part, this Report only assesses the information disclosure work of PPP projects, but not the quality of the information disclosed. For example, the Research Group has assessed whether the value-for-money report and financial affordability report were disclosed but without assessment of their quality. Therefore, the content of these key project reports should direct special assessment and analysis in the future, examining the standardized management of PPP projects in all regions and of all stakeholders.

Appendix Ⅰ Determination Matrix Survey for Experts

Engaged by the Asian Development Bank, the PPP Research Center of Shanghai University of Finance and Economics is undertaking the *2020 China PPP Market Transparency Assessment Report*, which involves preparing an index to holistically reflect the achievements and deficiencies in the information disclosure efforts within China's PPP market. In the process of index preparation, the amount of information contained in each specific indicator and its degree of importance vary greatly. Therefore, the Research Group intends to determine the relative weight among the influencing factors of information transparency of PPP projects through an expert survey (the hierarchy chart is shown in Figure 3–1).

To this end, the Research Group has designed the survey below based on the Analytic Hierarchy Process (AHP), which makes paired comparison on the importance of influencing factors at the same hierarchy. The measurement scale is divided into 9 levels, of which the values of 9, 7, 5, 3 and 1 correspond to absolutely more important, more important, relatively more important, slightly more important, and equally important, while 8, 6, 4 and 2 indicate that the importance is between two adjacent levels.

In the tables below, the left cells indicate that the factors on the left are more important than those on the right, and the right cells indicate that factors on the right are more important than those on the left. Please tick "√" in the corresponding cell based on your own understanding. Your judgment is critical to our scientific and rigorous preparation of the PPP market transparency index.

Thanks for your help!

Research Group of SUFE

January 8, 2021

In paired comparison, what is the relative importance of the two factors to the "total transparency index"?

	Comparison of importance																	
Disclosure in due time	9	8	7	6	5	4	3	2	1	2	3	4	5	6	7	8	9	Immediate disclosure

In paired comparison, what is the relative importance of the two factors to the "disclosure in due time"?

	Comparison of importance																	
Identification stage	9	8	7	6	5	4	3	2	1	2	3	4	5	6	7	8	9	Preparation stage
Identification stage	9	8	7	6	5	4	3	2	1	2	3	4	5	6	7	8	9	Procurement stage
Preparation stage	9	8	7	6	5	4	3	2	1	2	3	4	5	6	7	8	9	Procurement stage

In paired comparison, what is the relative importance of the two factors to the "immediate disclosure"?

	Comparison of importance																	
Identification stage	9	8	7	6	5	4	3	2	1	2	3	4	5	6	7	8	9	Preparation stage
Identification stage	9	8	7	6	5	4	3	2	1	2	3	4	5	6	7	8	9	Procurement stage
Identification stage	9	8	7	6	5	4	3	2	1	2	3	4	5	6	7	8	9	Implementation stage
Preparation stage	9	8	7	6	5	4	3	2	1	2	3	4	5	6	7	8	9	Procurement stage
Preparation stage	9	8	7	6	5	4	3	2	1	2	3	4	5	6	7	8	9	Implementation stage
Procurement stage	9	8	7	6	5	4	3	2	1	2	3	4	5	6	7	8	9	Implementation stage

Appendix Ⅱ Interim Measures for the Administration of Information Disclosure for Public-Private Partnership Integrated Information Platform

Circular on Issuing the *Interim Measures for Administration of Information Disclosure for Public-Private Partnership Integrated Information Platform*

(Cai Jin [2017] No. 1)

The financial offices (bureaus) of all provinces, autonomous regions, municipalities directly under the Central Government and cities specifically designated in the state plan, the Financial Bureau of Xinjiang Production and Construction Corps, and the Financial Supervision Commissioner Offices of the Ministry of Finance at all provinces, autonomous regions, municipalities directly under the Central Government and cities specifically designated in the state plan,

In order to further carry out the related requirements of the *Circular of the General Office of the State Council on Forwarding the Guiding Opinions of the Ministry of Finance, the National Development and Reform Commission and the People's Bank of China on Promoting the Public-Private Partnership Model in the Public Service Sectors* (Guo Ban Fa [2015] No.42), strengthen and standardize the information disclosure of Public-Private Partnership ("PPP") projects, cause various parties to the PPP projects to act in good faith and strictly honor their agreements, protect the public's right to know and promote fair competition and regulated development of the PPP market, we hereby formulate the *Interim Measures for the Administration of Information Disclosure for*

Public-Private Partnership Integrated Information Platform, which are issued to you for your implementation.

Ministry of Finance
January 23, 2017

Interim Measures for the Administration of Information Disclosure for Public-Private Partnership Integrated Information Platform

Chapter I General Provisions

Article 1 In order to strengthen and standardize the information disclosure of Public-Private Partnership ("PPP") projects, cause various parties to the PPP projects to act in good faith and strictly honor their agreements, protect the public's right to know and promote fair competition and regulated development of the PPP market, the *Interim Measures for the Administration of Information Disclosure for Public-Private Partnership Integrated Information Platform* (the "Measures") are hereby formulated in accordance with the Budget Law of the People's Republic of China, the Government Procurement Law of the People's Republic of China, the Circular of the General Office of State Council on Forwarding the Guidelines of the Ministry of Finance, the National Development and Reform Commission and the People's Bank of China on Promoting the Public-Private Partnership Model in the Public Service Sectors (Guo Ban Fa [2015] No.42) and other related provisions.

Article 2 The Measures apply to the disclosure of information about the PPP projects within the territory of the People's Republic of China that have been included in the PPP integrated information platform.

Article 3 PPP project information disclosure shall be conducted in the principles of objectiveness, fairness, timeliness and convenience.

Article 4 Local finance departments at all levels (hereinafter referred to as the "finance departments") will, in conjunction with the related departments of the government at the same level, promote, guide, coordinate and supervise the PPP project information disclosure work within their respective administrative region and carry out the following work in combination with local realities:

1. collect and sort out the PPP project information;

2. enter into, maintain and update the PPP project information via the PPP integrated

information platform;

3. organize to prepare the annual work report of their government-level PPP project information disclosure;

4. make available the PPP project information in other channels at the same time in accordance with laws and regulations and actual needs; and

5. other efforts related to the PPP project information disclosure.

Relevant government departments, project implementing organizations, corporate partners or PPP project company and other PPP project participants shall provide the PPP project information in a truly, complete, accurate and timely manner.

Chapter Ⅱ Contents Subject to Disclosure

Article 5 The PPP project information to be disclosed during the project identification phase includes:

1. summary of the implementation program, including: basic information of the project (including the project cooperation scope, cooperation period, project output specification, performance standards and other basic information), risk allocation framework, operation mode, transaction structure (including financing structure, return mechanism and relevant supporting arrangements), contracts, regulatory framework, selection of the purchase mode;

2. the value-for-money evaluation report that has been examined and approved by the finance departments and the competent industry authority, including: qualitative evaluation indicators and weights, scoring standards, scoring results; main indicators, methods, processes and results (including PSC value, PPP value), etc. (if any) for the purpose of quantitative evaluation; conclusions on whether value-for-money evaluation is passed or not;

3. the financial affordability assessment report that has been examined and approved by the finance departments, including: liabilities of fiscal expenditure of each year and total expenditure liabilities, total liabilities of fiscal expenditure of the PPP projects implemented by the government at the same level in current year and that of the PPP projects to be implemented for various years, and ratios of them in the general public budget expenditures of various years; measurement basis, key factors and indicators of the financial affordability assessment as well as others; and conclusions on whether the financial affordability assessment is passed or not;

4. Other basic information, including: proposals for new or renovated or expanded projects and approval documents, feasibility study report (including planning permits, siting opinions, land pre-review opinion, environmental impact assessment report and other supporting documents) and approval documents, design documents and approval documents (if any); historical materials of construction and operation maintenance of stocked public assets as well as the asset evaluation report issued by a third party and the employees placement scheme, claim and debt disposal programs, land disposal programs and others (if any) that may be involved in the transfer of stocked assets or equity.

Article 6 The PPP project information to be disclosed during the project preparatory phase includes:

1. the authorization documents of the government, including the authorization granted to the executive agency, the governments signing the PPP project contract, the government's investment representatives (if any) and others;

2. the examined and approved project implementation program (including the approval documents of the people's government at the same level with respect to the implementation programs), including: basic information of the project (including the project cooperation scope, cooperation period, project output specification, performance standards and other basic information), risk allocation framework, operation mode, transaction structure (including financing structure, return mechanism and relevant supporting arrangements), contracts and core boundary conditions; regulatory framework; selection of the purchase mode;

3. the value-for-money evaluation report that has been verified based on the examined and approved project implementation program, if any; and

4. the financial affordability assessment report that has been verified based on the examined and approved project implementation program, if any.

Article 7 The disclosure of information in the procurement process shall comply with the provisions on government procurement and other provisions, and the PPP project information to be disclosed shall include:

1. prequalification announcements (including prequalification application documents) and supplementary announcement (if any);

2. project procurement documents, including notes to competitors, PPP project contract (draft), review methods (including composition of the review group, the number of review experts and the producing way thereof, the review rules, etc.);

3. addenda (if any);

4. concluding observations with respect to the review of prequalification and response documents;

5. the list of prequalification experts, review experts and the working group of negotiation about confirmation;

6. announcement of pre-bid winners and transaction results;

7. the announcement of the bid-winning and transaction results and the letter of acceptance;

8. the authorization documents of the government updated and adjusted during the procurement process (if any), including the authorization granted to the executive agency, the governments signing the PPP project contract, the government's investment representatives (if any) and others; and

9.the document of the people's government at the same level on consent to sign the PPP project contracts, and the signed PPP project contract, listing main output specifications and performance indicators, the return mechanism, the price adjustment mechanism and other core provisions.

Article 8 The PPP project information to be disclosed during the project implementation phase includes:

1. registration of the project company (if any), capital subscribed by the shareholders and availability of the capital, increase or decrease of the capital (if any), qualifications of the project company (if any);

2. name of the financing institution, amount of funds raised for the project, the financing structure and particulars on the financing delivery;

3. review of the project construction permits, construction progress, quality and cost and others made based on the related agreements under the PPP project contracts;

4. the operation of corporate partners or the project company (especially major business or financial risks that may seriously affect the normal operation of the corporate partners or the project company) and satisfaction of the operational performance;

5. the project company's performance monitoring report, interim evaluation report, major changes or termination of the project, project pricing and previous price adjustments;

6. the financial report of the project company, including payment for the project, the government subsidy granted to the project, and the assets and liabilities of the project

company and others;

7. cost monitoring and review of the project company, alteration of PPP project contracts or signing of supplementary agreements;

8. major breach of contract and withdrawal of performance bond, handling of public complaints, etc.;

9. provisions or decisions made by the government at the corresponding level or its functional departments that may have a significant impact on the project;

10. major disputes, litigations or arbitrations with respect to the project or of the parties directly related to the project (mainly the contracting parties to the PPP project contracts), except those forbidden according to the relevant judicial proceedings; and

11. the directory of the PPP projects at the same level, pilot library thereof and changes to the projects as well as the budget, implementation and settlement situations of governments for the PPP projects as approved by the people's congresses at the same level.

Article 9 The PPP project information to be disclosed during the project transfer phase includes:

1. composition of the transfer working group, transfer procedure, transfer standards and other transfer programs;

2. list of the assets or equity or interests to be transferred, assessment report on the assets or equity to be transferred (if applicable), scheme on performance test, and the release of various security or interests on the assets or facilities to be transferred;

3. detection results on satisfaction of the transfer standards for project facilities; and

4. post evaluation reports (including evaluation for the project output, cost effectiveness, regulatory effectiveness, sustainability, PPP model applications, etc.), as well as the subsequent operation manner.

Chapter Ⅲ Manner of Information Disclosure

Article 10 PPP project information can be disclosed immediately or in due time.

Article 11 To make disclosure immediately refers to the automatic disclosure of the related information as stipulated by the Measures via the PPP integrated information platform made by the finance departments, in concert with the related departments, the project implementing organizations and others according to the different stages of the PPP projects and the corresponding entry time. The contents and requirements of the instant

disclosure are detailed in the appendix to the Measures.

Article 12 To make disclosure in due time refers to the disclosure of the relevant information as stipulated in the Measures by the finance departments, in concert with the related departments when the project enters into a specific stage or reaches a specific condition rather than automatic disclosure upon the entry of the relevant information. Except as otherwise provided in the Measures, the information during the project identification, preparation and procurement processes will be disclosed by the finance departments in conjunction with the relevant departments at any time within six months after the entry into the implementation phase of the project; The information during the implementation phase will be made available to the public by the finance departments in conjunction with the relevant departments at any time before April 30 of the year following the determining or completion of matters corresponding to the information. The information not made available to the public after the expiration of the foregoing period of time will be opened to the public automatically. The contents and requirements of making disclosure in due time are detailed in the appendix to the Measures.

Article 13 The PPP project information made available to the public according to the Measures may be inquired on the official website of China Public Private Partnerships Center (www.cpppc.org). Information on government procurement of PPP projects shall be published at the media designated by the finance department of a people's government above provincial level.

Chapter Ⅳ Supervision and Administration

Article 14 The Ministry of Finance will evaluate and supervise the disclosure of the PPP project information all over the country, and the provincial finance department is responsible for the supervision and management of the PPP project information to be disclosed in the said province. Where the finance departments at lower level do not enter into the PPP project information that shall be made available to the public on a truly, complete, accurate and timely basis, the finance departments at higher level shall order them to make corrections within a time limit; if they refuse to make corrections or the circumstances are serious, they will be criticized.

Article 15 The relevant government departments, project implementation agencies, corporate partners or PPP project company and other PPP project information providers

shall be responsible for the authenticity, completeness, accuracy and timeliness of the information provided. Once the information provided is untrue, incomplete, inaccurate and not provided timely, the PPP project information provider shall take the initiative to amend, supplement or take other effective remedial measures in a timely manner. If the provider of the PPP project information is confirmed with related materials produced by the finance departments or stakeholders not providing information in accordance with the provisions or falls under other improper circumstances, the finance departments may order it to correct within a time limit; if it refuses to correct without justifiable reasons, the finance departments can weed out the project from the project library. The project being weeded out may not be included into the PPP integrated information platform within one year since the date on which it is weeded out.

Article 16 The finance department shall, in conjunction with the relevant government departments, complete the annual report on the disclosure of information about the PPP projects implemented by the government at the same level for the previous year before February 28 each year, submit it to the finance department at the provincial level, which will report the information to the Ministry of Finance before March 31 each year after making summarization. The report shall include:

1. circumstances on disclosure of the PPP project information on an instant basis and made in due time;

2. major issues occurred during the disclosure of the PPP project information and improvements thereof; and

3. other matters that need to be reported.

Article 17 The personnel of the finance departments will be subject to corresponding liabilities according to the *Civil Servant Law, the Law on Administrative Supervision, the Regulations on the Penalties and Sanctions against Illegal Financial Conducts* and other related provisions of the State if they abuse their power, neglect of duty, play favoritism and commit irregularities and have any other violations during the supervision and management of the PPP project information disclosure; if they are suspected of constituting a crime, they will be transferred to judicial organs.

Article 18 Citizens, legal persons or other organizations may provide feedbacks to the PPP project information disclosure situation through the PPP integrated information platform, and the relevant information provider shall verify the same and handle it in a timely manner.

Chapter Ⅴ Supplementary Provisions

Article 19 The PPP integrated information platform consisting of three parts, i.e. project library, institution library and document library, refers to the PPP integrated information management and release platform for the whole country established by the Ministry of Finance according to the *Circular on Regulating the Operation of the Public-Private Partnership (PPP) Integrated Information Platform* (Cai Jin [2015] No.166).

Article 20 In the event that the PPP project information disclosure involves state secrets, trade secrets, personal privacy, intellectual property rights, which may endanger national security, public safety, economic security and social stability or harm legitimate rights and interests of the citizens, legal persons or other organizations, it will be handled in accordance with relevant laws and regulations.

Article 21 The Measures will come into force as of March 1, 2017.

Requirements for Information Disclosure of PPP Projects

Stage	Contents to be disclosed	Manner of disclosure	Time limit	Information provider
Identification of projects	Introduction to the project, the cooperation scope, the cooperation term, the operation mode, selection of the mode of purchasing social capital	Immediate disclosure	Within ten working days from the date of completion of the implementation programs	Project initiator
	Transaction structure (including financing structure, return mechanism and relevant supporting arrangements), project output specification and performance standards, risk allocation framework, contracts and regulatory system	Disclosure in due time	Within six months after entering into the implementation phase	Project initiator
	Value-for-money qualitative evaluation indicators and weights, scoring standards, scoring results	Immediate disclosure	Within ten working days after the report is finalized	
	Conclusions on whether value-for-money evaluation is passed or not (including opinions of the finance departments in concert with industry departments)	Immediate disclosure	Within ten working days after the issue of approval documents with respect to the implementation programs	

(continued)

Stage	Contents to be disclosed	Manner of disclosure	Time limit	Information provider
Identification of projects	Value-for-money evaluation report that has been examined and approved (including the approval documents issued by the finance departments)	Disclosure in due time	Within six months after entering into the implementation phase	
	Financial expenditure liabilities of the project and those of the PPP projects implemented and to be implemented in the year and annual budget arrangements, and the ratio of expenditure for all the PPP projects out of the budget in each year in the expenditure of the general public budget	Immediate disclosure	Within ten working days after the issue of approval documents with respect to the implementation programs	
	Measurement basis, key factors and indicators of the financial affordability assessment	Immediate disclosure	Within ten working days after the report is finalized	
	Conclusions on whether the financial affordability assessment passes or not	Immediate disclosure	Within ten working days after the issue of approval documents with respect to the implementation programs	
	Financial affordability assessment report that has been examined and approved (including the approval documents issued by the finance departments)	Disclosure in due time	Within six months after entering into the implementation phase	
	Proposals for new or renovated or expanded projects and approval documents	Disclosure in due time	Within six months after entering into the implementation phase	Implementing organization
	Feasibility study report (including a full set of supporting documents) and approval documents, design documents and approval documents (if applicable)	Disclosure in due time	Within six months after entering into the implementation phase	Implementing organization

(continued)

Stage	Contents to be disclosed	Manner of disclosure	Time limit	Information provider
Identification of projects	Asset evaluation report with respect to the stocked public assets or equity, and various programs and others (if applicable) that may be involved in the transfer of stocked assets or equity	Disclosure in due time	Within six months after entering into the implementation phase	Implementing organization
Preparation for projects	Authorized documents of the government, including the authorization of the parties to the implementing agency, the contracting parties of the PPP project contract, the government's investment representatives (if applicable), etc.	Immediate disclosure	Within ten working days after authorization	Local government at the same level
	Introduction to the project, the cooperation scope, the cooperation term, the operation mode, selection of the mode of purchasing social capital	Immediate disclosure	Within ten working days after entering into the procurement procedures	Implementing organization
	Transaction structure (including financing structure, return mechanism and relevant supporting arrangements), project output specification and performance standards, risk allocation framework, core boundary conditions, contracts and regulatory system	Disclosure in due time	Within six months after entering into the implementation phase	Implementing organization
	Government's approval documents with respect to the implementation programs	Immediate disclosure	Within ten working days after the issue of approval documents	Implementing organization
	Project implementation program as examined and approved and amendments thereto	Disclosure in due time	Within six months after entering into the implementation phase	Implementing organization
Procurement of projects	Prequalification announcements (including prequalification application documents)	Immediate disclosure	Within ten working days after the issue of the prequalification announcement	Implementing organization

(continued)

Stage	Contents to be disclosed	Manner of disclosure	Time limit	Information provider
Procurement of projects	Project procurement documents, addenda (if any)	Disclosure in due time	Within six months after entering into the implementation phase	Implementing organization
	Concluding observations with respect to the review report of prequalification and response documents, including the list of prequalification experts and review experts	Disclosure in due time	Within six months after entering into the implementation phase	Procurement authority
	List of the working group of negotiation about confirmation	Disclosure in due time	Within six months after entering into the implementation phase	Implementing organization
	Announcement of pre-bid winners and transaction results, the announcement of the bid-winning and transaction results and the letter of acceptance;	Immediate disclosure	As agreed according to the law and the procurement documents	Executive agency, procurement authority
	Signed PPP project contracts	Disclosure in due time	Within six months after entering into the implementation phase	Implementing organization
	Key terms of PPP project contract, listing main output specifications, return mechanism for performance indicators, and the price adjustment mechanism	Immediate disclosure	Within ten working days after the project contract is approved by the people's government	Executive agency and project company
	Government's responsibility confirmation documents for the expenditure of the project or the update or adjustment documents (if applicable) of the people's congress at the same level (or the NPC Standing Committee) including the financial expenditure liability of the project into budgets which span two years	Disclosure in due time	Within six months after entering into the implementation phase	Implementing organization
	Government's authorization documents (if any) for the adjustment and updates during the project procurement process	Immediate disclosure	Appendices to the project contract approved by the people's government within ten working days will be made	Implementing organization

(continued)

Stage	Contents to be disclosed	Manner of disclosure	Time limit	Information provider
Implementation of projects	Registration of the project company, capital subscribed by the shareholders and availability of the capital, increase or decrease of the capital (in applicable)	Immediate disclosure	Upon incorporation and within ten working days after the capital fund is obtained	Project company
	Financing limit, key terms and closing conditions	Disclosure in due time	Before April 30 of the year following the determining or completion of matters corresponding to the information	Project company
	Review of the project construction permits, construction progress, quality and cost and others made based on the PPP project contracts	Immediate disclosure	According to the PPP project contracts; if the PPP project contracts do not make any provisions, prior to April 30 in the next year after the end of corresponding activities	Executive agency and project company
	Annual operation of private capital partners or the project company and satisfaction of the operational performance	Immediate disclosure	According to the PPP project contracts; if the PPP project contracts do not make any provisions, prior to April 30 in the next year after the end of corresponding activities	Project company
	Project company's performance monitoring report, interim assessment report, major changes or termination of the project, project pricing and previous adjustments	Immediate disclosure	According to the PPP project contracts; if the PPP project contracts do not make any provisions, prior to April 30 in the next year after the end of corresponding activities	Implementing organization
	Cost monitoring and review of the project company, alteration agreements on the PPP project contracts or supplementary agreements	Disclosure in due time	Before April 30 of the year following the end of corresponding activities	Implementing organization Project company

(continued)

Stage	Contents to be disclosed	Manner of disclosure	Time limit	Information provider
Implementation of projects	Related contents of the financial report of the project company, including payment for the project, the government subsidy granted to the project, and the assets and liabilities of the project company and others	Disclosure in due time	Before April 30 of the year following the end of corresponding activities	Project company
	Major breach of contract and withdrawal of performance bond, handling of public complaints, etc.	Immediate disclosure	Within ten working days upon occurrence	Implementing organization
	Provisions or decisions made by the government at the corresponding level or its functional departments that may have a significant impact on the project	Immediate disclosure	Within ten working days after the issue of provisions and decisions	Implementing organization
	Major disputes, litigations or arbitrations with respect to the project or the parties directly related to the project	Immediate disclosure	Except as otherwise provided in the Measures, within ten working days upon occurrence	Project company
	Directory of the PPP projects at the same level, pilot library thereof and changes to the projects as well as the budget, implementation and settlement situations of governments for the PPP projects as approved by the people's congresses at the same level	Immediate disclosure	Disclosed or quarterly disclosed as required by the law (if any)	
Transfer of projects	Composition of the transfer working group, transfer procedures, transfer standards, and other transfer programs	Immediate disclosure	Within ten working days after the transfer program is determined	Implementing organization
	List of the assets or facilities or interests to be transferred, assessment report on the assets or equity to be transferred (if applicable), scheme on performance test	Immediate disclosure	Within ten working days after the list or report is finalized or after the end of the test	Implementing organization

(continued)

Stage	Contents to be disclosed	Manner of disclosure	Time limit	Information provider
Transfer of projects	Release of various security or interests on the assets or facilities to be transferred (if applicable)	Immediate disclosure	Within ten working days after the corresponding release	Executive agency and project company
	Detection results on the satisfaction of the transfer standards for project facilities	Immediate disclosure	Within ten working days after the issue of detection results	Implementing organization
	Post assessment report and the subsequent operation mode of the project	Immediate disclosure	Within ten working days after the post evaluation report is finalized or the subsequent operation manner of the project is determined	Implementing organization

Appendix Ⅲ List of PPP Information Disclosure and Regulatory Management Systems

No.	Issued on	Document No.	Document	Issued by
1	2013.12.19	No. 74 Decree of Ministry of Finance	Measures for the Administration of Government Procurement in No-bid Procurement Model	Ministry of Finance
2	2014.09.23	Cai Jin [2014] No.76	Circular on Issues Concerning the Promotion and Application of the Public-Private Partnership Model	Ministry of Finance
3	2014.11.29	Cai Jin [2014] No.113	Circular on Issuing the Operational Guidelines for Public-Private Partnership Model (Trial)	Ministry of Finance
4	2014.11.30	Cai Jin [2014] No.112	Circular on Issues Concerning the Implementation of the Demonstration Projects of Public-Private Partnership	Ministry of Finance
5	2014.12.30	Cai Jin [2014] No.156	Circular on Regulating the Contract Management of Public-Private Partnership	Ministry of Finance
6	2014.12.31	Cai Jin [2014] No.215	Circular on Issuing the Administrative Measures for Government Procurement under Public-Private Partnership Projects	Ministry of Finance
7	2014.12.31	Cai Jin [2014] No.214	Circular on Issuing the Interim Measures for the Administration of Competitive Consultation of Government Procurement	Ministry of Finance

(continued)

No.	Issued on	Document No.	Document	Issued by
8	2015.02.13	Cai Jian [2015] No.29	Circular on Promoting Public-Private Partnership Projects in Municipal Public Utilities	Ministry of Finance Ministry of Housing and Urban-Rural Development
9	2015.03.10	Fa Gai Tou Zi [2015] No.445	Circular on Relevant Work Concerning the Promotion of the Development Financial Support for Public-Private Partnership	National Development and Reform Commission
10	2015.04.07	Cai Jin [2015] No.21	Circular on Issuing the Guidelines for the Financial Affordability Assessment of the Public-Private Partnership Projects	Ministry of Finance
11	2015.05.19	Guo Fa Ban [2015] No.42	Notice of the General Office of the State Council on Forwarding the Guideline of the Ministry of Finance, the National Development and Reform Commission, and the People's Bank of China on the Promotion of Public-Private Partnership (PPP) Model in Public Service Sector	The General Office of the State Council
12	2015.06.25	Cai Jin [2015] No.57	Circular on Further Effectively Implementing the Demonstration of Public-Private Partnership Projects	Ministry of Finance
13	2015.12.18	Cai Jin [2015] No.166	Circular on Regulating the Operation of the Public-Private Partnership (PPP) Integrated Information Platform	Ministry of Finance
14	2015.12.18	Cai Jin [2015] No.167	Circular on Issuing Guidelines for Value-for-money Evaluation of PPP (Trial)	Ministry of Finance
15	2016.01		The Public-Private Partnership Law of the People's Republic of China (Exposure Draft)	Ministry of Finance
16	2016.05.28	Cai Jin [2014] No.112	Circular on Further Effectively and Jointly Implementing Public-Private Partnerships	National Development and Reform Commission, Ministry of Finance

(continued)

No.	Issued on	Document No.	Document	Issued by
17	2016.10.20	Cai Jin [2016] No. 92	Circular on Issuing the Interim Measures for the Administration of Finance for Public-private Partnership Projects	Ministry of Finance
18	2016.12.21	Fa Gai Tou Zi [2016] No.2698	Circular on Relevant Work Concerning the Promotion of Asset Securitization of PPP Projects in Infrastructure Sector	National Development and Reform Commission
19	2016.12.30	Cai Jin [2016] No. 144	Administrative Measures of the Ministry of Finance for the Public-Private Partnership (PPP) Expert Database	Ministry of Finance
20	2017.01.23	Cai Jin [2017] No.21	Circular on Issuing the Interim Measures for Administration of Information Disclosure for Public-Private Partnership Integrated Information Platform	Ministry of Finance
21	2017.03.22	Cai Jin [2017] No.8	Circular on Issuing the Interim Measures for the Administration of PPP Consulting Agency Database	Ministry of Finance
22	2017.10.19		Guidelines for Qualification for Asset-backed Securities' Listing and Information Disclosure in PPP Projects	Shanghai Stock Exchange
23	2017.11.10	Cai Ban Jin [2017] No.92	Circular on Regulating Project Database of the National PPP Integrated Information Platform	Ministry of Finance
24	2019.03.07	Cai Jin [2019] No.10	Guide of the Ministry of Finance on Promoting the Regulated Development of Public-Private Partnership	Ministry of Finance
25	2020.03.16	Cai Jin [2020] No.13	Guideline for Public-Private Partnership (PPP) Project Performance Management	Ministry of Finance

Appendix Ⅳ Ranking of Cities with Over 30 Projects in PPP Market Transparency Index

Ranking	City	Project quantity	Immediate disclosure	Disclosure in due time	Overall index
1	Dali, Yunnan	39	91.74	82.93	86.37
2	Jining, Shandong	76	90.82	81.60	85.20
3	Bortala, Xinjiang	45	87.36	83.06	84.74
4	Aksu, Xinjiang	56	87.88	82.48	84.59
5	Dongying, Shandong	32	88.77	81.21	84.16
6	Rizhao, Shandong	54	87.40	81.72	83.94
7	Yuxi, Yunnan	56	89.60	80.28	83.91
8	Honghe, Yunnan	53	89.39	79.97	83.64
9	Yantai, Shandong	38	89.37	79.72	83.49
10	Xuancheng, Anhui	34	88.87	79.52	83.16
11	Yiyang, Hunan	31	91.03	78.05	83.11
12	Xingtai, Hebei	40	84.56	82.01	83.00
13	Chengde, Hebei	59	88.78	79.05	82.85
14	Dezhou, Shandong	38	88.86	78.93	82.80
15	Kunming, Yunnan	62	89.18	78.70	82.79
16	Shijiazhuang, Hebei	37	85.12	81.14	82.69
17	Weifang, Shandong	93	89.03	78.59	82.66
18	Yulin, Guangxi	32	87.83	79.13	82.52
19	Cangzhou, Hebei	48	85.22	80.70	82.46

(continued)

Ranking	City	Project quantity	Immediate disclosure	Disclosure in due time	Overall index
20	Hengshui, Hebei	39	85.97	80.04	82.35
21	Qujing, Yunnan	44	88.21	78.47	82.27
22	Nanyang, Henan	81	86.14	79.13	81.87
23	Baoding, Hebei	42	82.01	81.26	81.55
24	Xinxiang, Henan	51	84.19	79.81	81.52
25	Heze, Shandong	63	86.68	77.65	81.17
26	Tangshan, Hebei	55	86.23	77.70	81.03
27	Handan, Hebei	46	84.38	78.84	81.00
28	Changchun, Jilin	47	83.76	79.12	80.93
29	Changsha, Hunan	43	87.33	76.80	80.91
30	Changde, Hunan	38	88.49	75.97	80.85
31	Dongguan, Guangdong	135	82.67	79.68	80.85
32	Xuzhou, Jiangsu	55	83.93	78.82	80.82
33	Qianxinan, Guizhou	48	86.85	76.53	80.56
34	Urumqi, Xinjiang	59	85.89	76.96	80.44
35	Wenshan, Yunnan	35	87.24	75.98	80.37
36	Bijie, Guizhou	70	84.19	77.59	80.16
37	Hulunbeier, Inner Mongolia	32	82.67	78.33	80.02
38	Bazhong, Sichuan	44	86.20	75.92	79.93
39	Nanjing, Jiangsu	86	86.77	75.44	79.86
40	Yichang, Hubei	40	82.63	78.07	79.85
41	Suqian, Jiangsu	40	84.18	77.03	79.82
42	Chuxiong, Yunnan	37	85.70	75.97	79.76
43	Xi’an, Shaanxi	81	85.14	76.10	79.62
44	Jiangmen, Guangdong	40	84.24	76.66	79.61
45	Pingdingshan, Henan	59	82.08	77.95	79.56
46	Jinan, Shandong	56	87.19	74.56	79.48
47	Luoyang, Henan	62	82.61	77.36	79.41
48	Changzhi, Shanxi	42	82.85	77.19	79.40
49	Jiujiang, Jiangxi	33	82.03	77.72	79.40
50	Jingmen, Hubei	33	84.53	76.06	79.36

(continued)

Ranking	City	Project quantity	Immediate disclosure	Disclosure in due time	Overall index
51	Linyi, Shandong	68	81.46	77.87	79.27
52	Chifeng, Inner Mongolia	52	85.03	75.54	79.24
53	Guiyang, Guizhou	49	82.15	77.36	79.22
54	Datong, Shanxi	33	81.60	77.32	78.99
55	Chengdu, Sichuan	58	84.70	75.21	78.91
56	Lvliang, Shanxi	49	84.27	75.39	78.85
57	Nanning, Guangxi	38	80.14	77.80	78.71
58	Fuyang, Anhui	61	83.94	75.23	78.62
59	Guangyuan, Sichuan	34	81.13	76.92	78.56
60	Tongren, Guizhou	32	79.94	77.51	78.46
61	Pingxiang, Jiangxi	34	82.87	75.55	78.41
62	Haozhou, Anhui	34	82.45	75.60	78.27
63	Leshan, Sichuan	32	80.28	76.96	78.26
64	Hangzhou, Zhejiang	68	84.02	74.34	78.11
65	Liupanshui, Guizhou	40	80.28	76.72	78.11
66	Quanzhou, Fujian	66	81.33	75.90	78.02
67	Taiyuan, Shanxi	37	82.58	75.04	77.98
68	Puyang, Henan	41	79.90	76.72	77.96
69	Zhengzhou, Henan	66	78.94	77.28	77.93
70	Wuhan, Hubei	70	80.43	75.86	77.64
71	Zhoukou, Henan	47	82.02	74.60	77.49
72	Chuzhou, Anhui	36	81.23	75.02	77.44
73	Xiangxi, Hunan	43	85.11	72.48	77.41
74	Lishui, Zhejiang	61	83.38	73.58	77.40
75	Ningbo, Zhejiang	50	82.67	73.90	77.32
76	Bayingolin, Xinjiang	51	78.99	76.20	77.28
77	Wenzhou, Zhejiang	82	79.52	75.78	77.24
78	Shenyang, Liaoning	31	82.94	73.45	77.15
79	Shangqiu, Henan	38	83.77	72.90	77.14
80	Ningde, Fujian	68	81.13	74.54	77.11
81	Kaifeng, Henan	37	77.74	76.70	77.11

(continued)

Ranking	City	Project quantity	Immediate disclosure	Disclosure in due time	Overall index
82	Zunyi, Guizhou	108	83.18	73.10	77.03
83	Anqing, Anhui	48	79.74	75.25	77.00
84	Linfen, Shanxi	57	79.96	75.09	76.99
85	Xinyang, Henan	55	79.20	75.55	76.98
86	Chenzhou, Hunan	31	77.80	76.28	76.88
87	Huai'an, Jiangsu	39	84.99	71.60	76.82
88	Suzhou, Anhui	40	81.29	73.96	76.82
89	Yibin, Sichuan	62	78.77	75.53	76.79
90	Zhumadian, Henan	69	80.31	74.39	76.70
91	Liangshan, Sichuan	40	82.92	72.66	76.66
92	Nanchong, Sichuan	37	85.43	70.86	76.54
93	Yuncheng, Shanxi	35	79.34	74.55	76.42
94	Shantou, Guangdong	31	77.95	75.38	76.38
95	Anyang, Henan	42	79.62	74.20	76.31
96	Huizhou, Guangdong	45	79.41	74.31	76.30
97	Zhangzhou, Fujian	60	75.74	76.09	75.96
98	Dalian Liaoning	48	79.77	73.44	75.91
99	Bengbu, Anhui	32	80.00	73.22	75.86
100	Fuzhou, Jiangxi	41	77.70	74.63	75.83
101	Jinzhong, Shanxi	50	81.08	72.10	75.60
102	Xinzhou, Shanxi	33	80.43	72.43	75.55
103	Qingdao, Shandong	74	80.88	72.07	75.51
104	Xianning, Hubei	33	81.03	71.80	75.40
105	Tianjin	112	79.70	72.61	75.38
106	Yichun, Jiangxi	58	78.87	72.86	75.20
107	Shangrao, Jiangxi	48	76.90	74.11	75.20
108	Ganzhou, Jiangxi	97	78.75	72.91	75.19
109	Taizhou, Zhejiang	62	78.65	72.74	75.05
110	Lu'an, Anhui	39	81.26	71.05	75.03
111	Chongqing	43	77.69	73.11	74.89
112	Xiaogan, Hubei	32	79.43	71.96	74.87

(continued)

Ranking	City	Project quantity	Immediate disclosure	Disclosure in due time	Overall index
113	Huzhou, Zhejiang	45	81.08	70.64	74.71
114	Liuzhou, Guangxi	35	78.12	71.65	74.17
115	Fuzhou, Fujian	53	75.37	72.63	73.70
116	Xiangyang, Hubei	44	76.67	70.66	73.00
117	Qiannan, Guizhou	54	72.43	72.46	72.45
118	Qiandongnan, Guizhou	56	75.38	70.47	72.39
119	Quzhou, Zhejiang	40	76.98	69.28	72.28
120	Jinhua, Zhejiang	41	73.22	71.05	71.90
121	Tianjin	177	73.65	68.53	70.53
122	Haikou, Hainan	48	65.98	64.20	64.90

Postscript

The *2020 China PPP Market Transparency Report* was prepared by the PPP Research Group under the Investment Department at Shanghai University of Finance and Economics (SUFE). The Research Group is comprised of the following leading members: professor Fang Fang, associate professor Zong Qingqing and PhD candidate Shi Cheng, all from the Investment Department of the School of Public Economics and Administration, SUFE. Based on the PPP Market Transparency Index prepared in 2017–2019, the Research Group has carried out investigation, analysis and evaluation concerning the information disclosure landscape of the Chinese PPP market by the end of 2020. During the evaluation, the Research Group has tried all the best to maintain the stability of the index system and index compilation methods, thus ensuring the comparability of PPP market transparency results in 2020 with those in the previous years. Meanwhile, the information disclosure of PPP projects in 2020 has also been put in comparison with that in the preceding years. The Group hopes that its work could accurately and objectively reflect the information disclosure status of the Chinese PPP market, thereby contributing to the healthy and sustainable development of the PPP in China.

The successful completion of the research project relies on the strong support and assistance of other organizations. First of all, School of Public Economics and Administration at SUFE has provided valuable financial support for the smooth implementation of the project. Second, the Group would like to thank China Public Private Partnerships Center (CPPPC) for its data support. However, it needs to be stated again that this Report, prepared independently by the Research Group, represents the academic opinions of the Research Group and doesn't represent the official opinions of

such institutions above.

Finally, gratitude should also be extended to Chen Chun, Chen Huijie, Chen Yusha, Chen Zihao, Cheng Ying, Li Shaotang, Li Xinyi, Liang Xiao, Lin Yuhui, Lin Zijian, Liu Yiting, Rong Jiaqi, Sun Yushi, Wang Jinghan, Wang Junqi, Wang Kaiyuan, Wu Yaning, Wu Hanqi, Zeng Wei, Zhang Zhijie, Zhao Han, Zheng Hao, Xu Mingxin and other postgraduates and undergraduates at SUFE, for their contributions to data collection, consolidation and other research assistance work in the project.

At the end, the Research Group would like to express our sincerest thanks to all parties for their support and assistance. We also welcome experts and practitioners from all walks of life to put forward valuable opinions and suggestions with regard to our work, with a view to formulating PPP market transparency index in a more scientific and rigorous manner in the future. Please contact our members for more details:

Zong Qingqing (email: zong.qingqing@mail.sufe.edu.cn)